JEFF GOODELL
SUNNYVALE

Jeff Goodell is the author of *The Cyberthief and the Samurai*. He is a contributing editor at *Rolling Stone*, and his work has appeared in *The New York Times Magazine*, *The New Republic*, *Wired*, and *GQ*. A fourth-generation Californian, he now lives in upstate New York with his wife and two children.

Also by Jeff Goodell

The Cyberthief and the Samurai

SUNNYVALE

The Rise and Fall of a Silicon Valley Family

SUNN

YVALE

JEFF GOODELL

Vintage Books
A Division of Random House, Inc.
New York

VINTAGE BOOKS EDITION

All rights reserved under International and Pan-American Copyright
Conventions. Published in the United States by Vintage Books, a division of
Random House, Inc., New York, and simultaneously in Canada by Random
House of Canada Limited, Toronto. Originally published in hardcover in the
United States by Villard Books, a division of Random House, Inc., New York,
in 2000.

Vintage and colophon are registered trademarks of Random House, Inc.

Library of Congress Cataloging-in-Publication Data
Goodell, Jeff.
Sunnyvale : the rise and fall of a Silicon Valley family / Jeff Goodell.
p. cm.
Originally published: New York : Villard, c2000.

ISBN-10: 0-679-77638-9

ISBN-13: 978-0-679-77638-3

1. Goodell, Jeff.   2. Sunnyvale (Calif.)—Social life and customs—
20th century.   3. Sunnyvale (Calif.)—Biography.   4. Sunnyvale (Calif.)—
Social conditions—20th century.   5. Goodell family.   6. Santa Clara County
(Calif.)—Social conditions—20th century.   I. Title.
F869.S86 G66 2001
979.4'73—dc21   00-068531

Author photograph © 1999 by Jonathan Barber
Book design by Mercedes Everett

www.vintagebooks.com

Printed in the United States of America

145052501

For Milo and Georgia

I like the Americans because they are healthy and optimistic.

—Franz Kafka

SUNNYVALE

1

As a kid, I always felt lucky. I had a mother, a father, a brother, a sister, four grandparents, aunts, uncles, cousins, two dogs, a surly cat named Princess, and a brand-new house in a brand-new world. Even the name of the town I lived in made me feel lucky: Sunnyvale.

I loved the word *Sunnyvale*. It was different from the names of towns around us—like San Jose and Palo Alto and San Francisco, which had a dreamy, old Spanish romance about them. And it was not a name like Silicon Valley, which Sunnyvale was right in the middle of, but which always made me think of breasts and robots. The word *Sunnyvale* had utopian flair. It suggested to me that I lived in a special place—a world of sunshine and progress, of new gizmos and old fruit trees, where life promised to be a rocket ride across friendly skies. Streets were named after birds and flowers, and I could walk all the way to school on beautifully curving sidewalks, and my fourth-grade class took field trips to buildings where people smashed atoms and built satellites. How could I not feel lucky? I lived in a place where, as my mother often counseled me after a hard day, "Everything will work out okay."

And for a long time, I believed her. The pictures on the TV news of bloody American soldiers being lifted into helicopters, the resignation of the president, the death of Elvis—none of that rocked me. Then one morning in the spring of 1979, my mother said firmly, "I have something I need to talk to you and your brother and sister about. Let's go sit down." I knew by the disturbingly unsunny look on her face that this was a serious matter. We tromped single-file into the family room.

I was nineteen at the time, the oldest of three kids in my family. Like most other seventies teenagers with social aspirations, I wore a puffy down jacket on even the mildest days and had let my hair grow out long enough that I could chew on my bangs. I wasn't a stoner, but I smoked dope at parties, especially if the party was at my friend Rod's house, where the nights often ended with *Dark Side of the Moon* blasting and everyone taking off their clothes and jumping into the pool. My brother, Jerry, was twenty-two months younger than me, a senior in high school with sun-bleached blond hair and a soft, gentle face that featured none of my adolescent cockiness. My sister, Jill, had just turned eleven and was a hazel-eyed girl whose bedroom was covered with posters of the Bay City Rollers.

My mother sat on the edge of our green plaid sofa. On good days, she looked a little like Liz Taylor without the movie-star glitz: dark hair, soft round face, a hint of tragedy in every smile. On bad days, like this one, her face looked like a thundercloud that was ready to burst from pent-up emotion.

As we waited for her to speak, the word *cancer* flashed in my mind. I'd been obsessed with the word lately. I often checked my body for lumps and lay in bed at night imagining tumors coiling through my body, their tentacles rooting into my liver and kidneys. Now I wondered whether these nightmares had been premonitions and our mother was about to tell us she was going to die. In that split second, I was already asking myself, "Why her?" I loved my mother. Not only that, she was an extremely cool person. She had been only nineteen when I was born—she felt practically like my older sister. She listened to Creedence and the Allman Brothers just like I did, danced with my friends at my parties, and never blew a gasket when she found an empty beer can in the backyard. Lately, she had been kicking up her heels a bit. She had frizzed her hair, started wearing paisley blouses and big beaded necklaces, and de-cided, for the first time in her adult life, that she wanted to get a job. In a town like Sunnyvale, which was stocked with engineers and their obedient wives, this was a revolutionary act. My mother had talked to a neighbor who was an executive at a data-storage company, and before long she was working in the file room.

My father was not thrilled. He liked the idea of my mother staying at home with us kids. For her to be off, working in an office at a big company that built computer stuff, just seemed wrong to him. He worried that people would think he could not provide for his family on his own.

My father's name was Ray. When I was a kid, I thought he was a big, noble man, my own Paul Bunyan. He was six foot two, with callused hands and a worn, slender, handsome face, dazzling green-gold eyes, and light brown hair that was so fine it danced with the slightest stirring of air—a closing door, a cough. He worked in the landscape-contracting business, building city parks and beautifying highways around the Valley, and was happiest when he had dirt under his fingernails. He loved to hunt and fish and tried to pass his love of the outdoors on to me. He taught me how to shoot a rifle and split kindling wood and thread a worm onto a hook. More than anything else, he loved to build things. He turned our garage into a family room, moved the location of the front door, built a carport, a workshop, a laundry room, and benches in the backyard. I could always tell when things weren't going well at work or when he was troubled by something at home, because that was when he started a new project. Pounding nails was his form of psychotherapy.

Of all his projects, however, the fireplace in the family room was the one he was most proud of. It was a massive brick and stone structure, more appropriate for a castle in the English countryside than a flimsy tract home in Sunnyvale, where the temperature rarely dipped below forty degrees. The firebox was large enough to roast an ox and sat on a two-foot-high hearth made of old cobblestones he'd dug up on a job in San Francisco. My father had laid every brick and stone himself, buttering them with mortar, stringing them along a plumb line. It had taken him months of weekends and evenings to complete and required a devotion that was as much spiritual as physical. Over the years, the fireplace radiated that devotion back to us in heat and light. It became our family totem pole, our mosh pit, our sacred site. It was where we opened our Christmas presents and sang "Happy Birthday to You" and talked about love and the threat of nuclear war.

Now I stared at those same bricks and stones, suddenly terrified of the bomb my mother was about to drop.

"Your father and I have decided to get a divorce," she said plainly and without tears.

Divorce! I exhaled, relieved. Unlike *cancer,* this was a word I could handle.

To me, divorce felt more like a step into the modern world than a breaking of a sacred covenant. In the late 1970s, it seemed like everybody we knew was splitting up—it was the romantic equivalent of the Pet Rock craze. My uncle Bob, who wore leather sandals from Tijuana and told jokes about traveling salesmen who got the clap, had ended his marriage with his go-go boot–wearing wife, Sheila, and taken up with a series of flashy women. My best friend's father, a building contractor who kept tightly rolled joints in the ashtray of his van, ran off with a dental hygienist. Even my uncle Dick, a strait-laced mid-level manager at Hewlett-Packard, split with his wife and took up with a succession of free-spirited female companions.

My mother did her best to make the divorce seem like a rational and sensible decision. She told us that it was no reflection of her feelings for us, that she and my father still loved us deeply, and that they would both continue to be parts of our lives.

Jill was the only one of us who showed any emotion: Her eyes welled up, and she ran out of the room. My mother followed her.

I looked over at Jerry.

"You okay?" I asked.

"Yeah, I'm fine."

We stared at the wall for a moment.

"This is no big deal," I said.

"Yeah," he said.

"It doesn't mean anything."

"I know."

Then Jerry went into his bedroom and put on a Van Halen album and that was the end of it.

Or so I thought. At some point, as I sat there in the family room, staring at those massive hearthstones, it dawned on me that there had been only four people present for the announcement, not five: Where was our father? He prided himself on always being there for his kids, no matter what. I couldn't believe he would dodge an important moment like this.

But he had. Later, my mother explained to me that my father was too torn up to face us and thought it'd be better for everyone if he wasn't around when she broke the news. I was not sympathetic. In fact, I thought it was cowardly.

When my father turned up the next day—he just pulled into the driveway in his white Chevy El Camino as if he'd run to the store for a carton of milk—he tried to act like it was no big deal, but even I could see how busted up he was inside. For a family man like my father, a man who had put all his eggs in one basket, so to speak, and carried that basket around for twenty years, this was the worst thing that could have happened to him. So he pretended it wasn't happening. He told us that he and my mother were "separating," but that he hoped things would work out. I nodded and shrugged and avoided looking him in the eye, afraid of what I might see. I couldn't believe that the man who often held me responsible for my actions was dodging responsibility for his own.

A few weeks later, Jerry and I took off on a trip to Europe that we'd planned for months. On the flight to London, Jerry and I hardly talked about the divorce. I think he believed that when he returned home, our mother and father would have worked it out and everything would be back to normal. I knew that wouldn't be the case. I knew it was over, but I didn't care. I thought breaking up a family was like breaking up with a girlfriend: There would be a few months of mooning and heavy hearts, then we'd move on.

Jerry got homesick and flew back after about four weeks in Europe. I stayed four months, rattling around with my backpack and Eurail Pass. I'd planned to go to India, but the farthest east I got was Istanbul; overland travel across Iran was extremely dangerous for Americans at the time, and I was too poor to fly. Instead, I spent a month crawling around ancient ruins on the Turkish coast. At a café in Marmaris, I ordered a peculiar-looking dish that I thought was roasted eggplant but might well have been decomposing eggplant, contracted dysentery, and headed home.

When I returned, I was greeted with a surreal sight: The family portrait was just as it had been when I'd left—big house, big fireplace, two dogs, my mother cooking dinner, Jill and Jerry battling over the TV—except my father had been airbrushed out of the picture.

Years later, I learned that when my mother had told my father she wanted to split up, his initial reaction had been disbelief. After all, he had just finished building a new upstairs addition, including a spacious bedroom suite. (It was a typically well-intentioned but clueless gesture, as if there were no problems in their marriage that a bigger master bath wouldn't fix.) He accused my mother of sabotaging their marriage and stealing his family from him, but his anger was brief and shallow because he knew it wasn't true. They were splitting up not because she had fallen in love with someone else but because she was bored. As my mother told me years later, "I wanted to dance." She meant that literally and metaphorically, and my father knew it. At one point, he fell to his knees and promised my mother that if she stayed, he would jazz up their lives; as proof, he offered to take her to Tahiti for a week. She declined.

Finally, my father decided that the best thing to do was give my mother some space. So while Jerry and I were in Europe, he moved into a two-bedroom condo in Cupertino. He believed his departure was only temporary—a matter of a few months, maybe—before my mother came back around. The condo was bike-riding distance from our house in Sunnyvale, but it was a different world—a lonely and anonymous place with a small kitchen window that looked out over a concrete side yard, and dark bedrooms with shag carpet and flimsy doors. It had no fireplace, just forced-air heating.

I was in no rush to visit my father after I returned from my trip. A week passed, then another; finally my mother practically begged me to stop by and see him. Out of respect more for her than for him, I agreed.

When I arrived, my father's eyes lit up. He invited me in, and we sat at the small rectangular table in the kitchen and drank instant coffee. He was still a young man—he'd just turned forty-three—but he looked as if he'd aged ten years in the four months since I'd seen him last. He was a person who thrived on fresh air and sunlight; in the condo, he lived like a caged bear. His shoulders were always brushing against walls, his eyes drifting toward the window, searching for soft, green space and finding only cyclone fence, concrete, and telephone wires.

"So you had a good time in Europe?" he asked.

I nodded and gave him a quick review of my trip—the Eiffel Tower, the midnight sun in Norway, the Alps. Recounting this for my father was all the sweeter because I owed him nothing for it—I'd paid for the trip myself, out of money I'd earned doing odd jobs. My father listened, slurped coffee, nodded. He didn't care about my trip. He cared that I was there, sitting across from him at his kitchen table, telling him about it.

When I finished, my father picked at a callus on his palm. I could see he was working himself up to something. Finally, he said, "What's new with your mother?"

What he really meant, I knew, was: "Do you think she's having second thoughts about the divorce?" The answer was no. My mother had blasted off Planet Marriage and was now orbiting other suns. But I wasn't going to tell him that.

"Not much," I said.

"How is she?"

"Fine, working hard."

"How's the house look?"

"Okay."

"Has she cleaned the leaves out of the gutter lately?"

I shrugged.

"Well, next time you talk to her, remind her, will you? She needs to do it before the rains start. Otherwise, the gutters will flood, and she'll have a real mess on her hands."

"I'll remind her," I said. Then I thanked him for the coffee and got out of there as quickly as I could.

2

A few months later, I stumbled into a job at a small company with a dopey rainbow-colored logo and a funny name: Apple Computer. This was long before the Macintosh was introduced, long before the company's two founders, Steve Jobs and Steve Wozniak, became as famous as rock stars, and long before the rest of the world cared about what was happening in Silicon Valley. I'd gotten the job at Apple not because I was a laser-brained hacker prodigy but because my mother worked there. She'd heard about Apple while she was working at the data-storage company and loved the fact that no one wore dresses or ties to the office and that there were beer bashes every Friday afternoon. When she learned there was an opening for an "area associate"—that's Valley-speak for *secretary*—she applied and was hired immediately.

Like my mother, I knew nothing about programming or engineering. Nevertheless, I was hired as an assistant to the assistant of the head of software development for a new computer called the Apple III, which everyone had high hopes for but was to be a spectacular flop. My job was to distribute memos, help with filing, and translate various documents the engineers had written into readable English.

To me, Apple was just a paycheck, a way to pay the rent while I figured out what to do with the rest of my life. I'd already washed out of one career. I'd raced motorcycles professionally for a few years during and just after high school—I had a wall full of plastic trophies, a part-time sponsorship, dreams of greatness, the whole bit. I'd given it up after I took a bad crash and nearly died from internal bleeding.

I had no idea what to do next. Going back to school might have been the obvious choice, but I'd already tried that. I'd attended a local junior college for a few semesters, taking classes in everything from business marketing to art history, then dropped out. Even after I quit racing motorcycles, I thought it was important to live dangerously, and school was never much of a thrill. Instead, I went skydiving and surfed at Shark's Cove in Santa Cruz and chased my best friend's wife. "A man ought not be tame" said a Spanish proverb I'd copied into my journal. I liked this idea, I realize now, largely because my father didn't. He believed in minimizing risk, in squirreling away money for a rainy day, in steel-belted radials, and in marriage until death do you part.

While I was working at Apple, my father often called and wanted us to do something together—go pheasant hunting in Manteca, or to a Stanford football game, or out to dinner at the Golden Dragon, his favorite Chinese restaurant. Sometimes I went, sometimes I didn't. I knew he was lonely and that I owed him some of my attention, but the truth is I found him unbearably difficult to be around. There's a particular smell that a broken man gives off that's hard to take, especially for his oldest son. One of my problems with Apple, in fact, was that the guys I worked with seemed to be a lot like my father: modest, socially inept, excessively decent. There were a few exceptions, like Woz, who seemed to be a total goofball. He wore Hawaiian shirts and ate lots of junk food and seemed to do nothing but play video games. I rarely saw Steve Jobs, but when I did he always looked distracted and lonely in his ripped and faded Levi's.

For the most part, however, the crowd I worked with at Apple was pretty dull—and when it came to sex, strangely immature. I knew engineers who could spend hours lost in glorious rapture with chips and code, but whenever a member of the opposite sex walked within twenty feet of them, their eyes fell and they blushed like fifteen-year-olds. Even the mail carrier—a jolly woman in her mid-forties with chubby cheeks—inspired panic whenever she dropped a pile of letters on the receptionist's desk and tried to strike up a conversation with a passing geek.

To me, this was just evidence of how out to lunch these guys were. They had their priorities all wrong.

After about five months at Apple, I decided to move on. Not just to a new job but to a new world. My main reason for leaving—although I would never have admitted this at the time—was to get away from my father, as well as from anything and everything that reminded me of him. Arrogant young genius that I was, I had no sense that by leaving Apple I was walking out of the biggest party capitalism has ever thrown even before the hors d'oeuvres were passed out. Quite the contrary: I felt like I was leaving behind a bunch of nerdy machine heads who were destined to live small, narrow lives empty of romance or mystery.

I gave my two-week notice to my boss, whose name was Ed. He was a brusque guy in his mid-forties with a Grizzly Adams beard and quarter-inch-thick glasses that made his eyes look fishy. When I told him I was leaving, he mumbled something about how sorry he was to lose me, then rushed off to a meeting. Thanks, Ed.

Then a few days before I left, Ed poked his head into my cubicle and asked me to lunch. I was stunned—no one at Apple had ever taken me to lunch before. I suddenly felt important, like I'd misinterpreted my place in the solar system. Then I remembered the pencils, paper clips, and yellow legal pads I'd been lifting from the storeroom, and my small burst of joy faded quickly into worry.

We went to a seafood restaurant called the Sandpiper, which was in the parking lot of a nearby shopping mall. There were fishing nets on the wall and lobsters with rubber bands around their claws in an aquarium near the bar. By the standards of Silicon Valley in those days, this was five-star elegance, several notches above the Good Earth, a health-food diner where most Apple employees went for lunch. I had no idea why Ed was taking me to a fancy joint like this, and I worried that he was going to hit me with a bill for the supplies I'd ripped off. I started to relax when I saw that he seemed genuinely curious about me. He asked me if I still lived at home, and

I told him I'd recently moved into a cheap apartment that I shared with a friend. He spoke warmly of my mother, whom he knew only in passing, and asked how long she'd been working at Apple. About a year, I told him, since just after my parents' divorce. He lifted his eyebrows at that—it turned out he was himself locked in a nasty courtroom battle with his wife. I explained to him that my mother and father had been married for twenty years but that their split was no big deal—no wars over who got what furniture, no lawsuits over child support, no screaming at each other on the phone. This was true enough, as far as it went. I could have added a few details about my anger and disappointment at my father, of course, but I resisted.

"You're lucky you have such a civilized family," he said.

I shrugged, which back then was my general response to everything.

Then Ed asked me why I was quitting.

"I'm not interested in computers," I said coolly. "I think they're boring."

"They're still in a primitive state," he told me, stabbing at his scampi. Then he explained how computers will evolve quickly in the years to come, becoming easier to use, faster, more efficient. They will turn the lights on and off in your house and run your car. They will be a powerful communications tool, enabling you to send large amounts of data to people in distant corners of the world. They will become an instrument for democracy and social good. They will empower the little man. They will destroy corrupt corporations. Basically, it was what I now recognize as Steve Jobs's riff, which had been bottled and passed around the Apple offices like sugar water.

I didn't believe it. When I thought about technology, I thought of HAL in *2001: A Space Odyssey*. Technology was Big Brother. Technology was the cold war; it was rockets and bombs and nuclear annihilation. It was IBM, men in suits, mechanical drones. It never occurred to me that most of the people at Apple felt the same way, that the whole point of building personal computers was to steal fire from the gods.

Apple, I thought, was just IBM with long hair, and I didn't want to be a part of it. I didn't know much about who I was or where I was going, but I knew I didn't want to spend my days in front of a computer screen. I wanted adventure. I wanted to climb mountains, swim in warm seas, argue loudly about books and movies, and have lots of sex.

I explained this to Ed in so many words.

This idea was so perplexing to him that the only way he could respond was to push his scampi around on his plate for a very long time. That was one of the tricky things about talking to engineers: They were always finding hidden complexities in the simplest statements, and they always felt like they had to resolve them—reverse engineer them—before they could go on.

Finally, he looked up at me with his fish eyes and said, "So, basically, you're a Luddite."

I'd never heard that word before. "What's a Luddite?"

He explained that Luddites were named after a movement of farmers in England early in the industrial revolution. They had been afraid machines were going to destroy their way of life (which they more or less did) and, in doing so, destroy humanity's fundamental relationship with the world (on this one, the jury's still out).

"I don't hate technology," I said, lying. "I just don't have any interest in it."

He nodded, then pushed his scampi around again for a few minutes and seemed to run through some silent calculations in his head. "Now that you're out on your own, have you thought about what you'd like to do for a career?"

"Not really."

It took him a minute to comprehend this. "Why not?"

"I'll figure something out."

"You can do well at Apple. There are a lot of opportunities here."

I shrugged. By "do well," I presumed Ed meant that someday, if I worked hard, I might be able to pull in forty grand a year. To me, it wasn't worth it. I wasn't against money in principle—I just couldn't see working fifty hours a week at a job I had no feeling for just so I could buy bigger speakers for my stereo system. At the time, I'd never heard of stock options or IPOs and had no idea that Apple was planning to go public soon—an event that was to turn men like Ed into overnight millionaires. But then, I doubt even Ed knew how lucky he was about to be.

"So what are your plans? Are you going back to school to get your degree?"

"Nah. I've been thinking about moving to Lake Tahoe," I said out of the blue.

"Why?"

"I like to ski. Maybe I'll be able to get a job dealing blackjack."

"And then?"

I shrugged.

"I like Tahoe," he said carefully but firmly. "It's a great place to visit. But the future is here."

"Your future," I said, smiling inwardly at my mildly clever witticism.

Instead of laughing, he gave me one of those tight little smiles that adults get when they're talking to children who they know are about to do something very foolish. And that only reinforced my feeling that I was doing the precisely right thing. A few weeks later, I tied my bicycle onto the roof of my Volkswagen and headed for the mountains.

3

It was twilight as my trusty VW rattled over Echo Summit on the eastern rim of the Sierra Nevada. The highway dropped quickly into the Tahoe basin, and I drove directly to Caesars at the end of the strip, locked up my car, and walked in to seek my fortune.

I'd been in the casino only about a half hour when I noticed a middle-aged Indian man in a pink turban and a white robe at one of the roulette tables. He was alone, expressionless, fantastical, a character out of *Arabian Nights*. He had a large, sagging face and heavy, dull eyes that seemed terribly bored, as if life were a movie he'd seen many times before. In front of him were stacks of black fifty-dollar and purple hundred-dollar casino chips. By my rough calculation, he had over fifteen thousand dollars piled on the green felt.

I pulled up a stool at the nearby bar and watched him through three gin and tonics. I'd never been in a casino before, I knew nothing about the rules of gambling, about hot streaks and cold streaks, about odds or long shots. But it was obvious that this guy was on to something. Whenever he lost—which wasn't often—he doubled his bet the next time. If he lost again, he doubled it again. Inevitably, he won. An elegant system, I thought. While I was sitting there getting drunk, he was getting rich.

I approached the roulette table. In my pocket was exactly $735, all cash, folded neatly. It was all the money I had in the world—enough to rent a room and feed myself until I found a job, but that was about it. The dealer, a middle-aged woman with a towering red wig and heavy eyeliner, smiled kindly. I exchanged a twenty for four five-dollar chips, then watched the dealer send the ball spinning. When the guy in the turban slid one hundred dollars onto red, I immediately pushed one of my chips onto the felt beside his. I glanced up at him, not sure if I was breaking some gambling protocol by copying his bet. He ignored me.

The ball clacked around, then stopped.

Red. We won. I felt a surge of adrenaline.

We bet again. We won. Again. We won. When we lost, I doubled my bet. If we lost again, I doubled it again. It was such a simple system and so elegant that I didn't understand why everyone in the casino wasn't doing it. Before I quite knew what happened, I had a mini-Manhattan of gambling chips in front of me.

Then I panicked. I felt that sudden hole-in-the-cosmos queasiness that you get when you know you're bending the laws of nature. I didn't know if my muse was tapped in to a higher consciousness or perhaps had a magnet in his shoe, but I suddenly understood I didn't want to hang around to find out. I scooped up my chips into a plastic bucket and racewalked over to the cashier, where a man behind steel bars counted out fifteen crisp, new hundred-dollar bills, two twenties, and a five.

I grabbed the bills and ran out of the casino before anyone could stop me. When I got outside, I took a few deep breaths and realized it was after midnight and I hadn't eaten in about twelve hours. I saw a sign in the window of a nearby casino advertising "The Biggest Lobsters in Tahoe!" So I took the elevator up to the restaurant on the eighteenth floor and ordered a two-and-a-half-pounder. I sat alone in a booth near the window, looking out over the black hole that was Lake Tahoe, watching the green light of a boat slide through the darkness. Gradually, it dawned on me that this was not a hoax or a daydream. I had actually won $1,545. It was legal. And no one could take it away from me.

When I finished eating, I left a lavish tip then headed back toward my car, noticing for the first time how a pocket full of cash helps you swagger. Instead of walking around the rear of the building to the parking lot, however, I decided to go back into Caesars and cut across the casino floor. And that was a big mistake.

The man with the pink turban was still at the roulette table, the stack of chips in front of him as high as ever. I said to myself, very clearly, "Don't be an idiot." But then I thought if I won another three or four hundred dollars, I could buy some new snow tires for my car and a ski parka, and I'd be set for the winter. What's the big deal? I'll bet a few spins, and if things aren't going well, I'll get up and leave. I'll still be richer than when I arrived.

I won't bother to recount the miserable details of my losing streak or the despair I felt at watching money fly out of my hands, always thinking, "This is the one, this is going to turn it all around." Every time I lost, I doubled up. I got a quick education in the wonders of geometric progression; at one point, I had $620 riding on a single spin of the roulette wheel.

I lost.

When I finally walked out of the casino, sunlight was just breaking over Nevada. Sugar pines cast long, cold shadows across the parking lot, and the thin mountain air was icy and quiet. My swagger was gone. I had exactly four dollars and thirty cents in my pocket. And I had that only because the minimum bet at the table was five dollars. When I left, the man in the pink turban was still there, still betting, undisturbed by our losing streak.

I slept for a few hours huddled in the front seat of my VW, shivering and cold, then woke up to the blazing noon sun. My neck was stiff. I was hungover and hungry. I drove to a pawnshop a block from the casino and hocked my typewriter for thirty-five dollars. Then I sat in my car and cried.

For the next week, I slept in my VW and survived on crackers and peanut butter. Once, I splurged at the Sahara's $5.95 lunch buffet. I stuffed fried-chicken legs in my pockets and bread rolls up my sleeves and ate them for the rest of the week. I grabbed the first job I could find—as a dishwasher and janitor at Harrah's, which paid $4.15 an hour. And I was grateful for every penny of it. I worked the swing shift, 8 P.M. to 4 A.M. I wandered around the casino floor in blue coveralls, pushing a cart filled with garbage, and scrubbed pots in the basement with a Cambodian refugee named Hao who had walked hundreds of miles across Pol Pot's killing fields and somehow managed to squeeze into America. He cleaned two pots to my one, never stretched his dinner break, never left a minute early, and sent half of every paycheck to his wife and two daughters in Cambodia. He dreamed that someday he would bring them to America.

When I told him I'd lost fifteen hundred dollars at the roulette table, he refused to believe me. "Nobody that stupid," he said, shaking his head.

"It's the truth, Hao," I said.

"You must be rich boy," he said in broken English.

"If I were rich, why would I be washing dishes?"

"If you not rich, why you throw away money?"

"I didn't throw it away," I said. "I lost it playing roulette. There's a difference."

"It's still gone, no?"

"It is, but—"

"You throw it away. Poof, it gone. Next time you do that, you give to me, okay?"

After a month of dish washing and garbage hauling, I made the leap to carrying change in the slot department. I strolled through rows of slot machines wearing a heavy belt of nickels, dimes, and quarters. I'd made enough money to get my typewriter out of hock, but that was about it. I rented a room in a cabin with two other guys and began a fast slide into oblivion. I worked all night, skied most of the day, slept a few hours, snorted crank to stay awake on the job, and drank green lizards in the morning with keno runners.

Through it all, I remained convinced that I was having a big adventure. Tahoe was my Paris, my Mexican jungle, my boxcar across the prairie. I often thought about those poor fools back at Apple. Every day, ass flat in the cubicle, pounding out meaningless code that sent meaningless bursts of electricity through meaningless silicon chips, all so that sales managers could keep track of their widgets. God, save me from that! I was poor, but at least I was out in the world, hacking through the kudzu of life.

About six months after my arrival in Tahoe, I decided to take my first trip back to the Valley. A friend was throwing a twenty-first birthday party that I didn't want to miss. As I left my cabin, I knew a snowstorm was blowing in, but I didn't give it a second thought. By the time I reached the California Highway Patrol checkpoint at the base of the mountain pass that leads out of Tahoe, however, snow chains were required on all cars. I didn't have chains and couldn't afford them.

"I'm a local," I told the patrolman at the checkpoint, hoping he'd let me through.

"No chains, no way," he said, not amused. "You'll have to turn around."

I thought it was absurd. It wasn't snowing that hard. Besides, my VW was excellent in the snow—it *never* got stuck. So I turned around and spent the next hour or so driving around on back roads, blasting through unplowed snow, until I finally found a road that dumped me out on the highway a half mile or so above the checkpoint. The highway immediately began a steep, twisting climb out of the Tahoe basin, hugging granite, the driver's side dropping off hundreds of feet in a sheer cliff. By this time, snow was falling heavily—it was nearly a whiteout. I hunched forward in my seat, squinting, searching for markers that told me where the road ended and the abyss began.

Forty-five minutes later, I made it up over the summit. A highway patrolman in a four-wheel-drive vehicle passed me going the opposite direction; I thought nothing of it. A moment later, a red light appeared in my rearview mirror.

I pulled over immediately. I thought he was stopping me because I didn't have chains and figured I could talk my way out of it. At worst, I'd get a ticket and be on my way.

I rolled down my window. Snowflakes blew across the patrolman's unhappy face.

"What the hell are you doing?" he bellowed.

"I'm heading home for—"

"Get out of the car," he demanded.

"Why?"

"GET OUT OF THE FUCKING CAR."

I got out of the fucking car. I stood there in the snow, shivering. The patrolman was so angry he was vibrating. I thought he was going to melt a hole in the snow.

"This road has been closed for an hour," he said, his face an inch from mine.

"I didn't know—"

"Bullshit."

"I'm on my way—"

"Bullshit! I know *exactly* what you're doing."

Then he reached into my car and grabbed my keys. "You can pick them up at the South Tahoe station tomorrow morning. Along with your summons."

He turned to walk back to his patrol car.

I panicked. I was alone on the highway in the middle of a blizzard, wearing nothing more than jeans and a sweatshirt. "How am I supposed to get home? You can't just *leave* me here!"

"There's a roadhouse a half mile up the highway," he said. "I suggest you start walking."

By the time I got to the restaurant, I was furious, vowing that I would bring a lawsuit against this cop. My nose and cheeks were numb, my fingertips white. The bartender chuckled and shook his head. I sat at the bar drinking coffee—I was too broke to get drunk—until 2 A.M., when the snow lightened and the road opened again. I hitched a ride back to Tahoe with the first truck that came along. As we passed my car on the side of the road, I saw it was buried in snow from the door handles down.

The next morning, I grabbed my spare key and a snow shovel and hitchhiked back to where my car was marooned. By the time I got there—the snow had continued most of the day—the car was invisible except for the radio antenna and part of the right front fender. It took me several hours to dig it out. Then the engine wouldn't start—it'd turn over, but it wouldn't catch. I kept trying until the battery went dead. I kicked a tire and screamed. Faces in passing cars floated by like strange underwater fish, creatures of a different world, safe and warm and purposeful.

That's when the hammer hit. Alone on the road, at that moment, watching the taillights of strangers disappear down the mountain. My big Tahoe adventure suddenly seemed very small. Who was I kidding? I had no money, no friends other than my ski pals and bar buddies and a coked-up cocktail waitress who I sometimes reluctantly called my girlfriend, and I was stuck on the mountain with this broken car that I could not afford to have fixed or towed. I felt desolate and cold, suddenly aware of the thin edge I was living on, heading nowhere, losing the days.

I returned to the roadhouse and called my father collect. This was not an easy thing to do, not only because of the severe judgment I'd passed on him since the divorce but because it's pretty hard to pretend you're a big man on a big adventure when you're calling daddy for help.

When my father picked up the phone, he knew immediately that something was wrong. "What's going on?"

"I'm having a little car trouble," I said.

"What's the problem?"

I gave him a brief explanation. I tried to make it sound like this was just a casual call, that I was in a bit of a jam, but if he was busy, no big deal. My father knew better.

"Where are you?" he asked.

I told him.

"I'm coming up," he said abruptly.

"You don't have to do that—"

"It's no problem," he said. Then he added, in a softer tone, "Don't worry. We'll get you fixed up."

He arrived in just under four hours—record time, given the road conditions. Relief spread over his face when he saw me standing in the parking lot. I think I'd given him the impression I was standing on the edge of a cliff, ready to jump. He got out of his El Camino in his familiar old jeans and blue Sears quilted nylon jacket and announced, "You look like hell."

"Sorry to drag you up here like this," I said, trying to preserve some shred of dignity.

"Don't worry about it," he said. "I was just sitting around the house, watching the boob tube." He said this with a kind of nonchalance, as if I had not asked for anything beyond what he considered his fatherly duty. And that in itself was an act of extreme generosity, given the shabby way I'd treated him lately.

My father had come prepared: toolbox, new spark plugs, wires, distributor cap. He was a practical man, and he loved it when he had a practical job to do. He had the engine purring in less than an hour. I thought that was a fairly stunning accomplishment. But what was most remarkable to me was what he *didn't* do: He did not give me a lecture, he did not tell me how stupid I was for driving on the highway in a blizzard with no chains, or for letting twenty thousand miles pass since the last tune-up, or for snorting up all my paychecks, or for treating him like a leper.

He just waited beside me until I started the car and he was sure that it was running smoothly. Then he drove off in one direction and I drove off in the other.

4

It was a nice gesture, and I appreciated it, but my father's rescue mission changed nothing. When he called a few days later to ask how the car was running, I spoke to him in a voice that was only slightly less frigid than usual: "It's running great," I said. "Thanks." At one point, he asked if I'd thought about how much longer I was going to stay in Tahoe. "For a while," I said, then changed the subject.

As if to prove to the world that I was not going to let my father ruin my big adventure, I burrowed deeper into casino life. I was promoted from change carrier to a position known as keyman, which meant that I wandered around the casino in a red polyester jacket watching for hustlers trying to jimmy the machines and paying jackpots to blue-haired ladies. When I got bored with that after a few months, I applied to a blackjack training school. I spent three weeks learning how to shuffle and deal and pay bets and then was let loose on the two-dollar tables.

I worked the graveyard shift at Harveys, black pants and tie, wrinkled white shirt, scuffed black shoes, the worst-dressed dealer in the state of Nevada. I leaned against the Naugahyde bumper on the blackjack table from midnight until 8 A.M., eyes propped open by artificial stimulants, flipping cards onto green felt. I witnessed outrageous examples of greed and despair every hour. A pink-haired woman in her sixties removed her pearl necklace, laid it on the table, and said, "Deal." A truck driver from Nebraska tipped me one hundred dollars after I dealt him three blackjacks in a row.

When a bald little man draped in gold nodded at a cocktail waitress and said, "I'm interested in her," I relayed his message to the pit boss because I knew he was a high roller, and in the casinos, high rollers get what they want.

I relayed the messages, that is, unless the waitress in question was Amy. Amy had wild blue eyes and a loud, silly, hiccupy laugh that echoed above the jackpot bells in the casino. She was a year younger than me and a high-school dropout from a twisted family somewhere in the San Fernando Valley. Most of my friends in the casino thought she was a ditz and advised me to keep away from her. Besides, she was living with another man, a traveling salesman for a kitchen-appliance company.

I pursued her anyway. I liked her bone-white skin and her cherublike ringlets of blond hair. She had a Carole Lombard quality about her, at once incandescent and vulgar. She was also fearless. Amy was completely unintimidated by the powerful men who ran the casino and considered sex with cocktail waitresses an executive privilege. Every time she saw Vinnie, the ill-tempered, gout-ridden, blow job–obsessed, sixty-year-old casino boss who struck terror in the hearts of everyone who worked beneath him, men and women alike, Amy asked, "You get your hummer last night, Vinnie?" And she'd say it with such a cackle that he couldn't help but smile.

I often entertained myself at 3 A.M. on winter nights when the roads were closed and all but the most die-hard gamblers were snowbound in their hotel rooms by watching Amy walk across the casino floor in her tiny purple-velvet uniform with rhinestones around the collar. You could tell which cocktail waitresses had been around for a while: They moved in a sluggish way and often wore heavy-duty ten-ply nylon support stockings that corseted their thighs and gave their legs a metallic glaze. Amy, on the other hand, wore sheer L'eggs and moved around the casino with a sprightly bounce. Unlike many of the other waitresses, she didn't give a damn about high rollers and paid as much attention to the little old lady at the keno bar as she did to swaggering jock with the Rolex at the craps table.

She was also the only person in the entire casino I ever saw reading a book in the employee cafeteria. We struck up a conversation one night on our 4 A.M. break when I saw her absorbed in a dog-eared copy of *Siddhartha*. I was on an Albert Camus binge at the time, and, as it turned out, she had just read *The Stranger*. "Isn't that a funny coincidence?" she said. During the next week or so, we discussed existentialism during our lunch breaks—"I don't believe in God with a capital *G*," she announced, licking her yogurt off a plastic spoon one morning, "but with a small *g*, I'm not so sure"—and before I knew quite what had happened, we were naked on the floor of the log cabin where she lived with the appliance salesman.

Amy had more fire and spark than anyone else I knew in Tahoe, but her background—no family connections, no high-school diploma—was shared by a lot of people I met in the casino, people who had come up to this lake in the mountains because they knew they could get a good job without much education or training and because it was a beautiful place to live—no smog, no traffic, no sky-high rents. Like me, many of these people were fleeing family troubles or looking for refuge from abusive relationships. Every night in the casino cafeteria, I heard stories about incest, sexual abuse, rape, murder, fathers who abandoned their children, wives who stabbed their husbands, husbands who beat their wives. Sometimes the entire Tahoe basin felt like nothing more than a melting pot of fucked-up kids.

By Tahoe standards, my family troubles were pretty boring. No rampant alcoholism, no wife beating (that I knew of), no sexual abuse (that I knew of), no suicides, no inexplicable, heart-stopping tragedies. Just another suburban family that didn't quite make it, another nuclear quintet that fell off Norman Rockwell's easel.

Amy's family portrait was much bleaker. She confessed a few tidbits to me, mostly about her father, whom she called "a complete fucking asshole, with the word *asshole* underlined in red ink." She hadn't seen him in years and had no idea where he lived. Her mother, she said, was a homeless person, "one of those women you see pushing a shopping cart full of tin cans around on the streets of L.A." She always wanted to tell me more about what had happened to her, but I did not want to hear it—I knew our relationship couldn't bear the weight of real intimacy. And the whole point of this run to Tahoe had been to escape, to leave all that family stuff behind like a bad dream on a hotel-room pillow.

The truth was, I knew from the beginning that Amy was a wild and unstable person whose long-term forecast was cloudy. But for a while her recklessness and mine intersected. We were both bodies in motion, escapees from other lives, willing to try anything. We smoked joints, swapped paperbacks, squandered money on hotel rooms and cognac. On hot summer days, we often threw a bottle of wine into my day pack and hiked up to a small mountain lake at the base of Mount Tallac, one of the highest peaks in the Tahoe basin, and swam naked in the icy, clear water.

One of Amy's favorite games was to play dress-up. She loved to dress up and go dancing or dress up and have sex or dress up and do anything. One morning, after a high roller at the craps table had been outrageously generous to her (turned on, I suppose, by the verbal abuse she undoubtedly heaped on him), we drove to the only thrift shop in South Lake Tahoe, which was filled with silk ties and sequined dresses that I imagined were pawned when luck turned bad. Amy said, "Pick yourself out a suit. I'm taking you out to dinner." I found a charcoal-gray number with narrow lapels and trousers that had probably been hanging on the rack since 1954. It made me look like an FBI agent. Amy bought a clingy orange sweaterdress that was indecently snug.

That night, we drove down to Sacramento, where Amy had made reservations at a fancy Italian restaurant. In the parking lot, Amy opened her purse and took out two tiny squares of paper—one for her, one for me. LSD. "An hors d'oeuvre," she said, and then flipped down the visor and stroked on some mascara. I swallowed, she swallowed, then we went into the restaurant, which was ridiculously stuffy in the way that expensive suburban restaurants sometimes are, straining for big-city grace and elegance and ending up with just a lot of big hair and elaborately folded napkins. I tensed up immediately, feeling a bad trip coming on.

"Oh, come on, this is hilarious," she whispered, and then

walked ahead of me toward our table. I noticed that as she walked, her sweaterdress clung to her thighs, and she sashayed in a deliberately provocative way, intending to make everyone in the restaurant notice. And they did. Chewing stopped, forks paused in midair, and a roomful of eyes focused on her lovely hips, at once awed and embarrassed by the way she moved through the world, by her willingness to flaunt her sexuality and be amused by it, and by the way she announced, simply by the way she walked, that she was not going to play the game by anyone else's rules or cruise smoothly along the middle lane of life. She possessed the kind of outrageousness that lights up a room and leads either to glory or ruin—and at that moment, on that night, it wasn't clear which.

I don't remember much about dinner, except that after the acid kicked in Amy and I became convinced that the shrimps on our plate were speaking to us. We complained loudly to the maître d', and after a few minutes of debate two large men in dark blue suits approached our table. In harsh whispers, they informed us that this was a private dining establishment. If we didn't leave, they would call the cops.

"That's very uncivilized," Amy sniffed, but we didn't argue. When we paid the bill, Amy insisted on leaving a fifty-dollar tip, "just to give them something to think about." Then we drove to a dark corner of the parking lot, and Amy hiked up her orange sweaterdress and climbed onto my lap.

On a cold weekend in early January 1981, my sister, Jill, came up for a visit. My mother and her boyfriend were taking a trip to Napa that weekend, my father was off pheasant hunting, my brother was playing a gig with his garage band, and my sister had nowhere to go. So she hopped on a bus and visited her big brother.

I'd picked up weird vibrations in Jill's voice on the phone earlier, but the changes in my sister didn't really hit home until I saw her step off the Greyhound at the South Lake Tahoe bus station. Maybe it was the eyeliner and mascara she was now wearing or her expensive feathered haircut. But I think it had more to do with the curiosity in her eyes and the way she smiled when she saw me walking across the station to greet her. It was a smile that suggested that, at age thirteen, she had suddenly figured out that the world is a complicated place.

"Hey, Gorilla, good to see you," I said, giving her a hug. I don't know where the nickname Gorilla came from, but my brother and I had been calling her that for years. She hated it, of course, which was exactly why I used it.

She gave me a look that told me she now considered herself too old for this kind of public display of affection, as well as a little blush that hinted that she was, despite her teenage cool, happy to see me. I was happy to see her, too. She was the one person in my family I had truly uncomplicated feelings about, the one person I regretted not seeing regularly.

As we drove back to my cabin, I asked her perfunctory questions about life in the Valley—how was Mom, had she seen Dad lately, what was new with the grandparents, how was school going. She gave her usual monosyllabic answers: "fine," "good," "okay," "great," sometimes adding shades of nuance with a phrase like "not bad" or "pretty good." But I sensed something was not right. She seemed more distant than usual, more closed up, as if she was struggling to keep something locked inside of her.

For the next couple of days, I avoided Amy and hung out with my sister. It was a frigid, stormy weekend, but that didn't stop us from spending most of our time on the slopes at Heavenly Valley. I taught her to snowplow, to use her poles when she was setting up for a turn, and to keep her weight on her downhill ski. We spent a lot of silent time on the lifts dangling above granite crevasses, the wind howling around us, turning our cheeks and the tips of our noses pink. I was surprised by how strongly I felt for her and how much I had missed her. She seemed taken aback by the excessive attention I paid to her, my random hugs, my abundant praise for her smallest triumphs on skis, but I wanted to be sure she understood that just because I'd run to Tahoe didn't mean I'd stopped thinking affectionately of her as my little sis.

Eventually, Jill opened up about what was bugging her. Mostly it concerned my mother and her boyfriend, Michael. "Michael's a jerk," Jill explained. I didn't disagree. I'd met him once, briefly, at my mother's condo. Tall guy, red hair, red beard, nervous manner, at once slender and burly, like a lumberjack on a Slim-Fast diet. He was a salesman for a tool manufacturer—he drove around the Valley in a red van, hawking wrenches, sockets, and screwdrivers to professional mechanics. The day I met him, he was watching the NCAA Final Four on my mother's TV. He sat on my mother's couch, pumping his fist in the air whenever Louisville sunk a basket, refilling his wineglass during commercials. We had nothing to say to each other, which was not surprising, given that the whole idea that my mother was going out with this guy was not something I wanted to ponder. Neither did Jill. Divorce, okay, she could bend her mind around that. She could not bend her mind around the extra toothbrush in the bathroom, the whiskers in the sink, and the late-night whispers and giggles.

My inclination was to take my mother's side in all this. I admired her for throwing her cards in the air, for refusing to suffer in silence, for insisting on her own right to be happy. And in the aftermath of the divorce, she'd done very well for herself—particularly careerwise. She'd started as a secretary at Apple but was now taking classes in computer-aided design (CAD) and learning the exacting art of designing printed circuit boards. For a woman without a college degree, it was a brave and remarkable move—she'd gone from housewife to cutting-edge technologist in a few short years. Where else but the Valley would a transformation like this have been possible? Now she was in her early forties, making decent money and free, finally, of her suffocating marriage—free to kick up her heels, free to be the wild teenager she hadn't allowed herself to be more than twenty years ago, free to reimagine an entirely new life for herself.

So why was she going out with a loser like Michael?

Jill was glum about it all. She didn't know what to do, whom to talk to. I asked the questions, but I didn't really want to hear the answers. The only consolation I could offer was that I didn't think Mom would marry this guy—she wasn't that dumb.

The next morning, I put Jill back on the bus to the Bay Area. Hugging her before she left, a surprisingly deep wash of sadness broke over me. I felt like I was sending her back to the gulag.

5

Shortly after Jill's visit, I found myself wondering—usually at 4 A.M., when the casino was empty and you could almost hear the snow striking the tinted windows—if I'd judged my father too severely. Or, more accurately, if he deserved some sympathy and kindness, even if my judgment of him was correct. So he wussed out at the big moment. But hadn't I done the same thing? By fleeing to Tahoe, I was fleeing hard truths, too. And I began to feel bad about it—and about how I'd treated my father.

Reading about Apple's IPO didn't help. All right, so a few of the people I'd worked with were probably out shopping for mansions in the hills right now. Big deal. I still thought they were all clueless machine heads, even if they were now *rich*, clueless machine heads. But it did make me feel a pang of sympathy for my father. It's one thing for your wife to leave you; it's another for your wife to leave you and then start a promising career at the Valley's most talked-about company. There was no question she had hitched herself to the ascendant culture and was going nowhere but up. My father's career, in contrast, was going nowhere but down.

He had spent most of his adult life working for the landscape-contracting company that my mother's father had started in the early 1930s. My grandfather—whom we all called Pop—had done spectacularly well in the business and intended to hand it off to my father. Unfortunately, before he retired in 1969, Pop hit a short-term financial crisis that led him to make a spectacularly poor decision:

He sold a portion of the company to a young Stanford grad named Howard.

For the next decade, my father and Howard engaged in mortal combat. Howard was a pampered rich boy who drove a blue Corvette and knew nothing about how to plant a tree, but he was right about one thing: The glory days of California landscaping were over, killed off by, among other things, the decline in government funding of public-works projects. Howard wanted the company to get into the business of erecting the concrete tilt-up office buildings that are the hallmark of the Silicon Valley boom. My father wanted to stick with plants and shrubs and city parks. Howard screamed at my father, told him he had his head in the sand; my father screamed back, telling him he didn't know shit about the business. This screaming went on for years, until my father suddenly sold his stake of the company. I don't know how much he got for it, but I know it was not even enough to buy us a new car.

This hit all of us hard, but it hit my mother hardest. Her father had started the company with just a shovel and a wheelbarrow and built it into one of the best-known firms in the Bay Area. He had worked with famous landscape architects such as Thomas Church, who was responsible for the cool modernist look of many residential properties in the Bay Area, and Joe Eichler, an architect and builder whose sleek, glassy, Frank Lloyd Wright–inspired tract homes are now highly sought after by IPO millionaires. Pop had known many of Silicon Valley's early pioneers—he'd landscaped Dave Packard's home in Palo Alto back when Packard and his friend Bill Hewlett were building electronic instruments in their garage—and was widely respected as a man of the highest integrity. The company was his legacy; it bore his name and had been built with forty years of sweat and toil. For my father to blow it, to lose control, to hand it over to this arrogant young guy who drove a Corvette—that was pretty bad. To add to his humiliation, my father had difficulty finding another job and eventually joined a three-person landscaping firm for an embarrassingly low salary. How could my mother help but measure him against her father and find him wanting?

Still, it's one thing to pass judgment on a man; it's another to kick him when he's down. By the time my mother started to rise at Apple, it was clear to me that my father was reeling from the double whammy of losing his career and his family. Holding a grudge against him began to feel mean and ungrateful, especially given the powerful feelings I'd had for him when I was younger.

So when Father's Day rolled around in 1981, I decided, for perhaps the first time in my life, to be a good son. My father had often talked about riding a motorcycle across the country someday. I don't know where he got the idea—besides messing around in the dirt with a trail bike, he had never ridden a motorcycle in his life. I think he liked the freedom associated with a cross-country motorcycle trip; it was carefree and unconventional, emblematic of the kind of life he'd never led but must have dreamed about. I couldn't afford to buy him a motorcycle, but I did have a friend who was the sales manager at a motorcycle dealership in the Valley who would let me take two bikes for "a test drive."

On Father's Day, I picked my father up at 7 A.M. By that time, he and my mother had swapped living arrangements: He'd moved back into the house, while she took the condo. Both were happier that way. My father loved to spend his Saturday mornings cleaning leaves out of the gutters and weeding; my mother was happy to be free of the expense and obligation of maintaining a big home.

I didn't tell my father what I had planned—I just told him to dress in jeans and a warm coat. He was puzzled. "I think you should tell me what's going on," he insisted, but I could see that he was looking forward to the surprise.

When we arrived at the dealership, I unlocked the door to the service department with the key my friend had sent me and wheeled out two brand-new 750cc motorcycles, gleaming chrome, with candy apple–red gas tanks and fenders.

My father's face paled. "What's this?"

"We're going for a ride," I said.

We strapped on two borrowed helmets and rode out of the parking lot, with me in the lead. It was the first time I'd been on a motorcycle in several years, and I was looking forward to a fast and fun cruise over to the beach. My father put an end to that fantasy. Although he didn't say anything, he was clearly terrified. For the first five or six miles, he never accelerated above 30 MPH. Fortunately, there weren't many cars on the road. I dawdled, waiting for him, impatient, restless. I thought, this is his whole life: too cautious to have fun, too afraid for his life to live.

When we stopped for gas, I noticed that he was drenched in sweat. "You okay?"

"I'm a little shaky," he said. "But I'll get used to it."

When we got off the main roads and up into the coastal mountains, he began to feel more comfortable. The air smelled of fog and redwoods. Except for an occasional bicyclist, we had the road to ourselves. The yellow line twisted into grayness, a wandering path we leaned into and out of in a crude mechanical dance.

I was dying to twist the throttle and let it fly. I pushed harder into the turns, enjoying the lean, then slowed down when the road straightened out and waited for my father, who always appeared in my rearview mirror in the exact center of the lane, sitting ramrod straight, well away from the dangerous edge of acceleration and excitement.

We stopped at an overlook above Palo Alto. We bought cups of coffee and stale Danishes from a catering truck parked at a crossroads, then walked over to a large rock that gave us a view of the valley below. It looked like the palm of an enormous cupped hand. The fog was just beginning to burn off, and we sat there for maybe fifteen minutes, watching the indistinct rectangles of suburban houses emerge through the haze. If you looked closely, you could see the low, flat roofs of the chip factories and PC companies that were rising along the flatlands near the bay. Cars moved along Bayshore Freeway like electrons in a giant fiber-optic cable.

Out of nowhere, my father said, "I'm a failure, and I'm sorry."

He said this to the fog, his eyes trained on some indeterminate spot in the middle distance.

I wasn't sure I'd heard him correctly. My father had never made any kind of emotional confession to me before; his strategy had always been denial and optimism. "What?"

"I've failed you, I've failed your mother, your brother, your sister," he said, the words tumbling out. "I've failed myself. I never wanted things to work out this way. I just wanted to say, 'I'm sorry.' I just wanted you to know."

I was so stunned by this confession that I was unable to move. I'd never had a raw emotional exchange with another man—not my best friend, not my brother, and certainly not my father. Wasn't it a little unseemly—a little *unmanly*—to talk about oneself in this way?

Not surprisingly, I responded to his confession with my own brand of denial and optimism. I said, "You're not a failure. You're just going through a rough time. It'll work itself out."

That's all I remember of the conversation. It did not last much longer. My father probably expressed regret at the pain the divorce had caused for me and Jerry and Jill; I probably assured him we would be fine, that we knew both he and my mother still loved us, and so on. Those words sounded as hollow then as they do now. But I had no other language in which to respond; I didn't know how to reach over and take his hand or simply tell him that I forgave him. He had taught me how to cast a fishing lure, how to pee into a toilet, and how to pound a nail, but he had not taught me how to speak from the heart.

So I left him dangling there, his guts wide open for the crows to pick at. He must have sensed my discomfort, because he didn't push the discussion any further. We said nothing to each other for a few moments. Then the sun came out, and we slipped on our helmets and rode down the mountain toward the ocean.

6

I'm sure my father was as surprised as I was to hear the word *failure* slip out of his mouth. It wasn't that the idea was unfamiliar to him—on the contrary, he knew the smell, texture, and color of failure as well as anyone. He'd grown up with it, but he had also once believed that he'd beaten it. Until everything started to fall apart, my father had thought of himself as a man who had been dealt a lousy hand in life but who through savvy card playing and plain good luck had ended up with a full house. This triumph had turned him into a hopeful man, a person who believed fate could be wrestled to the ground, who loved living in a place called Sunnyvale because it matched his own bright sense that if you live right and work hard, you will live happily ever after.

My father was born in 1936 in Clarendon Hills, Illinois, the second of three boys. He never spoke of his childhood with much warmth or affection, which is not surprising, given the chilly character of his parents—especially his father, Leonard, a stern New England Yankee and engineering genius. Leonard's grandfather and great-grandfather had been prominent Methodist preachers in Connecticut, and as they defined themselves as men of faith, Leonard defined himself as a man of numbers. He studied electrical engineering at Brown University, then went to work designing coils and transformers at Westinghouse when he was in his early twenties. He was tall, cocky, and extremely hardworking, a man whose every gesture said, "I'm Brilliant, I'm Important, I Understand the Mechanics of the Universe, and I Will Bestow My Knowledge Upon Ye."

My father's mother, Edie, revolved around Leonard like a distant moon. She was a short, blue-eyed woman from Newfoundland who had a big laugh but whose essential character was about as warm as the North Atlantic in December. Judging from the way my father talked about her, and from what I saw of their relationship in later years, she was a fine mom—dutiful and disciplined and always busy preparing meals and doing laundry. She was not, however, a mother who was very attuned to—or interested in—the emotional lives of her sons.

By all accounts, my father was a troubled kid. He was fat, for one thing. It wasn't that he ate more than his brothers or was profoundly lazy—his body just seemed marvelously, disturbingly efficient at transforming every calorie he consumed into blubber. His porkiness led to self-consciousness, which led to diffidence, which led to painful memories of being called "Fat Boy" by all the kids in the neighborhood.

Of Leonard's three sons, my father was the one who needed him most. By the time my father was five, however, the war was imminent, and Leonard had been put in charge of Westinghouse's entire Chicago operations. He became deeply involved in building electrical components for the military—turbines for submarines, electronic missile-launch equipment, generators for the merchant marine. He worked with Enrico Fermi, the brilliant Italian physicist, on designing and building one of the world's first cyclotrons—the atom-smashing device that eventually led to the construction of the nuclear bomb. He also met with military brass on a regular basis, flying to and from Washington several times a month. There was no time for help with homework, or playing ball in the street, or discussions with his middle son about how it felt to be the fattest kid in the class.

Leonard wasn't entirely hard-hearted, however. When he learned that his secretary, Elaine, often ate dinner alone in her apartment, he began inviting her over to eat with him and his family in Clarendon Hills. As he explained to Edie, "She's a single woman, and you know how tough it is to be single in a big city like this. I think she gets lonely."

Edie was happy to have her, and so were the boys. Elaine was a short, busty woman with a throaty voice that reminded my father of Marlene Dietrich, and eyes so blue and brilliant you wanted to pop them out and mount them on a ring. The daughter of Irish immigrants, she'd been born and raised in a rough neighborhood on the South Side of Chicago, and there was still something of the same street-smart city girl in Elaine. She sat at the big table with the family and talked with Edie about how she wanted kids of her own someday, and Edie shared recipes with her, and the boys gawked at her legs, which she liked to show off with skirts carefully chosen to draw attention to her muscular calves and nice ankles. She smoked, too, which was a thrilling sin for a woman to commit in the Goodell household. Edie never touched cigarettes or liquor.

The dinner invitations went on for several months, until Elaine was almost like one of the family. Taking her in felt like a small good deed, like giving shelter to a stray puppy. Everyone assumed that one day she would find a man and start her own life.

Then one weekend Leonard decided to take the family camping on Lake Michigan. They loaded up the car, drove an hour or so north to a quiet spot along the shore. They spent a few hours setting up the tent and rolling out their sleeping bags, then my father's older brother, Bob, went off for a hike along the sand dunes.

When Bob returned, he looked puzzled. "Hey Ma, what's Elaine doing here?"

Edie frowned. "What are you talking about?"

"Elaine—you know, Dad's friend. What is she doing at the beach?"

"I still don't know what you're talking about."

"I saw her sitting over there at a picnic table." Bob pointed a few campsites over. "She was all by herself. Like she was waiting for someone. What's up?"

Edie understood immediately that there was no innocent explanation for this, and her face blazed with fury. She grabbed Leonard and literally dragged him off into the woods. That must have been a sight, given that she was about a foot and a half shorter than he was. She didn't say anything to Leonard until they were almost out of earshot of the kids. Then she let him have it. My father heard her voice echoing in the trees. He couldn't make out the words, but he didn't need to.

A half hour later, they returned. "He looked like a beaten man," my father said of his father.

Leonard reformed. He became a better husband and dad. He worked less and was home with the boys more. He spent hours in the garage helping Bob rebuild a car engine, and Richard, the youngest, remembered the family attending at least one Cubs game. For my father, who felt like he had grown up until then without a father, those were good times.

Elaine, of course, was never seen in the house again.

One night, Leonard came home from work with big news: Westinghouse wanted him to move to the West Coast, where he would become regional manager. It was a big promotion for him, one he was eager to accept. "It'll be a new beginning," he told his family.

Edie and the boys weren't so sure. Leonard's treachery aside, they were happy with their lives in Clarendon Hills. They lived in a comfortable two-story brick house on a quiet, leafy suburban street. Edie had dug a large vegetable garden in the backyard and had worked hard repainting all the bedrooms. "I'd never been to California and had no particular curiosity about it," Edie told me years later. But the more she thought about it, the more appealing the idea became. It would, after all, put two thousand miles between Elaine and the family. And if you didn't have trust, maybe distance was the next best thing.

The family arrived in the Bay Area in the summer of 1950. Leonard had been out on a house-hunting trip a few weeks earlier and had found them a nice shingle-style house in Palo Alto, about a mile from the yellow sandstone gates of Stanford University.

SUNNYVALE

For my father, the move was wrenching. He was not the sort of kid who made friends easily, and his first few weeks at Palo Alto High School taught him that there were a lot of rich kids in those hills above Stanford, and none of them was too interested in a fat boy from Illinois.

Leonard immediately plunged into work. He was responsible for all five Westinghouse plants on the West Coast now—a big job. If he was home for dinner two nights a week, that was a lot. Often he traveled with a small suitcase packed with enough clothes for several days, all white shirts and dark suits.

Several months passed. The moving boxes were finally unpacked, the clothes put away. But something was wrong. Once, my father caught his mother crying in the kitchen. When he asked her what had happened, she said, "It's nothing."

A few weeks later, my father walked by his parents' bedroom and saw Leonard packing a suitcase. My father noticed it was a larger suitcase than usual. "Hey Dad—you taking a long trip?"

Leonard did not look up at his son. "Your mother and I are getting a divorce," he said, and then he closed the suitcase and walked out the front door.

It turned out, of course, that when Leonard had spoken about a new beginning in California, he was talking about his life with Elaine. She was waiting for him in the car at the curb.

7

Of Leonard's three boys, my father was hit hardest by the betrayal. Years later, I heard the pain in his voice whenever he talked about Leonard. I see it now in the pictures of him, age fifteen, standing on the lawn in front of the house in Palo Alto, a fat kid with his thumbs hooked in the pockets of his jeans, his head tilted to the side, his fine gold hair combed nicely but his eyes dulled with a kind of sweet, stunned glaze.

He graduated from Palo Alto High School in 1954. In his senior-class yearbook, there are exactly two autographs. One reads, "To the biggest chug-a-lug on campus. Good luck. Tom Jennings." The other is simply a name: "Ronnie Samuels." His future looked bleak. Because of his weight problem, he was 4-F from the military. He wanted to go to college, but his grades were low and his confidence lower. Besides, there was no money for that—Edie couldn't help, and Leonard wouldn't.

By this time, not only was my father fat but his skin had turned a sickly white, and he hardly got off the couch anymore. Edie finally took him to a doctor for a checkup, who referred them to a specialist, Dr. Walsh at Stanford Medical Center. After many tests, Dr. Walsh determined that my father was suffering from Cushing's syndrome, a rare and serious disease that involves tumors on the adrenal glands and interferes with the body's metabolism, causing severe weight gain, bruising, sleepiness, and other problems. My father was fat not because he was a sloth but because he was sick.

For my father, this was good news because it gave him a reason for his grotesque physical form; it was bad news because the only remedy was an extremely difficult and dangerous surgical procedure. Without surgery, the tumors would continue to grow, the metabolic dysfunction of my father's adrenal glands would increase, he would get fatter, and his muscles would continue to waste away. Eventually, his heart would give out, or his lungs would be overrun by pneumonia, and he would die. There was no other scenario.

But surgery was almost as perilous. The adrenal glands are buried deep between the lungs and the kidneys; the best approach is through the back, just below the rib cage. Even today, adrenal surgery is considered a complex, risky procedure; in 1955, it was almost unheard-of. Dr. Walsh explained that this highly experimental operation had been performed only eleven times in the United States; in five cases, the patients died on the operating table. One died shortly after. Five survived and, after long and difficult recoveries, went on to lead fairly normal lives—albeit without adrenal glands. And it just happened that Stanford Medical Center, which was five blocks from the Goodell house, was where two of those successful operations had been performed—and by Dr. Walsh, no less.

In effect, my father was being offered the chance to be a surgical guinea pig. In exchange, Dr. Walsh offered him a fifty-fifty chance at a new life. For my father, it was not even a close call.

Surgery lasted seven hours. Dr. Walsh made two footlong incisions in my father's back, on either side of his vertebrae, severing the thick muscles that support the spinal column, then using a small bone saw to remove two ribs on each side. The tumors were the size of lemons.

Recovery was long and brutal, but my father pulled through. Photos of him before the operation are like a cartoon flip book: fat, fatter, fattest . . . then bang, after the surgery, he's seventy pounds thinner. In those early photos, he just looks sick and wasted. But then you can see something coming alive in him, and even in old black-and-white pictures his eyes burn through the paper, and you can see a new man emerging. He grows muscular and strong looking. The fat melts out of his cheeks; his face is lean and angular. He becomes handsome. His chin drifts upward, a gesture that marks his increasing confidence. He gets a stylish flattop and begins to appear in a coat and tie, as if he were perpetually heading out on a date.

What my father did not know then, and what I have come to understand only recently, was that the surgery that saved his life also left him invisibly crippled. Without adrenal glands, his body could not produce adrenaline. No wonder he later seemed so maladapted to the world he lived in. Without adrenaline, he literally lacked the fuel that made Silicon Valley fly.

In February of 1958, my father went on a blind date with an eighteen-year-old girl named Arlene Schromm. I don't know what my father was expecting, but as soon as he laid eyes on her—my mother was not only beautiful, she was darkly, mysteriously beautiful, with big secretive eyes—he must have known that he'd hit the jackpot. My mother, too, was wowed. Years later, she told me that the first word that popped into her head when she saw my father was *handsome*.

They played charades with friends and went out for burgers. There were a lot of shy smiles and polite small talk. He asked her out the following weekend, and the one after that, and they began a brief, giddy, fifties kind of affair: dinner at the Blue Fox in San Francisco, Kingston Trio records, cruising in my father's cherry '54 Buick.

My father's feelings for my mother were strong and simple from the very beginning. I'm sure that ten minutes after he met her, he started thinking about when and where to propose. For my mother, it was more complicated. Their dates were fun, and she liked that my father opened the car door for her and pulled out her chair in the restaurant, and she liked the way he looked at her with his dizzying green eyes when she spoke. But nothing about him said This Is The One.

There was also the problem of my father's habit of dozing off during movies. Unlike people with functioning adrenal glands, he had nothing in his system to keep him perked up when the lights went down, but my mother didn't know that. She just thought he was working too hard. Or bored.

Though my mother's initial infatuation with my father started to wear thin, she nevertheless had a hard time saying no to him. Independence was not a highly valued commodity in her world; propriety was. The idea that she would tell a decent and well-intentioned guy like my father to buzz off was unthinkable. Plus, her family loved him—especially her father, Pop.

In my father, Pop saw an earnest, hardworking young guy who was crazy about his oldest daughter. Pop was not very interested in whether my father was rich or poor or in why he hadn't gone to college. What was important to him was that when he looked at my father, he saw a man who was alive with enthusiasm and gratitude, who had a second shot at life and was determined not to blow it.

For his part, my father was taken by Pop's warmth and gentle wisdom. Sure, Pop was a very successful man, but unlike Leonard, who thrived on mental jousting, whose goal in life was to demonstrate that he was smarter than everyone he met, Pop was a cowboy at heart, and like all cowboys he cared most about the people he shared his campfire with. Pop had been born in a sod hut in Valentine, Nebraska, and, perhaps because of that, was connected to the world in a very unmodern way: He could look at a horse's ears and tell you if it was healthy or sick, broken or wild, and he could glance at a dying tree and tell you exactly what nutrients were lacking in the soil.

When my father came over for dinner, Pop sat at the head of the table—his wife and his three kids on both sides, wearing his well-worn cowboy boots and big silver belt buckle—and told stories about rolling across Nebraska and Colorado in a covered wagon, and about the log cabin he and his father and brothers had built in the Canadian wilderness, and about picking prunes in San Jose when he was a teenager. And when my father saw how much Arlene loved her father and how warm he was to her and how Pop sparked up a Macanudo after dinner and was in no hurry to go anywhere, how he in fact seemed perfectly content, with the dirty dinner plates all around him, in the midst of the chaos of family life, telling stories about the American West . . . well, my father knew exactly what kind of man he wanted to be.

———

My mother and father met on February 15, 1958; by April 24, they were standing at the base of Vernal Falls in Yosemite Valley. My father, so nervous he was shaking, pulled a ring out of his pocket and dropped down on his knees and said, "Will you marry me?"

Why did he move so fast? Because he was young, eager, and in love. I also think he was scared. A part of him must have been afraid the midnight bells would chime and he'd be transformed back into the Fat Boy and my mother would run for the hills.

It was different for my mother. She knew the question was coming, and when it came she was both terrified and thrilled. She was right to be terrified: She was just a year out of high school. She'd never lived alone, never traveled any farther from home than the Oregon border. She knew nothing about life or about her own mind, much less about the kind of man she should marry. She had come of age at the tail end of the fifties, in those twisted, repressive years when the most likely future for a woman like my mother was a Betty Crocker fantasy of marriage and babies and tuna casserole. Had she been born fifteen years later, she might have headed straight to college. Instead, she dreamed of becoming an airline stewardess.

Other, more adventurous women were already breaking ranks. Joan Baez was one year behind my mother at Palo Alto High School. My mother remembers her carrying her guitar to class and sitting cross-legged out on the grass behind the school, her dark hair falling in front of her face as she sang.

Another acquaintance at Palo Alto High was Grace Wing. In her yearbooks, Grace has long brown hair and a fresh-faced wholesomeness that gives not the slightest hint of what was to come. She's dressed like all the other girls: modest skirt, sweater, saddle shoes. In one sophomore-class picture, Grace is standing beside my mother. They have the same fifteen-year-old brightness about them, the same innocence and anticipation. Looking at them, a stranger could never pick out which one was to go on to become a housewife in Sunnyvale and which was to become famous as Grace Slick, the lead singer in Jefferson Airplane.

My mother did not have rock-'n'-roll in her heart, however. Standing at Yosemite on that sharp April afternoon, with Vernal Falls thundering behind them, throwing a glittering mist into the air, she made her choice. She looked into my father's eyes and said, "Yes."

The wedding was set for the end of August—only four months away. Whatever second thoughts my mother might have had were pushed aside in the rush to order flowers and pick out a gown.

Then, on the morning of her wedding shower, she answered the phone and heard a voice that almost knocked her off her feet.

"Hello, Arlene?"

"Yes."

"This is Bob Schultz."

Bob Schultz was in the class of '54 at Palo Alto High, the same class as my father. Whereas my father had been a fat, friendless, lost soul during high school, Bob had been a jock. He had been on the wrestling team and had played varsity basketball.

My mother had met Bob during her senior year. They went out on four or five dates and were just getting to know each other when he shipped off to the navy. They wrote back and forth for a few months, sharing news and making plans for when he returned, but to my mother, who was only seventeen, that always seemed a long way off. Eventually the letter writing slowed, then stopped. By the time she started going out with my father, she hadn't heard from Bob in several months and just assumed he had met another girl.

"I'm home," Bob said happily. "I just got released from the navy. Can I stop by and see you?"

"Um . . . sure," my mother said, her heart thumping madly in her chest. "But there's something I need to tell you first. . . . I'm engaged."

There was a long silence.

"It's not a sure thing," my mother added nervously, not able to help herself. "Maybe you should come by, and I'll explain it all to you."

Bob took my mother out for a Coke in downtown Palo Alto. My mother told him—this was the first time she'd said this to anyone—that she wasn't sure she was doing the right thing in marrying my father. Especially now. Bob was a perfect gentleman about it and told her that he would respect whatever decision she made.

When my mother returned home a few hours later, she boldly announced to her mother she wanted to postpone the wedding. It wasn't that she didn't love my father, she explained, she just wasn't sure.

My mother's mother, whose name was Muriel but whom I always called Nan, was not happy to hear this. Nan was a warm, witty, good-humored woman with pale blue eyes and a girlish laugh that masked the hard drama of her early life. She'd been born into a poor family in San Jose, then given up for adoption, after her mother died, when she was six years old. Her stepmother had been harsh and cruel, beating her with a stick whenever she misbehaved; perhaps not surprisingly, as a child, Nan often dreamed of running away and becoming a Ziegfeld girl and marrying a rich man.

She and Pop never became rich exactly, but they did become quite prosperous and respectable. They had owned a nice ranch in Portola Valley, which was then, as now, where what Nan called "the well-to-do people" lived. Nan was president of her local sorority chapter and loved to pull on long, white gloves and attend fancy holiday parties. She was crushed when, a year or so before my mother met my father, Pop's business took a downturn and they had to sell their ranch and move to the flats of Palo Alto. For Nan, it was a social embarrassment. She did not want any more embarrassments.

My mother went into the bathroom and drew a bath. Before long, she heard footsteps, then a knock on the door.

"Arlene?" Nan called through the door.

"Yes?"

"I want to talk to you."

My mother slipped deeper into the water as her mother entered. She saw that closed-up look on Nan's face, and she knew exactly what it meant. "You cannot cancel the wedding," Nan told her. "We have a house full of women arriving in two hours for your shower, and I'm not going to tell them that the wedding is off and that they should all go home. By tomorrow morning, the whole town will be talking about us, and I just won't have it."

My mother covered her face in her hands and burst into tears.

On Sunday, August 24, 1958, a crowd of about 235 invited guests witnessed my mother and father take their vows at the First Methodist Church in Palo Alto. My father never knew about Bob Schultz or the crying in the bathroom or his bride's second thoughts. By the time her wedding day arrived, my mother told me years later, she had no regrets. My father certainly had none. In photos, his beaming face radiates excitement and joy. The fat kid who never thought he'd have a chance at romance had scored big, and he knew it. As he said to me years later, "I felt like the luckiest guy in the world."

8

When Amy stopped greeting me with her usual "Mornin', fuck-head," I started to worry. To make matters worse, I noticed her star-ing at me from the other side of the casino and scheduling her breaks so that we could have coffee together in the cafeteria. After work, she often waited for me in the parking lot, her nose glowing in the cold morning air, looking all too eager and expectant. Before long, she started writing me love poems. Well, not love poems, ex-actly, more like dopey rhyming couplets and sarcastic haiku. She scribbled them on napkins with a felt-tip pen then dropped them on the table where I was dealing as she scooted by with a tray of drinks. She also drew sexually explicit cartoons, featuring enormous penises and breasts. She'd drop a napkin on the table just as I was tossing a round of cards, and I'd have to snatch it up before one of the pit bosses saw it and sent us both home with a spanking.

One evening, I ran into her in the parking lot before our shift. She told me that she wouldn't be able to see me after work because her boyfriend had just gotten home from a three-week road trip and needed, as she put it, "some attention." She always spoke about him with respect and consideration, which, in her mind, never conflicted with the fact that she was screwing around on him. I presumed he was screwing around on her, too, and that they had worked out—to use the phrase that was popular in Tahoe—"an understanding."

Then she said, softly, coolly, "He's starting to bring up the *m* word again."

"What's that?"

"Marriage," she announced.

"What did you say?"

"I've decided he's a stupid fuck," she said sweetly. "He sells toaster ovens. I like you better."

That's when I knew I was in trouble. I tried to talk to Amy about the feelings I suspected she was having for me, but without luck. I'd say dumb things like, "The beautiful thing about our relationship is that it's so here and now"; or "I think love is an old-fashioned idea." She never disagreed. Still, that sparkle in her eye persisted, and it scared the hell out of me.

I know precisely the moment I made my decision to leave Tahoe. I had lied to Amy, telling her I was going to play volleyball with my friend Lance; instead, I was sitting at the Horseshoe Bar at Harrah's with a craps dealer named Lorraine. It was a Sunday morning, about 10 A.M., and each of us had already had two Bloody Marys, and I was thinking that things were moving in the right direction. Lorraine had lived in Tahoe for years and was known, unofficially, as the Queen of the Craps Dealers. She earned this title because she had been around so long, because she knew everyone, and because she wielded the croupier with a sexual panache that drew men to her as if it were Spanish fly. I had been chasing her for weeks, asking friends about her, small-talking her in the cafeteria. She was ten years older than me and seemed amused by my giddy attraction to her. Beyond her talent with the croupier, I can't say exactly why I was so captivated by Lorraine. There was nothing remarkable about her appearance—she was tall and athletic looking and had a deeply tanned face and long, straight brown hair. Her most interesting feature was her eyes, soft, brown lumbering animals that moved slowly and deliberately and radiated thoughtfulness, even wisdom.

As we talked at the bar that morning, I learned that her eyes lied. She was not thoughtful, just dull. She had once wanted to be an actress, but that hadn't worked out. She had thought about going into nursing, but that hadn't worked out either. Neither had her first marriage, to a pit boss, nor her second, to a real-estate agent. Now she made two hundred dollars a night at the craps table and spent her summer mornings learning to sail on her roommate's Hobie Cat.

"I only sail on nice days," she explained earnestly. "If a big wind kicks up, I head in. Why take the risk, you know? I'm not training for the America's Cup. I just want to have fun."

I knew that if I stuck around, she might invite me back to the house she shared with a cocktail waitress and a keno runner, where there would be nylons hanging over the chairs in the kitchen and a pile of unwashed dishes in the sink, and we would go out to the garage and have a look at her roommate's Hobie Cat, and then one thing would lead to another, and we would end up in her room doing something that approximated sex. And when it was over, I would lie back and stare at the ceiling and wonder why I was lying to Amy for this, why I was cheating on a girl I didn't even love, with a woman who had long since given up whatever modest dreams she'd once had.

And as I sat there chatting with Lorraine about the Hobie Cat, I felt myself sinking like an anchor. I thought, This is what my big adventure in Tahoe has come to. Compared to Lorraine, Amy was a Nobel laureate, a stand-up comic, a rocket ship of ambition, a Mother Teresa of sympathy and kindness. Lorraine seemed to me the final expression of what too many years in Tahoe could do to you, the way all that fun in the sun, all that freedom, all that twenty-four-hour-a-day neon-lit pleasure numbs you and hollows you out and leaves you with nothing but a slippery grip on a Hobie Cat.

And the worst of it was, I understood that after a few more months, a few more lies, I'd be just like her: unattached, nicely tanned, sailing only on nice days. I could just keep following the roulette wheel around and around, transfixed by the sound of the little steel ball whirling against the hardwood, and by the time it stopped I wouldn't care where it landed, red or black or double zero. I thought about my father and his confession on the mountain and wondered if failure was an inheritable disease, passed from generation to generation, hidden in a strand of DNA.

It was somewhere in the middle of this funk, between Bloody Marys three and four, that I saw my old friend Hao on the far side of the casino. I had not talked with him for over a year, since I'd quit my job washing dishes and moved on to bigger things. He looked exactly the same as I remembered—black hair falling across his eyes, full of nervous energy—except that he was not wearing his lasagna-splattered kitchen whites. He was dressed in black polyester pants and clean sneakers and a red nylon windbreaker. I presumed he had worked a few extra hours this morning and had just ended his shift—he was making a beeline for the back door.

I watched him go. He did not notice me. He did not leer at the roulette table. He did not turn his head when a jackpot bell went off. He walked like a man with a purpose. He walked like a man who believed that time was precious, who understood that actions have consequences and that there is a difference between right and wrong. His whole life was about one thing: saving enough money so that he could bring his family to America. And because of that, I understood in some fuzzy way that has become clear only over the years, his life had everything that mine didn't: purpose, meaning, context, faith.

That's when I decided I had to get out. I wanted Hao's life, not Lorraine's. It was a moral judgment, not a practical one, and I made it in a snap.

I paid the bar tab and said good-bye, leaving Lorraine more offended than disappointed. When I got back to my cabin, I called the admissions office at the University of California at Berkeley and asked them to send me an application for the upcoming quarter. It was a random act of desperation, unpremeditated, the only antidote I could think of for all those long nights in the casino.

I typed my admissions essay in my backyard on a sunny day, sitting in a lawn chair with the typewriter I'd once hocked. I called it "My Friend Hao"—it was a two-page, poorly punctuated account of our nights washing dishes together at Harrah's. When I was finished, I dropped the application into the mailbox with the same mix of arrogance and prayer that I saw on the faces of 4 A.M. drunks when they hit on a soft thirteen.

Six weeks later, a thin envelope from UC Berkeley appeared in my box at the South Tahoe post office. I knew before I opened it that I'd drawn a hot card.

———————

It took me a few days to break the news to Amy. "Fucking-a, who did you pay off?" she joked, but then she got a little teary eyed. When I talked about apartment hunting in Berkeley, I knew she was waiting to hear if I was looking for a studio or a one-bedroom. When I talked about how I was going to support myself, I could see that she was thinking it would be easier to pay the rent if there were two of us. But I never offered to take her along, and she never asked to go. For her, it was a point of honor, a silence borne out of dignity and pride.

I knew how much she wanted to come. I had crossed a line that she, too, desperately wanted to cross. She wanted to go over the Berlin Wall with me, to hitch a ride into a better world. I think she knew she wasn't going to get many shots at it: Her boyfriend the appliance salesman wasn't going anywhere; she didn't have the education or ambition to build a career for herself; there was no family inheritance coming down the road, no trust fund to steal from. Sure, people overcome far more daunting hurdles than the ones Amy faced, but for some reason she didn't have it in her to go it alone. She needed help, and she understood that I could give it to her. She knew as well as I did that for all my cocaine snorting and recklessness, I was better off than she was. Among other things, I had a father who drove up to rescue me in a snowstorm, a mother who cooked me dinner any time I stopped by, a sister whom I wanted to save from her troubles, and a brother whom I hadn't seen in too long. I had been loved and was loved, even if the people who loved me were a fractured mess.

Amy had none of that. She was weightless, bound by nothing, deeply alone, an angel in the void. She needed me.

But I never really considered taking her along. Instead, I slipped away as smoothly and as quickly as I could, telling her that we'd keep in touch, that she should come down to visit me at Berkeley,

yeah, sure, any time, it's only a four-hour drive, and then I took off
in my saggy VW with my clothes in the backseat and my typewriter
in the passenger seat beside me like a tired old dog.

I knew no one at Berkeley and was deeply unsure of my place in this
new world. Amy called several times to see if I was settled, we talked
for a few hours, and the next thing I knew she was driving down for
the weekend. We went through the motions of maintaining the same
frolicky relationship we'd had in Tahoe, but it was clear immediately that everything had changed.

For one thing, I no longer had idle hours to waste. My first
months at Berkeley were brutal. I studied three or four hours a
night—by my standards a tremendous effort—and by the end of the
third week I was hopelessly behind anyway.

When Amy visited, she tried to be helpful—she cooked and sat
quietly in the bedroom for hours while I read or typed an essay, but
it was no use. She'd eventually get bored and want to play and I'd
say, "Sorry, I've got too much work to do." Then she'd get pouty
and vanish back to Tahoe for a week or so. She'd return, bearing
flowers and take-out Chinese food. I didn't have the guts to tell her
to get lost; instead, I'd offer her coffee, talk with her, and eat the
food she brought, but I stopped sleeping with her. When she raised
her skirt or rubbed my thigh, I said, "I can't do this any more,
Amy," and moved to the other side of the room and opened a book.
An echoing canyon of bad feeling and resentment opened between
us. She often left in a fury, slamming the door. Other times she left
in tears: "Adios, Mr. College Boy. I don't need you."

I began staying at the library until late at night, reading Milton
and Chaucer in the stacks. I didn't want to go to my apartment because I didn't want to be there when Amy knocked on the door. I felt
cowardly and weak, slinking around this way, but I was desperate. I
believed strongly that I had a choice to make, that it was Amy or
Berkeley—I could manage one or the other but not both. I was on the
verge of falling hopelessly behind in my first semester, failing classes,
dropping out, ending up back in Tahoe, flipping cards on green felt.

I did not want that to happen. If nothing else, my father's confession that he felt like a failure had galvanized my ambition. Whatever else happened to me in my life, I did not want to end up like him.

One night on the phone, I tried to explain this to Amy. She understood instantly. "So this is the big heave-ho, right? You're telling me not to bother coming down to visit, not to call, just forget you ever existed, right?"

"Exactly," I said, holding nothing back.

"Thank you for your frankness, honey," she said and slammed down the phone. I felt not sadness, not regret, but relief. Now it was over.

Or so I thought. A week or so later, I was awakened from my sleep by a pounding at the door. I jumped up, thinking *fire*. Then I heard Amy's voice—"Hello? Hello? Anybody home?" Without turning on the light, I tiptoed to the door. I could see, even through the distorting peephole lens, that she looked bad—hair flattened out and dull, glistening eyes, accusing lips.

"Open up, please. I just want to talk to you."

Silence. Through the door, I heard her breathing—short, quick pants, punctuated by occasional sighs.

"I know you're in there," she said. She pounded on the door. I looked at the clock on my desk: 3:45 A.M. My toes curled off the cold wood floor.

"Don't make me beg," she said. "I just want you to open the door so I can talk to you. Five minutes. You don't have to fuck me. I don't even want to fuck you. I'm not interested. I just want to talk, okay?"

Longer silence. I felt like I was watching her drown, seeing her sinking away below the waves and doing nothing to help her. I knew that she was suffering for my selfishness as well as her own, but this was as far as I was going to go.

Amy began to sob. A moment later, her footsteps retreated down the hallway and out of my life.

9

At Berkeley, I got myself a proper girlfriend. Her name was Karisa, and she was so unlike Amy that she was practically a different species. Karisa was a solid citizen, raised in the church, groomed for success. She was tall and beautiful in a midwestern farm girl sort of way, with flawless skin and high, exquisite cheekbones, but she had no respect for her beauty and wanted to be loved for her brains alone. She had been valedictorian at her Sacramento high school, as well as class president and treasurer; in her senior yearbook, she was voted most likely to become a millionaire. She could trace her family back through four generations of South Dakota wheat farmers—a lineage as stable and solid as mine was fragmented and explosive. Her father was a math teacher at a Sacramento high school and leader in the Presbyterian church; her mother, a quiet, docile woman, taught grammar school and stitched quilts. Karisa thought they were both hypocrites but loved them anyway.

I met Karisa in a Marcel Proust seminar and was immediately taken by her cheekbones and professionalism. She managed her study time efficiently, kept class notes organized rigorously in color-coded binders, never overslept, and never wrote an essay that was less than very good. She was not joyless, nor was she a prude, but she did not have an irresponsible bone in her body. When there was work to be done, she might complain about it, but she did it, cleanly and efficiently. To her, life was a task that needed to be well managed. While these might sound like fantastically dull qualities in a twenty-one-year-old woman, in fact she was a wonder to me, simply because I was so clearly her opposite: disorganized, a slow reader, grammatically an idiot, and either unjustifiably arrogant in my opinions or perversely shy.

Unlike me, Karisa didn't have many friends whose parents had been divorced and could never completely shake the idea that I came from inferior stock because my parents had broken the vows they had taken at the altar twenty years earlier. Karisa was too discreet to ever say this explicitly, but I could see it in the look of disdain that sometimes crossed her face when I talked about the recent troubles in my family.

Nevertheless, Karisa and my father got along fairly well: She was sympathetic to his sad-sack eyes, and he was interested in her long legs. He was flirty with her. She usually hated flirtiness in men—she thought it disrespectful, a boorish male trait that degraded women and destabilized the hard-won balance of power between the sexes. But for some reason, when my father winked at her and told her how great she looked in a summer dress, she took it as a gesture of affection. I think she liked my father because, for all his problems, he radiated warmth and bigheartedness, which were precisely the two qualities her own father lacked.

Karisa never knew what to say to my mother, but she tried very hard to be pals with my sister—too hard, in fact. After I arrived at Berkeley, I did my best to reconnect with Jill and frequently invited her to come up and stay with me on weekends. Often, Karisa joined us for dinner or a movie. Karisa tried to be sweet and chummy with her, asking her about school and movies and her plans for the future, and my sister would stare at her with eyes that said, *Who does this prom queen think she is?* Jill hated her efficiency, her cheekbones, her girly chatter. Once, in a phone conversation, Jill snidely referred to "that Barbie-doll girlfriend of yours."

As for my brother, Jerry, well, to Karisa he could have been a poster boy for her ideas about What Divorce Does To Children. Not that she ever brimmed over with sympathy for him. For Karisa, the antidote to the emptiness of her suburban California roots was good books and fine wine; for Jerry, it was Aerosmith and a sixer of

Heineken. In the three years since the split, he'd turned from a shy, gentle teenager into a tough-assed young man. After high school, he'd attended junior college for a few semesters—he was a straight-A student—but gave it up to pursue his dream of becoming a professional musician. At the moment, he was a drummer in a garage band called Asylum, which played at high-school dances and private parties all over the Valley. Like most garage bands, Asylum was perpetually one cut away from a major deal with a minor label. Jerry had the rock-'n'-roll thing in spades: He ripped the sleeves off his T-shirts, brought a different girl home to my father's house every weekend, and often made brash pronouncements such as, "I'm either a genius or an idiot. My goal in life is to figure out which."

Karisa first met Jerry on a hot summer night at a club in Berkeley. As soon as Karisa and I walked in, I saw Jerry standing near the stage, a Coors in hand, dressed in shorts and a T-shirt, deeply engaged in conversation with a cocaine-thin woman with a ring in her nose and a tattoo on her shoulder.

As Karisa and I walked over to him, the woman Jerry was talking to melted away. "Hey, bro," he said when he saw us coming. "Glad you could make it."

Jerry immediately shifted his eyes to Karisa, who looked positively milk fed in this crowd. "I'm Jerry," he said smoothly, then extended his hand.

"Nice to meet you," Karisa said, shaking it.

Jerry gave Karisa the look—ass, breasts, lips—like he was taking sexual inventory. Then he wiggled his left eyebrow and nodded at me, a gesture that said, "She'll do."

I'd seen Jerry do this many times before, and I knew it was a joke, a caricature of himself as a hot, swinging dude. Karisa, however, didn't see it that way. She gave him an icy, drop-dead stare. Jerry held her eye for an instant, then let loose a big, devilish laugh that suggested that you had to be a real fool to take life too seriously.

On the way home that night, I launched into my standard defense of my brother's character. "Reserve judgment," I told her. When he's sober, I explained, he's charming, witty, gentle. I explained that his rock-'n'-roll sex-stud routine was just a mask for a more sensitive soul within. I told her that Jerry had read *War and Peace* when he was fifteen, and that in his celestial rankings the only person who scored higher than Mick Jagger was Charles Dickens.

I also told her about the time I'd crashed on my minibike in the middle of the wilderness, tearing a deep gash in my lower left leg. Jerry, age ten, had had the presence of mind to ride the four miles back to the cabin where we were staying and fetch our parents. "He might have saved my life," I said to Karisa, exaggerating only slightly.

"Big fucking deal," Karisa huffed. "He has a lot to learn about how to treat women."

"Lighten up, will you? It was a *joke*," I explained. "He thought he was being funny."

"I didn't think it was funny."

"Well, I didn't either. But that doesn't mean you have to be offended by it."

"He has that piggish male thing. I can spot it a mile away."

"What piggish male thing?"

"It's a derivative of the virgin/whore thing. He's one of those guys who can only see women two ways."

Eventually, I was able to wear Karisa down and get her to agree to spend a little more time with Jerry before she consigned him to eternal damnation. Before she got the chance, however, Jerry abruptly announced that he was moving to New York City. "If I'm ever going to get anywhere in the music biz," he explained, "I gotta be in the Big Apple." Within a few weeks, he quit his part-time job at a tuxedo shop, sold his car, packed his clothes into cardboard boxes, and bought a bus ticket to Manhattan. Karisa and I drove him to the Greyhound station in San Francisco.

That afternoon, Jerry was as sober and straight as I'd ever seen him. He was dressed in a red polo shirt and khakis, his face nicely tanned from a recent trip to the beach. The Coors haze was gone from his eyes, and he spent most of the drive up the Bayshore Freeway talking about how grateful he was to be leaving the Valley. He was tired of the perfect weather, the shopping malls that were springing up everywhere, and all the talk, talk, talk about computers and satellites. "It's gonna be so cool to live in a place where I'm surrounded by actual *human beings*," he said, meaning as opposed to geeks, whom he considered robots with appetites.

We both knew, however, that it was not the Valley of the Geeks he was running from but the whole postdivorce mess of our family life. I knew this because I'd run from the same thing.

At the bus station, I helped Jerry pull his two suitcases out of the trunk, then hugged him good-bye. "I'll be out to visit soon," I promised. Then he turned to Karisa, and I saw a look of horror flash across her face. I expected her to pull away. But she surprised me. I don't know if it was out of respect for him or for me or simply out of an unwillingness to be intimidated, but she allowed Jerry to give her a hug. Jerry never gave gentle hugs, and this one was an eye-popper. "Take good care of my brother," he said, patting her on the back with surprising affection. Then he smiled at me, and his eyes went glassy with emotion. He turned quickly and picked up his two bags and headed into the bus station.

Later, as we drove across the Bay Bridge to Berkeley, Karisa said, "What a sweet guy. I hardly recognized him."

10

As a kid, Jerry had small, delicate hands. I always admired them and thought they were beautiful, even if they were useless for throwing a football or basketball. To me they were proof of what I already knew: My brother was fragile. He was shy and quick to blush, and he cried easily. Even as a small child, he was never quite at ease with himself—he was always moving, fidgeting, uncomfortable. He was also a bundle of energy. When he was about five years old, our family doctor prescribed Ritalin, a drug often used to treat hyperactivity. After a few months, my mother saw no change, so she quit giving him the pills. She thought he'd grow out of it. On his Kindergarten Conference Record (November 12, 1966), his teacher wrote: "Tends to hold back on any show of emotions—Does not relax in class—Often tense—Excellent intellectual potential."

Fragile or not, however, I thought Jerry was a wimp. Not only was I twenty-two months older than him, I was bigger and stronger in every way. I had a limber arm and quickly became a starting pitcher on our Little League team. I was a decent basketball rebounder, an above-average horseshoe tosser, and I could cast a fishing lure as far as my father could.

Jerry was good at none of this. He was too short for basketball, too weak for horseshoes, too impatient for fishing. He participated in all these activities because this was what boys did in our family, but it gave him no pleasure. He preferred sitting alone in his room and reading the *Lord of the Rings* trilogy or pawing through back issues of his favorite magazine, *Famous Monsters of Filmland*. In our neighborhood, Jerry was hardly unusual. The sons and daughters of aerospace engineers were all lousy baseball players and lame free-throw shooters, too. They were interested in chemistry sets and ham radios and other hand-me-down garage gizmos. But whatever gene makes a kid seek transcendence through wires and circuits, Jerry didn't have. He was even more allergic to technology than I was.

Jerry found transcendence another way: by pounding on things. As far back as I can remember, he was always banging out a rhythm on the kitchen table, or a car seat, or the back of Jill's head. In fourth grade, when music lessons were first offered in our public school, Jerry naturally took up drums and spent hours beating out simple rhythms on a snare drum in his bedroom.

Before long, Jerry used his paper-route money to rent a drum set from a local music shop, but it was a piece of junk and expensive. He kept it for only a couple of weeks. Jerry dreamed about a set of his own, but the idea of saving eight hundred dollars—which is what the set he wanted cost—seemed impossible.

Then at Christmas one year, Jerry walked out into the living room and there beside the tree was a drum set. It was used, not new, but it was professional quality: a bass drum, two floor toms, a snare, and two Ziljan cymbals. This was by far the most expensive and indulgent gift my parents had ever given any of us. Jerry could hardly believe it was real. I still have home movies my father took that morning. In them, Jerry's standing beside the winking Christmas tree in his pajamas, sleepy eyed, the glare of the camera lights making him squint. Our golden retriever trots into the scene and nuzzles Jerry's hand. Jerry stares at the drum set, stunned. *For me? This?* He looks like he wants to cry. Instead, he gingerly sits on the stool, picks up the sticks, and crashes the cymbal.

From that moment on, the trajectory of Jerry's life seemed fixed. He set the drums up in a corner of the family room, then hooked up his stereo nearby, so that he could plug in headphones and play along with an album. He started with "Proud Mary" and "Hey Jude," then moved on to Led Zeppelin and Iron Butterfly. He spent months trying to master the three-minute drum solo in "In-A-Gadda-Da-Vida."

It drove us all wild, of course. Jerry was not just interested but obsessive: He often played two, three, four hours at a time, until his small hands were raw from the drumsticks, or until my father or my mother couldn't stand any more and made him quit. When Jerry was playing well, when he hit a riff just right, he was higher and happier than I ever saw him. That high would last for days—or until he tried to play the riff again and screwed it up. Then he'd get so angry that he'd throw his drumsticks across the room. I often found them stuck in our hollow-core doors like darts.

But Jerry's obsessiveness paid off. In junior high, he joined the school band and quickly distinguished himself on the timpani. Every concert in those days featured the opening fanfare of Richard Strauss's *Also sprach Zarathustra* used in *2001: A Space Odyssey*. During the beginning of the piece, when the timpani rise to a dramatic crescendo, all eyes in the auditorium were on Jerry. And he loved it.

Jerry and my father had more in common than either of them wanted to admit. Like our father, Jerry was a middle child; like our father, he had a quick temper; like our father, he was an emotionally needy kid; like our father, he was a loner. I don't know what my father saw when he looked into Jerry's dark eyes, but, whatever it was, there's no question that his relationship with Jerry was different than his with me or Jill. During the happy moments between Jerry and my father—and there were lots of them—I envied their closeness, the way they seemed to connect on a level that seemed deeper and easier than anything I ever felt with my father.

But there was a flip side to this. When they clashed, it was, as my mother often said, "like two mules butting heads." I saw this head butting most often at the dinner table when Jerry, a finicky eater, refused to touch his vegetables. My father went after him like a Marine Corps sergeant. "You're going to sit there until you finish your peas," he'd say, and Jerry would say, "No, I'm not," and my father would say, "Yes, you are," and on and on it would go until Dad shouted, "God damn it, I don't care if you have to sit there until midnight, you're going to finish your goddamned peas!"

It was a stupid war for my father to wage, but he seemed incapable of taking any other approach. Something in Jerry brought out the brute in him. And the harder my father pushed, the more determined Jerry became never to give in.

My mother rarely interrupted my father or disagreed with him while he was battling with Jerry. She believed it was important that she and my father show a united front. But I saw the strain in her face as she stood over the sink while my father yelled at Jerry, her fingers gripping the Formica, her shoulders tense. There was a certain look she always got when she wanted to say something but wouldn't dare: She focused hard on some inanimate object right in front of her and bit her bottom lip, and you could just feel the muscles of repression straining to keep down whatever urgent words threatened to leap out of her mouth.

My mother tried to make up for my father's harshness with Jerry in any way she could. She rarely raised her voice at him the way my father did and always stood up for him when I accused him of being a sissy because he didn't want to play war games with us. Jerry never left for school without kissing her good-bye—or if he did, as soon as he remembered he'd turn around and walk home, even if it meant being late for class.

———

The same year that Jerry received his drum set for Christmas, my father bought us a small Honda motorcycle. It was a gentle machine, meant for putting around campgrounds and exploring logging roads in the Sierras. My father thought it would give Jerry and me something to do on family camping trips. Instead, it gave us something to do for most of our adolescence. Jerry and I both liked the feeling of horsepower between our legs, and before long the Honda was traded in for a more powerful bike, then two more powerful bikes, and within a couple of years Jerry and I were outfitted in leather pants and knee-high leather boots and spent every weekend racing motocross, a sport in which about thirty racers scream around a dirt track laid out on a hillside. There are lots of bumps and jumps and ruts, as well as mud, dust, noise, howling engines, and spectacular wipeouts—pretty much all the things that make happiness for a teenage boy.

As was the case in other sports, I was better at this than Jerry was. Because I was bigger and stronger, it was easier for me to muscle the motorcycle around. Also, I was willing to take bigger risks, whereas Jerry, as much as he loved the sport, always proceeded with caution.

When we got involved in motorcycle racing, Jerry abandoned music. I don't know why. I can think of several possible explanations: because motorcycle racing was more of a thrill; because our mother and father were more supportive of us risking our lives by flying over whoop-de-doos at 50 MPH on dirt bikes than they were of Jerry's banging benignly on the drums, an activity neither of them comprehended; because he had dreams of beating me on the racecourse someday, of finally proving to himself and everyone else in our family that he was not just my equal but my superior.

Whatever his motivations were, there's no question that Jerry came to believe that because of my success on the racetrack, I was better built for the world than he was. He began to see me as the golden boy, the one who could do no wrong. From any more distant vantage point, of course, this was absurd. My excellence in sports was only of the most middling variety: I was not a baseball or football star; no one was throwing college scholarships at me. I could just make a motorcycle go fast around a bumpy dirt track. It was a skill that would take me exactly nowhere in life.

Nevertheless, Jerry both hated and envied me for my success. I didn't grasp just how deeply these emotions ran until one afternoon when he and I and my high-school girlfriend Susan were driving through downtown Sunnyvale in our father's El Camino. For some reason, Jerry and I started screaming at each other. I have no recollection what the fight was about, but I do know that by this time these kinds of battles between us were rare. I was about sixteen and beginning to realize that my brother was built of different material than I was; he was less resilient, less self-confident. Of course, that might have been one of the things that pissed him off. The only thing worse than being picked on by your big brother is being considered too weak or sensitive to be picked on by your big brother.

Anyway, Jerry and I were shouting at each other about something, and Susan was in the middle, screaming, "Shut up, you guys!" when all of a sudden my jaw went numb, and I almost drove off the road. I wasn't sure at first what had happened . . . *my brother had punched me in the face.* He had never done anything like that before. I looked over at him, and he was almost as shocked as I was. But at the same time, there was something new in his eyes, something that said, *You ain't such hot shit, big brother.*

After that day, he more or less stopped competing with me and started living his own life. Among other things, he quit riding motorcycles and took up drums again. Although he'd been weaned on seventies suburban rock—Aerosmith, Led Zeppelin, Jeff Beck—his musical tastes soon broadened to include Dave Brubeck and Miles Davis. He and his friends sat on big paisley pillows on the floor in Jerry's bedroom and debated the merits of various albums for hours, playing the same track over and over until they had dissected and analyzed every note.

I have to say, this bugged me. Because my own ear for music was so unsophisticated—give me catchy lyrics and a strong back beat, and I'm happy—I couldn't make my own judgment about how good Jerry really was. Was he truly gifted or just obsessive? I had no idea. But he got enough acclaim from others that I knew he had some talent. And I was jealous of it. It made my own talent for going round and round on a motorcycle seem extremely juvenile. It was like he'd suddenly made a leap not only in another direction but beyond me, into a realm of human experience that was full of *real* danger, not just the simple physical kind.

11

From the beginning, there was something too good to be true about Jerry's reports from New York. He called me (collect) the day he arrived at Port Authority Bus Terminal, high as a kite: "I finally made it to the Big Apple—can you believe it? This is *my town,* man. This is *my city.*" Over the next several weeks, I received a half-dozen postcards from him, each with a brief note on the back, updating me on his progress in New York: One week, he found a job as a delivery boy for a midtown deli; the next, he met a guy who played guitar, and they were thinking of starting a band; another card described a night at a Greenwich Village jazz club. It said simply, "Village Vanguard, One A.M., life doesn't get any better. Your bro, Jerry."

When I pulled these postcards out of the mailbox in Berkeley, my life seemed to shrink a little. He was out there, making a go of it in Manhattan, while I slogged through *The Rape of the Lock.* I took an extra-heavy course load every semester, which, combined with summer school and junior-college credits I'd transferred, would allow me to graduate in two years. Not soon enough, as far as I was concerned. I was glad to be there, but I was determined not to spend the rest of my life in a stuffy classroom.

A couple of months after Jerry arrived in New York, Apple sent my mother out to Boston for a seminar. Before she returned, she flew down and spent a weekend with Jerry. He still hadn't found an apartment for himself and was living in a cheap, cockroach-infested hotel off of Times Square. My mother and Jerry toured the city together—

the World Trade Center, the Empire State Building, Ray's Pizza. My mother wasn't thrilled by the fact that her son was living in a filthy hotel room, but she understood the romance of Jerry's life in New York. The way she described it, Jerry'd gone boho. "I've never seen him so happy," she gushed to me. "He's on top of the world."

And she was right. Even in our twice-a-month phone conversations, I could hear an exuberance and enthusiasm in Jerry's voice that I couldn't explain. I wasn't sure if it was the adrenaline rush of Manhattan and the sense of liberation he must have felt living so far from the Valley, beyond the reach of family ghosts, or if it was a result of the clarity of mind he felt after finally deciding to make a go of it as a musician.

Whatever the explanation, Jerry certainly sounded as if he was having the time of his life. In contrast, I remembered how I felt when I'd arrived in Tahoe—a much less dramatic move, with much less at stake. I'd been a mess of highs and lows: exuberant and cocky one day, lonely and withdrawn the next. Jerry didn't seem to be going through that cycle of doubt and despair—which didn't necessarily mean anything. Maybe he really had found himself, I thought. But in our family, what is *not* said is often as important— if not more important—than what *is* said. And with Jerry, I was beginning to get the feeling that there was an awful lot he was leaving out.

Before long, I learned via postcard that Jerry had found an apartment in Chelsea. He seemed thrilled—"my roommates are ultracool," he wrote—and for the first time he invited Karisa and me out for a visit just before New Year's.

－ － － － －

On the phone, Jerry insisted that he'd meet us at the airport—"I have a little surprise for you," he said. But when we stepped off the plane at Kennedy Airport after midnight, he was nowhere to be found. I pushed through the crowd at the boarding gate and scanned the long corridor, with its slouchy guards at the X-ray machine and late-night business travelers leaning into the pay phones on the wall. No Jerry. I wondered if I'd given him the wrong gate information or if something had happened on the way to the airport. "Maybe he got held up in traffic," I said to Karisa, but she just rolled her eyes at me, as if I was hopelessly naive.

We headed down to the luggage carousel, thinking maybe he'd meet us there. We waited. Other passengers who had been on our flight grabbed their luggage and disappeared. Before long we were alone amid the circulating steel of the carousels. Suspicious-looking men in droopy pants and Nikes hovered behind pillars, eyeing us like jackals.

"Maybe we should take a cab," I said.

"What if he's not at his apartment when we get there?" Karisa said. "I'm not really in the mood to stand out in the street in the middle of New York City and wait for your brother. It's after midnight already, it'll be one A.M. by the time we get to his apartment, maybe it'll be two A.M. by the time he gets back. Let's just get a hotel somewhere and call him in the morning."

"Let's give him five more minutes."

Ten minutes passed. Karisa sighed heavily.

"Okay, let's go," I said.

As I bent down to pick up our suitcase, I felt a sudden crushing weight on my back. An arm clamped around my neck, trapping me in a headlock with surprising violence. I staggered, expecting the flash of a knife. Beneath me, I saw purple suede shoes. A crackhead, I thought. It was so predictably New York, so right-out-of-the-headlines, that it almost felt scripted. I thrashed around, elbows flying, trying to break free.

Suddenly, I was released.

"Hey, bro!"

I recognized the voice instantly—Jerry. I wanted to slug him. "What the fuck is going on?"

"Take it easy," he said, patting me on the shoulder as if I were a frightened child. "I'm just jiving you. Thought I should give you a proper New York welcome." Then he smiled his Hollywood hustler smile, a smile so mixed with emotions other than happiness—jealousy, rage, fear, apprehension—that it chilled my blood.

"Jesus Christ, what an asshole you are," I said. I looked him over, hardly recognizing him. He was dressed in tight white jeans, a flowing purple silk shirt, and purple suede shoes. To me, he looked like a Vegas lounge singer. His hair was slicked back with some greasy cream, his face pale and uncharacteristically thin. I also saw that he was a little woozy. Not just woozy—drunk.

Jerry ignored my outburst and turned to Karisa. "Nice to see you again," he said in a voice that was perfectly balanced between sarcasm and sincerity. "Sorry for the delay. There was an accident on the L.I.E. I got here as quickly as I could."

Karisa stared hard at him. "Glad you finally made it," she sneered.

He chuckled good-naturedly, as if to say, "Oh, we're gonna have fun together," then grabbed our bags. "Let's go. I've got a limo waiting—it's costing me big bucks."

I thought he was kidding, but then we stepped outside and there it was: a long black limo. The driver sat inside, thumbing through a wrestling magazine.

"This is absurd," I said, standing on the sidewalk. "I'm not getting into that thing. Why can't we just take a cab?" I felt a slam-bang of conflicting emotions: I was still pissed at him for jumping me, but another part of me was thrilled to see this black car at the curb. I'd never been in a limo before. And the idea that my brother, who probably didn't have five hundred dollars to his name, would do something so outlandish for Karisa and me was a sign of . . . I wasn't sure what. Affection, maybe.

So I shut up, and we got into the limo.

Inside, we were greeted by surprise number two: a blond woman sipping a glass of champagne. She was in her early twenties, long hair tumbling over her shoulders, wearing heavy mascara and eyeliner, a black sweater, and black jeans. Jerry flopped beside her. "This is Carol, my girlfriend," he said, as if it were an accomplishment. She did not look like his girlfriend. In fact, she did not look like she knew him very well at all. My first thought was that she was a prostitute, but she seemed too uneasy, too unsure of herself. She glanced at Jerry, looking like an actor who had forgotten her line. He squeezed her thigh. Then she looked at Karisa and me and said unconvincingly, "Nice to meet you."

Okay, maybe she *is* his girlfriend, I thought. Maybe they had a fight on the way to the airport and the weirdness I was picking up was its lingering fumes. I shrugged it off. We settled in, Jerry tapped on the glass behind the driver's head, and the limo pulled away from the curb.

As we headed out onto the Van Wyck, Jerry reached for a bottle of Korbel champagne that had been chilling in a silver ice bucket, sent the cork ricocheting off the ceiling of the limo, then poured four glasses of bubbly, spilling a little each time we hit a pothole. Karisa and I looked at each other. She was just as confused as I was. Jerry passed the glasses around, then raised his for a toast. "Welcome to New York," he said, smiling broadly. We clinked glasses. He downed his in a single gulp, then poured another. Karisa looked like she wanted to climb out the window, she was so edgy.

There were a few minutes of awkward conversation about our flight and the weather and Mom and Dad before it became clear that Jerry was too far gone for conversation. I tried to keep him talking, thinking that it would distract him from pouring himself another glass of champagne. It didn't. He finished the bottle, dropped it on the floor, then said, "Fuck! That's the last bottle."

I looked at Carol, trying to divine some meaning from her about what was going on, but she revealed nothing.

We rode in silence for a while. I caught Karisa's eye and laughed. I couldn't help it. A limo into Manhattan! My brother loaded! Purple suede shoes!

She was not amused.

As we approached the Williamsburg Bridge, Jerry gazed out the window at the Manhattan skyline for a long, complicated moment. His face was silhouetted by the city lights; his long eyelashes seemed to brush the sooty rooftops of East Side apartment buildings. He said, "There it is, man—isn't it beautiful?" And then he leaned over and kissed Carol, and she put her arms around him, and he pulled her close, and their lips did not part the rest of the way into Manhattan. They fell into the corner of the backseat, and he slipped his hand under her sweater, exposing her belly and more.

My smile faded. I turned away, embarrassed, my gut roiling. I watched the Empire State Building slide across the window, wondering what had become of my brother.

———

Jerry's apartment was above a fish market on Tenth Avenue in Chelsea. Karisa and I slept on the floor in the front room, awakened by the delivery trucks that arrived at 5 A.M. with clangs and rumbles and the briny stink of mackerel and mussels. The apartment was a dingy one-bedroom on the second floor of a brownstone; Jerry shared it with two guys named Bryan and Zane, both struggling actors, both strikingly handsome, both obviously gay. The three of them slept in bunk beds in a small room with a window onto an air shaft. Jerry introduced Karisa and me to them the next morning. They said hello, then disappeared.

I thought nothing of it. I was so bewildered by what had happened the night before that the presence of Jerry's roommates barely registered. Over the next three days, Bryan and Zane moved like cats, slipping in and out at odd hours, eyes averted, as if they were waiting for a signal from Jerry that it was okay to engage in conversation. It never came. During our entire stay in New York, we never exchanged more than ten words with them. I just thought they were shy.

As for Jerry, I didn't know what to make of him. The morning after our arrival, he brought Karisa and me bagels and orange juice and coffee on a tray and said, "Sorry about last night, man. I just got carried away. Things with Carol are just . . . I don't know. They're wild. I'll explain it to you later."

But he never did. In fact, he hardly spent a minute with Karisa and me that day or the next or the next. A few weeks before we'd arrived, he'd taken a job bartending at a midtown restaurant. He worked the lunch shift every day, 10 A.M. to 4 P.M. I thought he'd take at least one afternoon off while we were in town, but he didn't. His evenings managed to be equally busy.

I visited him once at the restaurant. It was an upscale bistro filled with men and women in expensive suits. Watching him behind the pine bar, I saw a completely different person than the one who had jumped me at the airport. Here, I could see the exuberance that I'd sensed in his letters; he looked confident and strong, a man in his element; I could see the hump of his newly pumped-up biceps as he shook martinis. (He'd been working out at his roommates' gym.) He smiled at me, kept my beer glass full, stopped by once in a while to wipe his hands with a towel and talk. He liked to think of himself as a real New Yorker already and was full of tips about the best pizza in the Village and how to find the mummy room at the Met.

Whenever I tried to turn the conversation toward his life or Carol or music or anything beyond the simplest chitchat, he immediately remembered he had something to do: restock the sweet and sour mixes, ring out the cash register, cut limes.

On the final night of our visit, New Year's Eve, Jerry, Carol, Karisa, and I planned to call out for Thai food and sit around the apartment together and watch the ball drop on TV. Karisa and I waited at the apartment until 10 P.M.—he was supposed to meet us there at eight—and then finally ordered without them. Jerry and Carol stumbled into the apartment a few minutes after the food arrived, both of them giggling like seven-year-olds. Karisa and I didn't even have a chance to dish out the food before they were horizontal and half naked on the couch. They were obviously blissed-out on something—champagne, poppers, coke, 'ludes, who knows. Karisa and I slipped out to the bar at the corner and celebrated New Year's by ourselves.

"Jesus, what is going on with your brother?" Karisa asked. I couldn't explain or defend Jerry's behavior. I said, "Maybe we're catching them at a bad moment." And: "Maybe it's a drug thing." And: "Maybe he's really in love and doesn't want to admit it."

Karisa didn't get it either. "I don't understand how a woman can let herself be groped like that."

Neither of us made a connection between Jerry's aggressive display of heterosexuality and the simple fact that he was living in a small bedroom with two gay men.

In fact, the thing that was most troubling to me during our stay was not his sexual smoke signals—I missed those entirely—but the conspicuous lack of talk about or evidence of his budding career in music. It was obvious that after six months in the city, he'd found no work as a drummer, he wasn't playing in any pickup bands on the Lower East Side, he wasn't renting studio time, and he didn't even have a practice pad in his apartment. I may not have seen the elephant in the room, but I knew there was something he wasn't telling me.

12

During the next few months, Jerry sounded tired whenever we talked. He complained that it was too expensive to live in New York, that he was working too many hours just to pay the rent, that he didn't have time to practice drumming, and that if he couldn't practice he'd never be a good enough musician to make a living at it. Then he had a quarrel with one of his roommates, who apparently accused Jerry of stealing money from him. I have no idea if he did or not. I was busy pounding out my thesis and listened with only half an ear.

Still, I was hardly surprised when he called a few weeks later and said, "I'm sick of this place. I'm coming home." He did not sound angry—he sounded broken. I knew how hard this was, returning with his tail between his legs, his big-city dream in tatters. I told him he'd learned a lot about the music biz, that he could always go back, that just by going there in the first place he'd shown more courage than most.

"Yeah, I know," he said. Then, trying to cheer himself up, he said, "This city hasn't seen the last of me yet."

Jerry took a bus back to the Valley and moved into his old bedroom at our father's house. I did not see him until graduation day, about a month later. We had talked on the phone a few times, and I could tell by his cutting asides about "college boy's big day" that he was not going to take my graduation easily. I presumed he'd find some reason to skip it, which was fine with me. I could live without seeing the look on his face as I stepped down off the podium, degree in hand. Jerry always drew sharp lines between winners and losers, and on this day we both knew what he'd be thinking. All brothers are competitive, but Jerry was insanely so. Sometimes it seemed like his only goal in life was to one-up me.

Whenever we talked, I played down the whole idea of my graduation, saying that I didn't really care much about the degree, it was only a piece of paper, a sign that I had jumped through the right hoops and pushed the right buttons. He understood exactly what I was doing. "Don't lie to me, bro. It's a major accomplishment. Why don't you just admit it and be happy about it? If I were you, I'd be doing fucking cartwheels."

Graduation day was obscenely sunny and bright. My mother put on her best red dress, and my father wore a tie and a brown corduroy sport coat. Even Jill, who usually turned sour at any family occasion, preferring honest distance to false intimacy, seemed bouncy and happy. To my surprise, Jerry showed up. He wore a yellow polo shirt and Levi's; I could see that he wasn't stone sober, but neither was he slurring his words.

After the ceremony, Karisa threw a party in the white bungalow on Ashby Avenue where she was one of several boarders. Karisa had learned a lot about life from *Bon Appétit* magazine, and this party was an expression of her acquired wisdom. It was very civilized, very Berkeley. There were maybe forty people in attendance—friends, professors, relatives. We threw open the doors and windows of the house and drank beer and champagne and picked at gorgeously arranged plates of cheeses and fruit. I was burned out from finals, coasting on the afterglow of too much caffeine and adrenaline, but I have to say I forgot all the bullshit about ratification from an establishment I didn't respect and simply enjoyed the heavenly presence of the blue sky above us. My father was as happy as I'd ever seen him, and my mother had that giddy air about her that she gets when things are going well.

I'd had a couple of glasses of champagne and was talking with one of Karisa's friends about a trip she was taking to Europe that summer when I noticed my mother cutting quickly through the crowd toward my father. She took him aside and whispered in his ear. I knew by the look on her face that something was seriously wrong. My first thought was that there had been an accident on the street in front of the house. My father spoke to her for a moment, nodded, then disappeared out the front door.

"What's going on?" I asked my mother.

"It's Jerry."

"What?"

"He's upset."

"About what?"

She wanted to protect me. "Nothing. I'll explain it to you later."

I looked over her shoulder, out the open door, and saw Jerry standing on the lawn. His face was red and wet with tears. My father stood beside him, his brown tie loosened, his hand on Jerry's shoulder, consoling him. It took me a split second to assemble the pieces, but when they came together it was like a blow to the stomach: Jerry was crying because of me. He was crying because he felt I had somehow copped all the good luck in our family, leaving him with the dregs.

I wanted to run over to him and shake him by the shoulders and tell him it wasn't true, that happiness is not rationed in the family genes, that life is not a zero-sum game, but my mother held me back. "I think it's best if you leave him alone right now," she said quietly.

In the coming months, Jerry's life began to unravel. He took a job as a waiter, was fired; he took another as a prep cook, and was fired again. He moved out of our father's house, lived with a girlfriend in Marin County for a few months, then moved back in with our father. And he drank—mostly beer, not hard stuff. Still, after five or six Heinekens, instead of simply getting loud or jolly, Jerry's darker side emerged. He'd often call me in the middle of the night and list my father's character flaws. "Do you realize what a fucked-up person our dad is?" he'd say. "He hates his job, he lost his family, all he does is sit at home every night and watch fucking TV until he falls asleep. What a life, man. And Jill, oh god, you should see how he spoils her. Whatever she fucking wants, Jill gets. He's so guilty about fucking up the family that he's trying to buy her love."

And so it would go on. Then my father would call, and he'd tell me about the pile of beer cans he'd found stashed under the bathroom sink, and how every time he came home from work Jerry was in his bedroom, playing his stereo "loud enough to rattle the windows." Jerry would disappear for days at a time, then come home with a mysterious wad of cash. "I'm afraid he's dealing drugs," my father told me.

"He's not dealing drugs," I said.

"How do you know?"

"I just don't think he is," I said.

"Where is he getting his money then?"

"I have no idea."

By default, I became the middleman between Jerry and my father. When my father lost his temper, I tried to talk him down, telling him that Jerry was just going through a rough time, that he just had to be patient, give him a break, he'll straighten out. And I told Jerry that he should forget about our father's problems and concentrate on his own, that he needed to get a job and move out on his own and get back into music. Yeah, he'd crashed and burned in New York. Yeah, that was tough. But it wasn't like his life was over—he was only twenty-three! "Yo, Jerry! How about a reality check here?" I'd say to him. "It's not like you've got a tumor growing in your ear."

"I know, I know," he'd say.

"You have a ton of talent."

"I know."

"You're, like, the most talented person I know."

"Don't bullshit me."

"I'm not bullshitting you."

Sometimes, this kind of talk would buoy him for a few days; sometimes it wouldn't. Inevitably, he'd call again and tell me that his life was in ruins and how ashamed he was of it all. During these confessional moments, he never talked about sex or his sexual identity—which now makes me think that that may have been what it was all about.

My many long midnight conversations were motivated by more than just brotherly love. I also wanted to assuage my own guilt. Deep down, I was afraid Jerry might be right: I had drawn too many winners from the deck, leaving him with deuces and spades.

13

After graduation, Karisa and I moved into an apartment in San Francisco near Golden Gate Park. It was small, but it had built-in window seats and shiny hardwood floors. From our bedroom, we could hear foghorns on the bay, and we often woke to find our entire block wrapped in silver mist.

Like many fuzzy-headed liberal-arts grads, I lived a schizoid life: By day, I waited tables; by night, I dreamed of becoming a writer. It was not a particularly vivid or promising fantasy, since the sum total of my creative output at Berkeley was three or four short stories, all of which were born onto the page like two-headed frogs and died quietly in the bottom drawer of my file cabinet.

By this time—the summer of 1984—I was well aware of what I'd given up. The Macintosh had been introduced with great fanfare at the beginning of the year, and Apple was on its way to becoming one of the most talked-about companies in America. Whenever I visited my mother, I was astonished at the changes: Every month, the company seemed to be expanding into yet another new glassy building, and the parking lot became more and more crowded with vintage Mercedes and Mustang fastbacks. Everyone had places to go, people to see, a meeting they were late for, a chunk of code that absolutely positively had to be written by tomorrow morning. They were building the new world, and they knew it.

Not me—I knew nothing except that I liked putting words on a page. And so, not long after graduation, I began work on a novel. It was, of course, loosely autobiographical, a story of a moody, confused kid who goes to work for a computer company very much like Apple, finds himself terribly bored, and spends a lot of time ruminating about technology and the machinery of the cold war.

If nothing else, my book had a slam-bang opening scene. It was based on the real-life story of Dennis Barnhart, who had been the CEO of Eagle Computer. The forty-year-old ex–fighter pilot had scratched and clawed and fought to make Eagle a success, and on the day the company went public—June 13, 1983—Barnhart reaped his reward: His shares of company stock were worth nine million dollars.

That afternoon, Barnhart hung around the company offices in Los Gatos along with the rest of the employees, drinking champagne and eating celebratory pizza. At about three o'clock, Barnhart went for a drive with a friend in his red Ferrari 308 Quattrovavole, which he had bought a few months earlier to celebrate his imminent success. Barnhart pulled out of the parking lot, hung a right onto University Avenue and punched the throttle. The Ferrari accelerated like a jet. As the road curved, Barnhart somehow lost control and flew through the guardrail, over small trees and bushes, and landed upside down, several hundred feet below. Barnhart was dead at the scene; his passenger was severely injured. Police estimated later the car had been traveling over 70 MPH on a curve that was marked at 35.

I read about Barnhart's accident after it happened and became weirdly obsessed with the story. Over the next year or so, I often visited the curve in the road where he had lost control. The skid marks were still there, as were a few shards of shattered glass on the hillside below and a newly installed guardrail. I lingered over these details with ghoulish obsession. There was something deeply comforting in Barnhart's death; it played out like a cautionary tale of a man who worshiped a little too reverently the false idols of money and speed and material gain. He was Silicon Valley's own Icarus.

Unfortunately, not even a mythological figure in a Ferrari could save my novel, and I abandoned it after several hundred pages.

Jerry visited our apartment in San Francisco once or twice, but Karisa was never very happy to have him around. Jerry's recent troubles just convinced her that she'd been right all along about him: He was a deeply flawed human being, and the sooner everyone admitted that, the better off we'd all be. She was also afraid of him. One day, Jerry showed up drunk and unannounced while I was at work. Karisa refused to let him in, which threw Jerry into a violent rage. When I came home that night, I noticed kick marks on the bottom of the door. Karisa was ashen faced.

"He scared the hell out of me," she said.

"Why?"

"You should have heard him screaming while he pounded on the door."

"What did he say?"

"Oh, I don't know—about how he expected unconditional love from his family, but he wasn't getting it. I don't know, it was hard to understand. But he knew I was in here, and it drove him crazy that I wouldn't open the door. I didn't know what to do, if I should let him in or not."

"He's not your brother," I told her. "You have no obligation to him." But then I added, almost an apology, "You know he'd never hurt you."

"I'm not so sure about that," she said.

"He's not a violent person," I said.

She looked at me like I had just landed from Mars. "I'm not so sure about that, either," she said.

Jerry's rages were always followed by periods of guilt and repentance, and, sure enough, a few days later Jerry called, sober, and insisted on talking to Karisa. "I really made an ass of myself," he said. She was reluctant to come to the phone, but then Jerry said to me, "Tell her I'm groveling on my knees, begging her forgiveness." I repeated the message to her; she rolled her eyes and grabbed the phone. She talked with him for twenty minutes or so, and by the time she hung up she was smiling.

For Mother's Day that year, Jerry was in the mood for another small act of kindness. A few days before, he'd called and proposed that he and Jill and I cook dinner for Mom together. I thought he was joking at first.

"I'm serious, man. I was thinking this morning about what it means to be a mother. I mean, she grew us in her womb. She fed us with her body. She *made* us. She *hatched* us. We emerged from her flesh."

"This is why you want to cook Mom dinner?"

"Well, I've treated her pretty badly lately," Jerry confessed. "I feel like I owe her something. This would be a start." I didn't argue, and I made arrangements to pick him and Jill up at our father's house early Sunday afternoon. We'd then go shopping together before heading over to our mother's condo for dinner.

When I arrived, the house was oddly quiet. No dogs, no cars in the driveway. Jill was sitting at the kitchen table curling her hair. "Where is everybody?"

"Dad took the dogs to the park," Jill said coolly.

"What about Jerry?"

"Dad kicked him out last night."

"Why?"

"He found another stash of empty beer bottles in his bedroom. Then when Dad asked him if he'd been drinking, Jerry said no. You know how pissed Dad gets when you lie to him. Well, he started screaming at Jerry. Told him he is not allowed back in this house, ever, unless he's sober."

So much for Mother's Day dinner, I thought. Jill and I went grocery shopping anyway, then drove to our mother's condo. All I had to say to my mother was "Jerry couldn't make it," and she understood. She didn't ask for details, although I could see that she was hurt. Every time I saw my mother now, she was heavier, both of body and soul.

Jill and I cooked pasta together, and then the three of us sat down to eat at the small oak table in my mother's kitchen. It was a fine meal—my mother talked about a deep-sea fishing trip she'd recently taken with some of her friends from Apple, and Jill and I compared notes on movies we'd seen. I knew this kind of peaceable gathering was a precious thing to my mother; it gave her hope that we might eventually learn to live together like any other suburban American postdivorce, postnuclear family.

Jerry called while we were drinking coffee and eating Tofutti for dessert. I happened to answer the phone, and he gave me his version of his battle with our father, then told me that this was the last straw, he was going to give up drinking. "It's fucked me up enough," he said. He'd come to similar conclusions before, but this was the first time I'd ever heard him admit it so baldly, with such desperation in his voice. "I'm very glad to hear you say that," I told him.

"It's so fucking obvious," he said. "I've had enough of this bull-shit. I'm going to turn my life around." Then he said, "Let me talk to Mom."

I passed the phone to her and watched her eyes well up as they chatted. I couldn't hear what Jerry was saying to her, but they were undoubtedly sweet words of repentance and love. Then she handed the phone back to me.

"I need my address book," he said. "Could you drop it by on your way back to the city?" I told him I would. He gave me directions to a room in a hotel on El Camino Real, the main drag in Sunnyvale, that he had apparently checked into after my father had kicked him out of the house.

After we finished the dishes, I drove back to my father's house, grabbed Jerry's address book off the nightstand, and drove over to the hotel. It was a decent place, by Silicon Valley standards, a business hotel pitched at midlevel managers in town for marketing seminars—a funny place for Jerry to stay, I thought. I walked through the lobby and punched the elevator button. The doors opened and standing in the elevator was a heavy, middle-aged man I pegged immediately as a drug dealer. He was nervous, fidgety, dressed in a very unbusinesslike way: tennis shorts, a Vuarnet T-shirt, and, inexplicably, women's sunglasses. "Hey, I was just coming down to find you," the man slurred. "What the fuck took you so long, man?"

It wasn't until he finished the sentence that I realized he was my brother.

I stepped onto the elevator. I looked him over: He'd put on thirty pounds since I had last seen him; he was unshaven, sweaty, suspicious looking. "You look like shit," I said.

"And you look like Robert fucking Redford," he joked. He pushed the button for the third floor. Up we went. There was so much to say, we said nothing for a moment. I felt like I'd slipped into another dimension. "I don't know if I told you this," he said coolly, "but I'm a gigolo. This chick pays me good money."

Of course I did not believe him. Jerry was an artful liar. Plus, I couldn't imagine any woman would pay to sleep with a man in his condition.

"In your dreams," I said.

"You don't believe me?"

"No, I don't," I said.

The doors opened. "Follow me."

We walked down the long, anonymous hotel corridor. He knocked on a door.

A woman's voice: "Hello?"

"It's me," Jerry said.

A middle-aged women in a business suit opened the door. Dark hair, plain looking, nervous. Wedding ring on her left hand.

"This is my brother," he said, motioning to me. "He brought me my address book."

"Nice to meet you," the woman said.

I nodded at her and mumbled.

"He's leaving now," Jerry said with a chuckle, then stepped into the room.

As he closed the door, he winked at me, as if to say, "Ain't this a hoot?"

14

Jerry did not volunteer much about his life as a gigolo. Sometimes, he claimed that he had no such life, that that woman in the hotel room was just a friend; other times, he claimed he was clearing several grand a week by, as he put it, "baby-sitting the wives of all these hot-shit engineers." The truth, I presumed, was somewhere in between: He probably accepted money for sex sometimes when he was down-and-out, but it was not a regular business for him. I think he did it not so much for money as for revenge. It was his way of proving that although he didn't have a vintage Mercedes and a house in the hills, he had something that many guys in the Valley didn't: the attention of their wives.

For me, seeing Jerry close that door in the hotel was like official notification that he was in deep trouble. And so I began a series of earnest attempts to convince him of this obvious fact. I'd meet him at my father's house, and we'd take the dogs down to the high-school field, and I'd say, "Jerry, you've really gone over the line here, you gotta face this, you can't keep going in the direction you're going. You gotta get help, you gotta go to AA, you gotta do something." If he was sober, he'd say, "Those days are over, man. I'm gonna get my shit together." If he was not sober, he'd say, "Drinking is not my problem. My screwed-up family is my problem. I can stop drinking anytime."

And so it went for months, me talking, him talking, both of us getting nowhere. He drank, and I talked again, and then he drank some more, and I talked some more. Nothing changed.

A month or so after my encounter with Jerry in the hotel, I happened to stop by my mother's condo on a Saturday morning to say a quick hello. I was surprised by how tired she looked. There were wrinkles under her dark eyes, and the corners of her lips sagged. The deliberate cheerfulness she often strained for was missing. She sat at her small kitchen table stirring a cup of black coffee. Like many other objects in her condo—Christmas ornaments, key chain, T-shirts, sweatshirts, her plastic ID badge—the coffee mug was emblazoned with the rainbow-colored Apple Computer logo. On mornings such as this, the logo contrasted mightily with the decidedly unrainbow-like expression on her face.

"What's wrong?"

"Your sister was out all night," she said. "She didn't get home until three A.M. I was worried sick about her."

"Where was she?"

"I have no idea. She didn't tell me she was going out. She just vanished."

I poured myself a cup of coffee.

"I just don't know what to do about her," my mother said. "I told her if she was going to go out, I wanted her home at ten P.M. Not a second later. She says, 'Okay, Mom, I promise.' Then she waltzes in at three A.M. She says that her friend's car had a flat, and they couldn't get anyone to fix it. I said, 'Well, why didn't you call?' and she said, 'I couldn't find a phone.' I said, 'Jill, there are phones everywhere,' and she shrugged and said, 'Not where we were.' God, that girl infuriates me. I talk to her until I'm blue in the face. It has no effect. She just ignores me."

That was my mother's favorite expression: *until I'm blue in the face*. It suggests a mix of love and exasperation, which pretty much summed up her attitude toward family life in those days.

I went upstairs to say hello to Jill.

Her door was closed. I knocked. "Hey, Gorilla, what's up?"

Silence.

"Hey, Jill, you in there?"

A reluctant groan.

"Can I come in?"

"I'm asleep."

I opened the door—trespassing on sacred ground, I knew, but I did it anyway. I was astounded by what I saw: not a messy bedroom but a nuclear explosion contained within four walls. Clothes strewn three feet deep all over the floor. Empty Coke cans, gum wrappers, bits of potato chips. A whiff of stale beer and cigarettes. Piles of cassettes on the stereo beneath a Duran Duran poster. I had a hard time determining where the bed started and stopped, and if indeed anyone was in it. Eventually, a blond head rose out of the debris like a serpent from the deep.

Mascara-stained eyes blinked open. She looked at me, focusing slowly. *Ah, you.* "Get out!"

"I just wanted to say hello."

"Get out! This is my room. I did not invite you in here."

"I didn't mean to intrude, I just thought—"

"I don't care what you thought," she said, and then with disturbing quickness she jumped out of bed and shoved me violently toward the door.

"What's going on?"

"Out!" she shouted. "Out!"

I wondered what there was in the room that I hadn't seen. I looked around but saw nothing more incriminating than a pack of cigarettes on the nightstand.

"Keep the fuck away from me, okay? I didn't invite you in here! Just keep the fuck away from me!"

Then she slammed the door.

I walked back down to the kitchen. My mother looked up at me, expectant.

I shrugged. "I don't know what's going on."

———

Next thing I knew, my mother was attending counseling sessions at Jill's high school. Jill was skipping class once or twice a week, neglecting homework, flunking tests. The principal of the school called my mother, concerned. "I'm afraid if this goes on, she may not make it through the year."

The counseling sessions were not productive. "She won't say a word," my mother told me on the phone one night. "She just sits there with her arms crossed and this look on her face. What am I supposed to do? I can't make her talk. I can't make her do her homework. I can't tie her down and tell her, 'You must do this.' You know how stubborn your sister is. If she doesn't want to do something, she's not going to do it, and nothing anybody says is going to change her mind. I'm really getting worried about her."

"What about sending her to a different school?"

"Like where?"

"I don't know. Maybe a private school, where they'd take more interest in her."

"I can't afford that. Besides, her school seems fine."

"What about a tutor?" I suggested.

"She doesn't need a tutor," my mother said. "She's very smart. She's just lazy."

"So what are you going to do?"

"I have no idea."

"What does Dad say about this?"

"Oh, you know your father," my mother said with thinly disguised disgust. "He's not very thoughtful about this kind of thing. He thinks I should ground her until her grades come up—not let her go out with friends, not let her watch TV at night. That's easy to say when you don't live with her, when you don't have to look at her moping around the house all day and night. You know Jill—she's very good at making me suffer more than her."

"Well, what about trying—"

My mother interrupted, "Hold on a second." I heard a door open in the background and a male voice. "Hi, come on in," my mother said in a tone unlike the one she was using in her conversation with me. This voice was bright and untroubled. "I'll be off the phone in a minute."

When we continued our conversation, her bright tone remained.

"Sorry about that. A friend just dropped by. We're going to the boat show up at the Cow Palace tonight."

He wasn't a friend—he was a boyfriend. Which one, I wasn't sure. "You're buying a boat?"

"No, no. It's fun to look, though."

I said nothing.

"Would you do me a favor? Jill is going to be home alone tonight. I told her not to invite anyone over and that she is not to leave the condo under any circumstances. She's got plenty of homework to do, and she can watch TV if she gets bored. Would you mind calling to check up on her? We'll be back by midnight."

"Yeah, I'll call," I said, even though I didn't like her cheery new voice. It was a voice that said, *I've been a mom for twenty years. Now I want to be something else.*

I called at 8 P.M.; the line was busy. I called at nine, ten, and eleven, and the phone just rang and rang.

—————

After that, I took Jill on as a project. I might not be able to bring Jerry back from the brink, but I thought I could help her. So I began calling her once or twice a week, just a friendly checkup, just a big-brotherly chat. It didn't go smoothly: Jill was too smart not to know that my calls always had an agenda. Plus, my frequent late-night conversations with Jerry had already sucked my sympathy tank dry. With Jill, I was often abrupt, impatient, and condescending. I tried too hard to dispense advice and guidance, which of course she resented. "You're not my father," she often snapped at me. If I was just chatty with her, however, I felt like I wasn't doing enough or like I was indulging her.

And, my god, she could be moody. Sometimes I talked to her on the phone and she would hardly say a word—the entire conversation would consist of me saying, "Jill, are you there?" And she'd say, "I'm here." And after about the sixth time, I'd get exasperated with her and say, "If you don't want to talk to me, just say so." And she'd say, "Okay, I don't want to talk to you" and hang up.

Early on, I made the mistake of asking her straight-out about school. She clammed up immediately. With a fifteen-year-old, I learned, you have to think strategically. You have to find an angle, a bank shot, a trapdoor.

Eventually, I figured out that all I had to do was mention Apple, and Jill opened right up. It worked every time, no matter how sullen her mood. To me, Apple had been a colony of inarticulate geeks; to Jill, it was the magic kingdom. She had been hanging out at Apple since she was in the seventh grade, when, instead of going home to the condo after school, Jill often walked the dozen or so blocks down to the company's offices in Cupertino. While my mother finished working—by that time, she was a full-fledged CAD designer, plotting the intricate circuitry for new PC boards—Jill hung out in the cubicle next to her, playing video games on a spare Apple II. Jill had no reservations about technology, no awkwardness in front of the machine, no fear. She just loved computers: simply, wholeheartedly, instinctively.

She also loved the people who worked with them. Whenever she was bored or thirsty, she headed over to the company fridge, which was always stocked with Cokes and Odwalla juices and various snacks. On the way back, she'd wander through the maze of desks, visiting her pals: hardware engineers, software coders, other CAD designers. They invited her into their cubicles, chatted with her about work and school, brought her T-shirts when they returned from out-of-town junkets. Many of them didn't have kids yet themselves—they were all working too hard to bother with families—and having Jill around was a kind of interesting novelty, a reminder of life beyond the cubicle walls. Before long, Jill was spending so much time at Apple that she started to think of these people as her aunts and uncles. Apple was the big, happy family that replaced her own dark, fractured one.

Jill loved the parties, too. At Apple, no event was too small to celebrate: the shipping of a new piece of software, a profitable quarter, somebody's promotion. The only Apple parties I ever attended were a few Friday beer bashes, and I felt as uneasy at them as I did in my cubicle. Not Jill. At Apple, she was a party animal. She and my mother had even trekked down to San Bernardino for Woz's infamous US Festival, a dusty feel-good concert with bands like INXS and Oingo Boingo that was supposed to be a California Woodstock, a spontaneous combustion of music and good vibes, but that is remembered by most who attended for the long lines at the port-a-cans.

And as far as Jill was concerned, the US Festival had been nothing compared to Woz's son's first birthday party the year before. To Jill, that was the coolest event that ever took place on the planet Earth. At the time, Woz lived in a stone mansion in the hills above the Valley, and this party had the festive air of a Renaissance celebration. There were jugglers, magic acts, puppet shows, costumed clowns, hot-air balloons, and llamas. Jill spent most of the afternoon in Woz's private game room, which was up in one of the turrets of the house and was stocked with all the latest video games: Tempest, Space Invaders, Dragon's Lair.

Jill talked about that party for years. To her, it was like something out of a fairy tale, and she desperately wanted to be a part of it. She must have said a thousand times, "When I grow up, I'm going to work at Apple Computer." She announced it as if it were a fact, a predetermined fate.

"I bet every person you know at Apple has a high-school diploma," I said to Jill one night.

"So," she said.

"So if you want to work there, you need to do well in school. They don't hire dropouts."

"Steve Jobs is a dropout."

"From college."

"So."

"That's different."

"Besides, I'm not a dropout."

"Well, I'm worried about you. You're such a smart girl. If you put your mind to it, I'm sure you could be a straight-A student."

"Yeah, right."

"It's true."

"I hate school," she said.

"Why?"

"It's so boring."

"Not all your classes are boring, are they?"

She sighed. "I really don't want to talk about this."

"Why?"

"I just don't, okay?"

"Maybe I can help you."

"No, thanks."

"I really think this is important—"

"I said I don't want to talk about it."

"But Jill—"

"Good-bye, Jeff," she said, and hung up on me. Again.

———

My mother had dated Michael the tool salesman for nearly two years. After that ended, she had gone out with a paranoiac who walked around her condo with a gun strapped to his belt and who, when dining in restaurants, refused to sit with his back to a window. Then there was a brief thing with a captain in the Palo Alto Fire Department who claimed to be a torch for the mob, and a slightly longer thing with a good-natured Italian guy with a silver van and matching speedboat who took my mother and my sister waterskiing on Lake Comanche.

Not surprisingly, Jill hated all these men. She hated them, in fact, before she ever met them. She hated even the idea of them. Whenever my mother tried to introduce her to a man who she thought held some promise, my sister glared and scowled and treated his every word as if it was the stupidest utterance to have ever escaped the mouth of a human being.

Sometimes Jill called me when my mother was out on a date and she was home alone. "Where's Mom?" I'd ask.

"Out," she'd say.

"Out where?" I'd ask.

"Just out," she'd say.

"What time will she be back?" I'd ask.

And then Jill would get exasperated: "I don't know! I'm not her baby-sitter!" Then my mother would come home, and no Jill—no note on the fridge, nothing. Just gone. Later, she'd find out Jill was cruising El Camino Real with her friends or eating French fries and smoking in a corner booth at Denny's at 2 A.M.

Before long, Jill was wearing spiky black high heels, crucifixes in her ears, and rubber O-rings as bracelets, as well as dyeing her hair orange and red. I thought it was pretty cool myself, but it drove my mother crazy. She'd call me and say, near tears, "What do I have to do—put bars on the window? Change the locks? Why can't I control your sister?"

Whenever I'd try to suggest to my mother that her own late-night adventures might not set the best example for Jill, she'd say, "You just don't understand me. You don't understand what I'm going through." And she would say it in a tone that told me she resented the fact that I passed judgment on her, that I would presume to tell her how to live her life—and, even worse, to pin the blame on her for Jill's troubles.

And she was right, of course. I didn't understand what she was going through. I was twenty-five years old—what did I know about love or loneliness? But she was my mother, and so I held her to an impossible standard. She was supposed to be infallible and saintly and unselfish. Divorce or not, she still belonged to us. Her own freedom was not up for consideration.

———

"You should have called," my mother snapped when Jerry, Karisa, and I arrived at her condo for Thanksgiving dinner that year. We had stayed at my father's house too long, listening to our wisecracking uncle Bob tell jokes about masturbating priests and traveling salesmen; by the time we arrived at my mother's place, we were two hours late. The turkey was dried out, the stuffing needed to be reheated, the rolls were going stale. My mother took holidays seriously, especially Thanksgiving. It was a celebration that was all about food, which she loved; more important, the holiday gave her a chance to show off her turkey collection. Three hundred and sixty-four days a year, her collection of ceramic turkeys and turkey napkin holders and turkey salt-and-pepper shakers sat quietly and unobtrusively on her bookshelves. And then, once a year, they descended and transformed the condo into a feathery celebration of gobblers.

Plus, this year she had a new boyfriend she wanted us to meet, so she really went all out with the cooking and the decorations. Dwight was a tall, broad-shouldered guy in his mid-sixties—too old for my mom, I thought—with a silver beard that made him look like Kenny Rogers. He'd recently retired after a career selling life insurance and now spent most of his time flying around California in a private plane and playing golf and poker with his pals. He was quiet and gruff. I immediately disliked him.

For a while, I behaved myself. My mother lit the candles, and we settled down to eat. We had hardly gotten the reheated turkey onto our plates when the conversation turned to Jill's troubles in school. By now, she had all but quit going to classes and was working part-time at Cool Licks, a yogurt shop nearby. I don't recall exactly how the topic came up—maybe my mother mentioned that she talked to Jill's counselor again or that she'd had another conference with her teacher. I just remember my mother looking at Jill and saying gently, "I think Jill understands how important school is."

And that's when I popped my cork. My explosion was the predictable result of months of biting my tongue, of saying not exactly what I thought, of tiptoeing around other people's feelings. At the time, I believed—as only a twenty-five-year-old can believe—that I was bravely speaking my mind and therefore helping, in my own small way, to open my family up to more honest dialogue. My rant lasted about ten minutes, but the gist of it went like this: "Let's cut the bullshit, Mom. You say you have so much concern for Jill, but I don't see you spending your Friday nights sitting home helping her with her homework. I don't see you making a whole lot of sacrifices in order to make sure she stays in school. I think the only thing that's on your mind right now is trying to hook up with a new husband. Why don't you at least be honest with yourself, and with us, about what is really important to you?"

And so on. In some families, this kind of confrontation is routine dinner conversation. Not in ours. I remember my mother looking at me with melting eyes, like she couldn't believe it was me saying this to her, that I would be so heartless.

And Dwight, the poor guy, he walked into a real shitstorm. When he interrupted and suggested, in a gentlemanly way, that I was out of line in talking to my mother this way, I said, "Excuse me, but this is none of your business." He stared at me long and hard, suggesting that were it not for his respect for my mother, he'd grab me by my arrogant little Berkeley-educated throat and yank me outside and knock some humility into me. (I didn't know until later that he was an ex-Marine who'd spent a few months on Guadalcanal.) Instead, he lifted his napkin off his lap, folded it on the table, and went into the living room to watch TV.

By that time, my mother was in tears. "I want you to leave," she told me at one point. "I want you to get out of my house."

"I'm not leaving until I've finished saying what's on my mind," I said.

Jill muttered, "God, you're all such jerks," then got up from the table and ran upstairs to her bedroom and slammed the door.

I stared at the cold food on my plate. Blood pulsed in my temples. My mother sniffled, trying to regain her composure. She dabbed her eyes with her napkin and said, "You should eat something."

And I did. I stuffed myself.

15

"I have a quote I want to read to you," Jerry said when I picked up the phone.

"What? It's three A.M.," I groaned. "I'm asleep."

"Who needs sleep?" he said. "You can sleep when you're dead. I want to read you something."

"Can't it wait until morning?"

"Just listen, okay?"

"I'm listening," I mumbled.

"Okay, here it is: 'Does wisdom perhaps appear on the earth as a raven which is inspired by the smell of carrion?' "

"What is that supposed to mean?" I asked.

"You tell me, college boy," he said. "I'll give you a hint: It's Nietzsche."

"Nietzsche . . . oh god, no. Tell me I'm dreaming. . . ."

"Don't be such a wuss, man. Don't you realize how brilliant this is?"

"Not at the moment, no."

"It's exactly what I've been thinking about lately. It's so fucking right on. I was just thumbing through this book of quotations I found in the closet, and there it was. I opened the page right to it. I was blown away."

"Great, Jerry. Glad to hear it. Now can I go back to sleep?"

"Man, you don't understand what I'm getting at, do you?"

"No."

"You remember the other day you asked me why I drink?"

"Yeah."

"Well, here it is."

"I still don't get it."

"Because there are limits to rationality, man. If you want to understand the world, if you really want to get deep, to understand the essence of things, you gotta push the envelope. You gotta let yourself go."

"And that's why you drink?"

"Yeah."

I had heard this—or a version of this—before. I agreed, there were limits to rationality—like rationalizing alcoholism as a path to enlightenment.

"Look, you want to drink, drink," I snapped. "You don't have to explain it to me. You don't need my approval. It's your life. Do what you want with it."

"Thank you, I will," he shot back. "Now, go back to bed, Mr. Sobriety."

Jerry knew I was tiring of the endless loop of sin and repentance in his life, and his wild stories about why he had to quit this job, or why he had become a gigolo, or why this or that woman had dumped him. I was tired of hearing about how our father had let him down when he was eleven and missed his Little League playoff game, or about how my mother had never put as much peanut butter on his sandwiches as she had on mine. And I think Jerry sensed that I was losing that essential faith that he could turn himself around by simply turning away from the bottle.

Besides, I had plenty of my own troubles. I'd just spent a year writing what I had come to recognize was a very bad book. It was bad for many reasons, but the main reason it was bad was that I so desperately wanted it to be good. I spent days rewriting the same sentences over and over, retyping them until they were so compressed and bloodless that they turned to dust on the page. In this way, they were not unlike my sex life with Karisa, which had devolved into a series of grinding, ritualistic moves that we performed together a couple of times a week and that usually ended with her turning toward the wall and crying and me getting up in the middle of the night and staring out the window at the fog rolling in over the treetops.

Karisa believed I was scarred emotionally by my parents' divorce, that I resisted intimacy with her because I was subconsciously afraid of repeating my parents' mistakes, and that it was a way of protecting myself from the inevitable breakup with her that I knew was coming.

She was probably right. But there was more to it than that. Our troubles—my troubles—had a lot to do with Jerry. The farther out of control his life spun, the deeper my need became to remain in control. The more he drank, the less I could stomach it; the more he lied, the more interested I became in telling the truth; the deeper he went in search of his inner demons, the less I pursued mine. In trying not to become him, I became something equally perverse: his depressively sober opposite.

In Tahoe, when I didn't know where to turn, I'd solved my problems by filling out a college application; now, when I felt boxed in again, I made the same move. Despite the fact that my novel sucked, I still had thoughts of becoming a writer. It was an unexamined impulse, not linked in my head to the fact that I came from a family in which silence was the golden rule. And like Jerry with his garage band, I labored under the illusion that I was one song away from a contract with a major label.

Instead of finding my rhythm, however, I was playing a lot of fuzz and feedback. I thought more lessons might help. So I applied to graduate writing programs at Columbia University, the University of Virginia, and Boston University. My main criteria for choosing these schools was that they were all a long way from Silicon Valley. Boston turned me down, Virginia said yes, and Columbia said yes and offered me a substantial fellowship.

Accepting the offer from Columbia should have been a no-brainer, but I was worried about Jerry. New York City was his dream, not mine. If I moved to New York, I knew it would be devastating to him. But was I willing to spend two years in Charlottesville in order to spare his feelings? That seemed stupid and self-destructive. I considered turning both schools down.

Karisa wasn't much help in the decision. My going off to graduate school was a delicate subject with her, given how chilly our relationship had become. She was beginning to think about going to law school or becoming an architect and was busy making connections in San Francisco. Also, I knew she was getting some heavy backroom lobbying from her parents and her sister to dump me. They saw me, justifiably, as a vacant lot that had been polluted by family toxins. I had no money. My career prospects were zip. "A smart girl like you deserves better," I imagined her mother whispering to her.

One afternoon, I drove over to Berkeley to discuss my dilemma with a former professor, Leonard Michaels. Michaels had been one of the big shots in the English department while I'd been at Berkeley. His novel *The Men's Club* had been published about that time to flattering reviews and was now being made into a movie. During my first year at Berkeley, I'd submitted a writing sample to him on a lark—a sugary short story about a boy who finds a love letter in the debris of an airplane crash. To my amazement, I was admitted into his class.

As a professor, he was brutal. He had a raspy, drawling voice that suggested he was fatigued by the small stupidities of life. Nothing slipped by him. He sometimes read aloud the first sentence from a story that had been submitted to him by a student, then he would stop, look up, and say, "Need I go on?" He despised sentimentality and artifice. He had grown up on the Lower East Side and still carried the attitude of the New York streets with him. He wore tweed coats on summer days and loafers in the rain and believed it was his job to discourage as many students as he could from thinking of themselves as writers.

I thought he was brilliant. I read every word he ever published. I even sent away for his Ph.D. thesis on Lord Byron. I ate black bread, butter, and onion sandwiches, just like the characters in his short stories. I told friends that the biggest regret in my life so far was that I had not been born Jewish. Other students thought he was an intellectual sadist, taking pleasure in the pain of his students, but I was drawn to him because he was the opposite of innocent and because I believed he was a truth teller.

Professor Michaels and I were not friends. We had never discussed anything of an even remotely personal nature before. In fact, when I walked into his dusty office on the top floor of Wheeler Hall, I wasn't sure he even remembered me. Typically, he did not offer any greeting or pleasantries. "I'm about to quit fucking around with this psychological stuff," he said as soon as I walked in the door. He waved a couple of pages of a manuscript in the air, as if he were shooing away flies. At the time, I had no idea what he was talking about but later gathered that it had something to do with the screenwriting hell he had recently been through on *The Men's Club*.

I got down to business immediately. "You enjoy moral dilemmas," I joked. Then I told him about the decision I had to make about graduate school. I offered a brief sketch of Jerry's adventure in New York and his subsequent troubles.

When I was finished, he blinked at me like an owl. "I understand your concern," he drawled.

"My brother—"

He waved the manuscript in the air again. "Whatever happened to him in New York, it had nothing to do with you. You're not responsible for him." Then he sighed, as if he were sorry that he had to be the one to break the news to me. "Nobody ever wants to talk about this," he said. "But selfishness is a greatly underrated virtue."

"Do you consider yourself a selfish person?"

"Monumentally," he said. "I think of selfishness as a kind of duty. I think of it as a calling."

That was really all I needed to hear. We chatted for a few more minutes, then I ran out of his office like a jewel thief.

Only now, as I write this, does it occur to me that maybe Professor Michaels didn't mean what he said quite as literally as I took it. He was, after all, quite capable of saying more than one thing at a time. And for all his arrogance, he struck me as a profoundly unselfish person. The question of what we owe to others is, in fact, the central theme of his writing. One of his collections of short stories is titled *I Would Have Saved Them If I Could*, a phrase he lifted from a letter Lord Byron wrote in 1817 after he'd witnessed a beheading in Rome. It's a coolly ironic line, suggesting the shallowness of good intentions and the silent rush of relief one feels at having absolved oneself from responsibility for others. At the same time, the line is full of sorrow, pity, and regret.

Which was exactly what I felt. *Sorry, Jerry. I would have saved you if I could. But I can't, so I gotta go now. Take care of yourself, all right?*

A few days later, I sent a letter to Columbia, accepting their offer. For several weeks, I did not tell my mother or my father about what I had done. If I did, I knew Jerry would hear instantly. I wanted to tell him myself. I anguished about it for days. Why had I even applied to Columbia in the first place? Did I have some subconscious desire to show my brother up? Finally, Jerry mentioned that he was coming up to San Francisco to watch a tennis tournament; he suggested we meet afterward in a bar near my apartment.

He was tossing back a shot of Cuervo Gold when I arrived. He offered to buy me a round, but I said, "You know I can't drink with you anymore."

"Come on, man, a single shot. What good are brothers if they won't drink with you?"

I sat on the bar stool beside him and ordered a Coke. I hated doing this—it made me feel like a preacher—but drinking side by side with him made me feel worse. I ran through my usual ten-second appraisal of his mind and body: a ratty leather jacket, Levi's, a Led Zeppelin T-shirt. Unshaven. Unshowered. But he was not swaying on the bar stool, which was a good sign. Pupils normal sized. No clenching and unclenching fists.

"I'm moving to New York," I announced. I said it as simply and unemotionally as I could. I told him about Columbia, the fellowship I couldn't turn down.

"Great, man," he said, not missing a beat.

I tried to round off the corners. I told him that he could come out and live with me, once I got settled. He shrugged it off, as if his own adventure in New York were a forgotten episode in his life, not even worth a moment of reflection. "Nah, I'm gonna stay around here," he said brashly. "I wanna go for the big bucks. Fuck New York. Fuck music. That's a loser's dream. Hey, we're living in the middle of Silicon Valley, right? This is a happenin' place. Why not take advantage of it? If you've got two fucking brain cells to rub to-gether you can make a million bucks. So I've decided I'm gonna go into sales. If I can seduce women, I can seduce customers. And if I can seduce customers, I can get rich. By next year at this time, I'm going to be driving around in a Porsche 911. A black Porsche 911."

He seemed to be waiting for me to tell him he was crazy, that he was wasting his talent as a musician, that he should stick with what he loved.

Instead, I lied. I said, without enthusiasm, "I'm sure you'll make a great salesman."

"Fucking-a I will. I could sell a hula hoop to a kangaroo."

Then he let loose that devilish, belly-rolling laugh of his, a laugh that boomed like thunder from some mysterious place inside of him and vaporized any bad feelings in the vicinity. I often thought that if he could just harness the engine that drove that laugh, everything else would take care of itself.

After he calmed down, he said, out of nowhere, "You know what I was just sitting here thinking when you walked in?"

"What?"

"How great it is to be human."

"As opposed to?"

"I mean, to open your heart. To feel things. That's how you know you're alive. God help the poor sap who cruises through life without any ups and downs, without feeling the rise and fall of everyday life. Whatever happens to me, I've lived, you know? I've tried things, I've felt things. You know what I mean?"

He looked at me strangely. I had the odd sensation that he was talking not about himself but about me. Like he was offering me advice. "I know what you mean," I said.

16

That summer, Karisa spent six weeks in Europe with one of her girlfriends. She wanted me to go with her, but I declined—I told her I needed to save my money for the move to New York. That was true, but it was also true that things between us had become unbearably stiff and bleak. She had decided to move east with me because she still wasn't sure what she wanted to do with the rest of her life, and because she was not ready to write off our relationship yet. We allowed ourselves to believe that maybe things would be different once we got to New York.

They weren't, of course. The instant Karisa stepped off the plane at JFK, we both knew it was over. There was a flicker of hesitation in her eyes and a new coolness in my greeting. I wondered what had happened in Europe, if she'd had a soul-lifting encounter with a stranger on a train, but I never asked, and she never told.

At first, Karisa distracted herself by trying to brighten up the dark one-bedroom apartment we lived in on the corner of 115th Street and Riverside Drive, a block from the Columbia campus. It was graduate-student housing, full of Naugahyde furniture, industrial carpeting, and metal kitchen cabinets. Karisa bought flowers, cooked elaborate meals, hung Edward Hopper prints on the walls. She also started scanning the help-wanted ads. She had come to New York solely to be with me and had no idea what she was going to do with herself while she was here.

Meanwhile, I fell in love with New York City. The noise, the traffic, the bobbing sea of faces on Fifth Avenue, the soot on the subway tiles, the steam rising from the sidewalk grates, the majestic brownstones in Harlem, knishes on the Lower East Side, the flutter of pigeon wings, the rush of kamikaze taxi rides. Unlike Sunnyvale, there was nothing innocent about New York. It was not a city that dreamed of itself in a utopian gown, nor did it have any faith that there is reason and logic in the universe or that tomorrow is going to be any better than today. It made no promises, told no lies. It was simply itself, a glorious ruin of a city.

I was less thrilled with Columbia. I spent four hours a day typing short stories in the basement of our apartment building (it was quieter down there), then emerged to attend classes taught by accomplished writers and editors. Some had intelligent things to say, some were simply tedious, but none seemed worth the many thousands of dollars it was costing me to attend. My fellowship covered only a portion of the tuition; my father wanted to help, but I refused to take any money from him. Instead, I took out student loans and began sinking deeply into debt.

One morning, I opened my apartment door and there was a UPS guy holding a big white box with a rainbow-colored Apple on it: a Macintosh. My mother and father had gotten together and purchased it for me, thinking that it would be a big improvement over my typewriter. A thoughtful and generous gift, but one I'd been dreading. I knew this machine was going to wheedle its way into my life somehow.

In principle, I wanted to hate it. I wanted to find it useless and ugly, a glorified toaster, a microwave for the mind, a confirmation that personal computers were never going to amount to anything more than fancy checkbook-balancing machines. But, of course, the opposite happened: I fell in love. I spent hours moving the cursor around on the screen and playing with silly paint and drawing programs. I wrote letters to people I didn't care about, simply to have something to type, and in a fit of nerdy elation I composed odes to our Naugahyde couch and plastic shampoo bottle. The Mac was nothing like the computers Apple had been building when I worked there, which were cold looking and hard to use; this suggested to me that maybe my problem with technology was not technology itself but the way it had been packaged. With the Mac, I felt a human response. I wanted to touch it, fondle it, whisper secrets in its ear.

It also conjured up memories of my days at Apple. I thought about those pale-skinned men who seemed to know so little about the world, who reduced every question to a sequence of bits and bytes, who never showed the slightest interest in the wind or the rain or the magenta bands of light over the Santa Cruz Mountains at sunset, whose idea of a good time was to spend hours blowing up asteroids in digital space—to think that those guys had built this beautiful machine! Maybe they had poetry in their souls after all.

The magic of the Mac, however, did nothing to change my views about graduate school. Six months after I arrived at Columbia, I was ready to drop out. I was down about everything: my stuck-in-the-mud life with Karisa, my sterile apartment, my new debt. I was already ten thousand dollars in the hole, and the idea of attending seminars for another year and a half and then graduating thirty thousand in the red did not seem like a smart move.

I mentioned all this one night in a phone conversation with my father. It was difficult to talk to him about my troubles at Columbia, partly because my decision to become a writer completely baffled him, but also because if I brought up money, I knew it would make him feel bad that he could not afford to help me out. But I was adamant about not taking money from him: If I was going to do this, I was going to do it on my own.

I told him that I'd recently applied for a teaching assistantship in the English department. It was a long shot, but if I got the job it would take care of my tuition fees, and I'd stay. "If not, I'll probably quit," I said.

"And do what?"

"Get a job," I said.

"Doing what?"

"Waiting tables, delivering pizza. Whatever I can find."

"Don't be ridiculous."

"I'm not being ridiculous. I just don't feel that the things I'm learning here are worth saddling myself with a thirty-thousand-dollar debt. I'm just being honest about it."

"Well, I hope you'll give it some serious thought."

"I already have," I said.

Two days later, he called me back and announced, "I'm coming out for a visit."

"Why?"

"I just want to come out. Do I have to have a reason? United has cheap fares. I'm flying in a week from Friday, I'll stay the weekend, then fly home Monday."

I was worried. Jetting into New York for the weekend was very unlike him. I told Karisa that I thought something was wrong, that he was sick, or that he had some bad news he wanted to break to me in person.

"You're crazy," Karisa said. "He just misses you."

A few nights before my father arrived, Jerry called. That did not surprise me. Not long after I'd left for New York, Jerry decided that a black Porsche 911 wasn't so interesting after all and that he, too, needed to make a big move—so he packed up and headed for Hawaii. Why Hawaii, I have no idea. He liked the sun and beaches, but I think he mostly liked the fact that he put a whole lot of ocean between himself and a woman named Olga.

Olga was the forty-nine-year-old wife of a NASA engineer. Jerry had met her as a gigolo. They had fallen in love, or something that Jerry described as love, although she was still married and the mother of three grown children. I'd met her once before I left for New York. She was thin and intelligent looking, with big eyes that, as her mood changed, could fade from gold to black in a split second. She had been born in Mexico, had slipped over the border when she was thirteen, had her first child when she was sixteen, and had spent her twenties raising her kids and working in the lettuce fields around Fresno. Then she divorced her husband and moved to the Valley, where she met a successful aerospace engineer and married him. At some point along the way, she went to college and got a degree in nursing; she now worked as an RN at Stanford Medical Center.

Jerry was always very cagey about the details of their relationship. He talked about how bored Olga was with her husband, "a wirehead who works fifteen hours a day, doesn't know the first thing about how to satisfy the tiger he has at home." There was a lot of sex and a lot of alcohol in their relationship, as well as drama about whether she was going to leave her husband for him or not. One of the reasons he moved to Hawaii, I think, was to escape confronting that question. For all his romance with sin, Jerry did not take lightly the idea of breaking up a fifteen-year marriage.

Jerry had never visited Hawaii before, had no job lined up, and knew no one. He was just going to rent an apartment on Waikiki Beach and start all over. Quit drinking. Quit Olga. Quit obsessing about how unfairly he had been treated as a child. All he needed was a change of scene, and it would all be different.

For Jerry, it went bad almost immediately. Three days after he arrived, he called me in New York (collect) to tell me that he'd just had $1,600 ripped off and he had nowhere to stay. I was suspicious. For the past year, he had not had a job for more than a few weeks at a time, and I presumed his gigolo nights ended when his relationship with Olga began, so where would he have gotten $1,600? Worse, he was drunk when he called, and when he was drunk he was a shameless liar. "I just set my backpack down and turned around—when I turned back, it was gone," he told me, slurring his words. He said he was desperate, needed money wired to him "right now, tonight," and wanted me to lean on my father. "I can't do that," I told him.

"Why the fuck not?"

"If you want him to send you money, you ask him. It's not my business."

"Well, fuck you, then," he said and slammed down the phone. He'd hung up on me enough that it didn't bother me anymore. I figured he'd call back in a few hours or in the morning, having forgotten what he'd been mad about.

My father called a few minutes later. "I suppose you heard from Jerry," he said.

"Yes. Did you send him the money?"

"Nope. He was lying to me. I could smell it."

"Yeah, me, too," I said. "What's he going to do now?"

"Call your mother, I suppose. Sooner or later, he's going to hit bottom and sober up."

My mother didn't give him money either. Finally, he called Olga, and she wired him some. Exactly how much, he never said, but enough to get him through.

For months after that, Jerry brought up that $1,600 whenever we talked. To him, it was evidence that he was unloved by his family. "How can you say that?" I argued. "You call us up, drunk, and expect us to believe this story about your $1,600? Since when does money equal love? Besides, Dad never charged you a penny for rent at the house or for all the food you ate. He let you use his car. You could still be living there if you weren't drinking—"

"Don't get me started on Dad," he said.

"*Unloved* is an outrageous thing to say."

"Forget I said it."

"But you did say it."

"*Forget it, asshole.*"

When my father arrived at the door of my apartment in New York, I hardly recognized him. I knew that he had a new girlfriend—a woman named Bev whom I'd never met—and that she had inspired him to start working out and dieting. Still, I didn't expect such a transformation. He looked like he'd lost about fifty pounds and gained a boatload of charisma. He was dressed in a stylish white sweater, a tan leather jacket, and new cowboy boots—a far cry from his usual Mervyn's jeans and Reeboks. He looked positively handsome. We hugged, and he gave me a big slap on the back and then kissed Karisa and said, "Hey, it's great to see you!"

He threw down his bag, and he sat down in the Naugahyde chair near the window and said, "Mind if I smoke? I have this bad habit." A two-pack-a-day bad habit, it turned out. He cracked open the window and lit up a Salem. I was stunned. When I was a teenager, he had often talked to me about the evils of tobacco, and although I knew he'd smoked in his twenties and early thirties, I thought he'd kicked it for good. Now he sat there waving his cigarette and babbling like a teenager about his adventures with Bev— "my special lady," he called her—and how much fun they were having "enjoying the finer things in life together." He had lost so much weight that his face was drawn and his ears looked big. I had the eerie sensation for a few hours that he was actually a different man, an impostor.

That night, he insisted on taking Karisa and me out to dinner. "Any place you want to go, you name it, that's fine with me," he said, waving his hand. "Price is no object." And that was when I started to worry again that my father had come out here to deliver some bad news, because as long as I'd known him price had *always* been an object. I'd seen him drive miles out of his way to buy grass seed on sale. I'd seen him deposit rolls of pennies in his bank account. I'd seen him change the lightbulb in the bathroom from sixty watts to forty because it would save him a few cents on his electric bill.

After much debate, we finally opted for a small French bistro in the Village. It was not an expensive place by New York standards, but the bill would be big enough for my father to feel good about paying it, which was all he really wanted.

"I suppose you're wondering why I came all the way out here on short notice," he said with a melodramatic flourish not long after we settled into the restaurant.

"Yes, I am," I said.

He made fatherly eye contact. "I'm here to ask you to stay in school."

I didn't get it at first. He came all the way out here to ask me to stay in school? We'd talked about this dozens of times on the phone. I'd been very clear to him that this was my decision, that I was going to stay or not stay based on what I believed was the right thing to do.

"Whatever you need, I'll try to give you. Money, whatever."

"Dad, I've told you—"

"This is important. Please listen to me. I don't care what you do after you graduate, but you have to stay in school." I knew what the next line was going to be. I wanted to cover my ears. "Education is the one thing that no one can take away from you."

If we'd been in California, I would have gotten up and left. I had explained to my father a thousand times before that having or not having a degree meant nothing for a writer, that no one cared what schools were on my résumé, that there was no reason to sink myself into debt if I wasn't learning anything, and on and on and on. None of it had made any impression on him, apparently. I knew that he genuinely wanted what was best for me, but I also understood that this was more about him than me. He deeply regretted the fact that he had never gone to college, and he believed it had held him back in his career. And perhaps it had. But that didn't have anything to do with my life. And I certainly wasn't about to do anything as idiotic as stay in school just to please my father.

I decided that tonight was not the time to fight a pitched battle over this, however. He had come all this way, taken us to a nice restaurant. So I said, half joking, "I'll finish the year at Columbia if you quit smoking. Deal?"

"That's easy," he said. "I'll quit tomorrow. Cold turkey."

"Sure."

"You watch me."

I didn't see him light up again the rest of the weekend. He did, however, go through about ten packs of gum each day, and I suspect he snuck a few smokes at night while Karisa and I were asleep, because in the morning there were always traces of ashes on the windowsill.

Given my lousy spelling and frequent abuse of the rules of proper English, I figured I had about as much chance of getting the teaching assistantship I'd applied for as I had of landing a seat on the space shuttle. As Karisa enjoyed reminding me, I may have been the only student since the university had been founded in 1754 to misspell the word *Columbia* on my graduate-school application. (I'd spelled it with an *o* instead of a *u*, like the country in South America.) Nevertheless, when the list of new teaching assistants was posted, my name was on it.

I was surprised, but I still wasn't sure I was going to hang around. Then a week or so later, I participated in the annual Columbia real-estate lottery, in which hundreds of graduate students hoping to upgrade to better apartments stick their hands in a hat and draw out numbers between one and one thousand. The lower the number, the better choice of real estate you have. I drew number four, which allowed me to trade in our cramped little bat cave for a sunny one-bedroom with a view of the Hudson.

The new apartment tipped the scales. If there was one thing that I'd learned in all those hours flipping cards in Tahoe, it's that when you've got a hot hand, you don't walk away.

17

Michele caught my eye because she always dressed in silk scarves and brightly colored clothes. One day, she arrived in the cobwebby dankness of Dodge Hall wearing a gold miniskirt and bright red, expensive-looking lipstick. Very unwriterly, very un-p.c. Her green eyes seemed to absorb all the light in the room and then project it back with laserlike intensity. She was small, thin boned, edgy—not my style at all. I dismissed her as a poodle—a rich, flashy, well-kept New Yorker. Then I read the first sentence of a short story she'd written: "My mother was afraid my father was making a bar slut out of me." That charmed me. After that, I noticed that whenever she opened her mouth, she had something cutting to say and was never bashful about duking it out with anyone. One afternoon, Michele and I got into a lively debate about Henry James in one of our seminars. I don't remember anything about the discussion, but I do remember feeling awfully sure that whatever I'd said was insightful and wise. When class was over, I wandered out of Dodge Hall with a friend. I heard the clatter of high heels behind me, then felt a tug at my elbow. It was Michele, her green eyes blazing like machine guns. She said, "I thought what you said in class today was incredibly condescending," then spun around and walked off.

Slack jawed, I watched her go. I was, of course, completely taken with her.

In the following weeks, Michele and I ran into each other at a few parties, and eventually I invited her to lunch at a lousy Chinese restaurant near campus. Everything I'd presumed about her was wrong: She was not a pampered New Yorker but a middle-class Jersey girl who happened to be going out with a rich TV writer who was making her miserable. She'd gone to Yale, graduating magna cum laude in three years, then dropped out of the Ph.D. program in English at UCLA and spent most of her early twenties going to clubs and listening to punk bands in L.A. Like me, she'd enrolled at Columbia because she didn't know what else to do with herself.

The fact that Michele and I were both involved with other people didn't slow things down a bit. Karisa and I had been living on borrowed time for a while now, and I wasn't exactly wracked with guilt when I spent six hours in a bar swapping life stories with Michele while Karisa was back at the apartment cutting out fabric for a new bathrobe. Besides, this didn't feel like cheating exactly. It felt more like an exit strategy. Despite the little buzz of excitement I felt whenever I looked into Michele's obscenely alive eyes, I did not see her as the one who would torpedo my bachelorhood. She was too sprightly, too complicated, too much an unfamiliar type. I thought of her as a novelty. I figured we'd have fun for a couple of months, and then we'd go our separate ways.

Nevertheless, my hubba-hubba for Michele required me to suggest to Karisa that we take the train out to Montauk for the weekend. We rented a room in an inexpensive hotel near the beach and went for long walks, and I told her in my shamelessly sensitive California way that things were not working out and that I thought it would be best for both of us if she got a place of her own. "A trial separation," I called it, even though I knew, and I'm sure she knew, that this was the end. Not a noble performance on my part. And the worst of it was, Karisa let me get away with it. She didn't fight me, didn't tell me what a jerk I was for not figuring this out before I dragged her all the way out to New York. Instead, she cried a lot and wondered what she had done wrong. I told her it was not her, it was just that our lives were changing, et cetera. I may even have used the phrase *I just need more space*. I certainly did not mention a word about Michele.

The semester ended a few weeks later, and Karisa had still not

moved out. By then, she knew I was running around with someone
else—how could she not?—and she was pissed. Good for her, but
messy for me. By now, she was calling me "asshole" over morning
coffee.

While she packed her things, I decided to go visit a friend in Tuc-
son. I didn't want to subject myself to hourly attacks as she boxed
up pots and pans and sorted through pictures. Plus, I was a little
spooked by how powerfully I was drawn to Michele. The last thing
I wanted to do was confuse the end of one relationship with the beginning of another. So I scrounged up a cheap ticket to Arizona,
hung out with my friend for a week, then took a bus down to Mexico and sat on the beach and watched the sun go up and down and
tried not to think about Michele.

It didn't work. Nevertheless, when I got back to New York, I did
not call her right away. I busied myself with moving my books and
clothes into my new apartment. I met Karisa once for coffee. In two
weeks, she had gone from hot to cold. No more anger, no more
"you asshole." Now it was, "I'm doing fine. Here's my new number.
Oh, and by the way, I'll be gone for a few weeks."

"Where are you going?"

"Cancún."

"With who?" I asked, surprised.

"What does it matter to you?" she replied, giving me a look that
suggested that our breakup was in no danger of sending her into a
nunnery.

Still, I didn't call Michele for a few days. I knew that if I didn't
want to get in deeper with her, I'd tell her it was fun but the timing
was wrong, blah blah blah.

I still had not made up my mind what to do when the phone
rang. It was Michele, of course. She was calling from the restaurant
at South Street Seaport where she waited tables a few nights a week.
She just wanted to know how my trip to California was, she said.
Right.

"What are you doing tonight?" I asked.

"Working."

"What time do you get off?"

"Midnight. As usual."

"We need to have a talk," I said. "How about if I stop by later?"

I could tell by the brief silence that followed that the phrase *have a talk* had a nasty ring to her—and I wasn't sure what I meant by it myself. But as soon as I hung up the phone, I felt a little lift of joy. That voice! I loved how sharp and lively it was. As soon as I heard it, I knew I was a goner.

I don't know how Michele handled things on her end, but before long she had dumped her rich TV-writer boyfriend, and we were spending twenty-four hours a day together. We watched John Ford movies on her tiny TV in her apartment way out in the wilds of Brooklyn. She cooked me buckwheat pancakes for breakfast, and when she was sick I made her chicken soup. Once, when we wanted to go out for dinner, we opened the Brooklyn phone book, I stabbed my finger at a restaurant, and we ended up out at Sheepshead Bay, drinking cheap champagne while a lounge singer crooned and a line of middle-aged Italian women with big hair did the Chicken on the dance floor. I loved how smart and adventurous Michele was. I loved her deep feeling for Lou Reed and her pale white Irish skin and the way she never averted her eyes when a foul-smelling street person approached her on the subway. Most of all, I loved her ruthless honesty. I knew she was a person who would let me get away with nothing and who would keep nothing from me.

18

In the fall of 1987, I was assigned two sections of Logic and Rhetoric, each with twelve freshmen, who were each required to write two essays a week. That meant I assigned and graded forty-eight papers every seven days, which worked out to about seven each night, if I was disciplined about it, which I was not, largely because I preferred having sex with Michele to scribbling warnings about dangling modifiers. By the time Thanksgiving break rolled around, Michele was spending four or five nights a week at my apartment, and our mindless fling continued to fly.

By now, I fully acknowledged the fact that I had fallen hard for Michele. I kept telling myself that this was all rebound action, that I would come to my senses soon enough, that I was using my feelings for Michele as a way of covering up the pain I was supposed to feel after my breakup with Karisa. Except I didn't feel much pain, only relief and occasional dark currents of sadness. It never stopped me from feeling a little jolt of excitement whenever, sitting at my desk late at night with the window open, I heard the clatter of Michele's high heels as she turned the corner on Riverside Drive and 116th Street, heading to my apartment from the subway station. I made up a list in my head of reasons why we were not ideal mates: She was too full of nervous energy for a California boy like me; she was too prickly; she was a writer (one writer per bedroom is enough); she was from New Jersey, and, even worse, she'd abandoned Bruce after *Born to Run*; she didn't have a trust fund I could mooch off for the rest of my life. But the clatter of her heels always swept away those objections.

A few weeks before Christmas, I learned that Michele's parents were going to London to spend the holidays with her brother. Michele had nowhere to go; at the last minute, I invited her to come west with me. I was hesitant, not because I thought this was a step toward something more serious, but because I figured she would take one look at my train wreck of a family and run screaming for her life.

Jill and Jerry were to meet us at the San Francisco airport. Although Jill and I had talked plenty on the phone, I hadn't seen her in almost a year. She never did go back to high school, but she had quit her job at the yogurt shop and was now working as a receptionist for a company called Airco, which supplied toxic chemicals such as arsenic and hydrogen chloride to semiconductor companies for use in the manufacturing of silicon chips. It was the first real job she'd ever had, and she was rightfully proud of it. She was dressed in black with a sweater tied around her waist, her blond bangs falling over her face, a dozen bracelets dangling on her wrist. We hugged, and I introduced her to Michele. "Where's Jerry?" I asked.

"In the car asleep," Jill said. I wasn't sure if she meant asleep as in passed-out drunk, or asleep as in tired. I glanced at Michele—I'd warned her that the potential for ugliness this holiday was high. She seemed unperturbed. When we got out to the car, Jerry was reclined in the driver's seat, dressed in shorts and a bright Hawaiian shirt, and completely zonked. I noticed immediately that he'd gained a lot of weight since I'd last seen him: His thighs, tan from the Hawaiian sun, were heavy, his face chubby. He must have weighed two hundred pounds. I shook him awake, and his eyes reluctantly fluttered open. They looked clear and sharp.

On the ride home, Jerry sat in the passenger seat while Jill drove. He insisted that we keep the heater blasting, even though it was fifty-five degrees outside. To my surprise, he and Michele hit it off—he bantered with her good-naturedly about how she wound up dating a guy as dorky as his brother and was obviously entertained by the fact that she was not intimidated by him. As we drove down the freeway in the darkness, I had a real surge of affection for Jerry. With all his late-night ranting recently, I'd forgotten how smart and sweet he could be and how fast he was with a laugh.

Jill dropped us off at our father's house, then offered to take Jerry to Olga's apartment, where he was staying during his visit. I wanted Jerry to come in and hang out with us for a while, but he said, "No, thanks, man, I'm not up for that tonight." So Michele and I went in by ourselves. My father was living here alone now, and it felt like it. The house was dark, depressing, gloomy. I felt like we were standing alone on a windswept Scottish moor, not in the warm embrace of the house I grew up in. When I ran the tap to get a glass of water for Michele, the water emerged gray and chemical smelling. She refused it. We moved into the family room, where I showed Michele the massive fireplace my father had built. Looking at it, I remembered how raw and cracked his hands had become from handling those hundreds of bricks, and I remembered the fine dust of mortar that covered his face, giving him a ghostly look. What a crazy project, I thought. It was as if he had been trying to hold the family together with brick and mortar.

Then the sliding-glass door in the kitchen opened, and my father stepped in as if he'd been cued offstage.

"Hey, Dad," I said. I noticed immediately that he was not in a good mood.

Michele stood up to meet him.

He didn't even look at her. "Where's your goddamned brother?" he asked me.

"Jill's dropping him off at Olga's, I think. Why?"

"That damn kid broke into my liquor cabinet again."

He pulled open the door, showed me a bottle of vodka and a bottle of bourbon. Both were half empty. "This is how I know when my son is in town," he said angrily. "I come home, and my liquor cabinet is empty."

"Why don't you change the locks on the door?"

"It doesn't matter," he said, and his face clouded over with that closed-up fury that always came over him whenever he was angry at Jerry, a face that indicated that Jerry touched some deep, irrational part of him, the black pit of all his blackest emotions. "The god-damned kid comes in through the windows or jimmies the sliding-glass door. It really ticks me off. He comes in, grabs the booze, blasts the stereo, pisses all over the toilet seat in the bathroom."

I glanced over at Michele. She looked spooked. My father had not even bothered to say hello to her yet.

"Dad," I said firmly. "I want you to meet my friend Michele."

He blinked at her as if she had suddenly materialized in the room like Captain Kirk.

"I'm sorry," he said. He shook her hand. "My son just gets me a little wound up sometimes."

The next day, we had dinner with my mother and her boyfriend, Dwight, in her condo. That went fine, my mother was cheerful and sweet to Michele; more surprising, Michele and Dwight positively hit it off, especially when he told her he did needlepoint. "He's six foot three! An ex-Marine!" Michele laughed as we were driving back to my father's house. "And he does needlepoint! That's the sweetest thing I've ever heard."

Michele and I also attended a family reunion for my father's girlfriend, Bev, whom he had been seeing now for several months. My father had insisted that we stop by. This was, of course, his way of signaling that things were getting serious between them.

The reunion was held in the rec room of a 1970s apartment complex in Sunnyvale; a Ping-Pong table was folded up against the wall, and the smell of a heavily chlorinated swimming pool seemed to seep into everything, including the bacon-onion dip. Bev, it turned out, had eight children of her own and who knows how many grandchildren. There were about fifty people at this party, lots of screaming kids, suntans, and blond hair. My father was in the middle of it all, dressed in a brown corduroy sport coat, enjoying the chaos. He waved Michele and me over to him and introduced us to Bev. She was attractive enough—dyed blond hair, blue eyes, lots of curves. "Oh, it's so nice to finally meet you," she said, planting a kiss on my cheek. Her perfume smelled of lavender and loneliness.

"Your father has told me so much about you." I introduced her to Michele, and the three of us talked for a few minutes. Bev was bubbly and excessively cheerful, in the manner of many California divorcées. (She'd been married twice before.) I immediately felt bad for my father. There was something unattractively coarse about her. She was a little too loud, and there was a little too much cheap gold jewelry dangling from her wrists and neck. She told us she was in the real-estate business, but then confessed sotto voce that she was really a poet at heart and that she had a book of poems she'd like to show me someday.

That's when we excused ourselves and headed for the door.

As soon as we got in the car, Michele shrieked, "Oh my god, those people!"

"What?"

"They're so decadent!"

I was confused.

"Every one of them is on their third or fourth marriage. It's all anyone was talking about. 'My second husband this,' 'My third wife that.' How bizarre!"

"Welcome to California," I said.

———

The following afternoon, I gave Michele a tour of my world. I showed her the high school a few blocks away that I'd attended, the shopping mall where I'd shoplifted a zillion candy bars and balsawood gliders, and the last few acres of apricot trees that remained, against all odds, on a busy street corner a few blocks from my house. I had powerful memories of the delicate white blossoms that covered those old trees in early March, and of halved apricots lying on drying racks under the bright summer sun. "They were beautiful, like a carpet of gold," I rhapsodized to Michele.

She rolled her eyes. She'd lived in L.A.; she'd heard the sad story of California paradise being paved over a million times. As we drove around, she kept saying, "I'm sorry, sweetie, but this place is butt ugly. It doesn't even have the charm of L.A."

When I drove her by the Apple campus, however, her face lit up.

Michele was anything but a technology junkie, but she had played with my Mac a few times and had fallen in love with it. She was also curious about the machine's chief architect, Steve Jobs, whom she had recently met at a book party in Manhattan.

During her first year at Columbia, Michele had interned at *The Paris Review,* where she had met and become friends with the writer Mona Simpson. At the time, Mona was writing her first novel, *Anywhere But Here,* about a young girl whose father has disappeared, leaving her and her crazy mother to fend for themselves. Mona had some experience with lost fathers and crazy mothers in her own life and had long assumed that she was an only child. Not long before she and Michele became friends, however, Mona had discovered she had a brother who had been given up for adoption: Steve Jobs.

When I met Michele, she and Mona jogged together in Riverside Park three or four times a week, and the three of us often went out to dinner or a movie together. This was not long after Steve had been booted from Apple after his battle with John Sculley, the former Pepsi executive whom Steve had recruited to help manage the company. Although Mona thought she could keep her relationship with Steve a secret (a notion she later abandoned), she was never shy about talking about him with us. I heard about many late-night calls between her and Steve and about his imperiousness, his drive to do great things in the world, his manipulativeness, and his ruthlessness. I had shaken his hand a few times at Apple but had never had any inkling of his Shakespearean character, so full of contradictions, as weak as he was strong, as cunning as he was naive.

The way Mona talked about Steve, I realized, was not so different from the way I talked about Jerry. Like me, Mona was often exasperated by her brother's late-night calls and by his unusual mix of arrogance and vulnerability. Like me, she seemed to love her brother deeply and want to shoot him at the same time.

I sometimes thought about how much Mona's brother and my brother had in common. Steve was seven years older than Jerry, but they grew up within a couple of miles of each other, both drank the same water, breathed the same air, went to schools in the same district, ate food from the same grocery stores, and were raised by blue-collar fathers and stay-at-home mothers (although Steve grew up with adoptive, not biological, parents). And yet their lives could not have taken more opposite paths. Where was the fork in the road? What's frightening to consider is not the fine line that exists between the winners and the runners-up, but the equally fine line between those who walk away with all the chips and those who walk away with nothing.

On Christmas Day, Jerry and Olga arrived at my father's house looking like they were dressed for church. Jerry was steady and calm and more or less sober, in khakis and a long-sleeved white shirt that had been nicely pressed. Olga looked surprisingly old and disturbingly thin. Jerry had told me that she had a son who was older than he was, but the inequality in their ages had never impressed me before. It did now. The lines on her face were deeper; she looked worried and weak. She couldn't have weighed more than ninety pounds. Next to Jerry, who was starting to get positively fat, she looked like a waif.

She was obviously in love with Jerry, however, and hardly took her hands off of him the entire day. Jerry snuggled affectionately with her, calling her by kooky endearments like "snoogums" and "my little sweet potato."

After we exchanged presents, my father built a big fire in the fireplace, and Jill gathered up all the wrapping paper and tossed it into the flames. Then Bev came over with one of her daughters, and we all sat at the dining-room table and ate a big family breakfast. I learned that Bev not only wrote poetry but also sang New Age spirituals. In fact, she had considered a career in music before choosing real estate. "After I left my second husband, I needed to do something a little more practical," she explained.

Michele seemed amused by Bev. In fact, she seemed to take my entire family in stride. She thought Jerry was a charmer, treated Jill like a peer, and wasn't put off by her first meeting with my angry father or his overbearing holiday cheer. Admittedly, she hated where I lived, but she didn't hold that against me either. I thought at first it was just good manners, but then I realized that she was not the kind of person who could have made it through the holidays on good manners alone. I had known Michele for only about six months, but I already recognized that she was a fairly transparent person—her emotions ran close to the surface. And the fact that she was able to embrace my messy, complicated family was a remarkable thing to me. I'd never met such a lively mind packaged with such a strong heart.

After breakfast, I noticed Jerry sitting outside under the mulberry tree. My father had transplanted this tree from a one-gallon can after we first moved in; now, its trunk was as thick as my waist, and the limbs of the tree spread over the backyard like angel wings.

"Hey," he said.

I sat down next to him. He had a crooked, bemused smile on his face. "What a trip, huh?"

"What?"

"Bev."

"Oh god," I said, rolling my eyes.

"I think Dad's pretty hot for her."

"It'll blow over."

"I don't know. I bet he marries her."

"No way."

Jerry shrugged. "I'm telling you. Just watch."

We listened to the voices in the house for a moment.

"You look good," I said.

He patted his belly. "Too many of Olga's tamales," he said.

"In Hawaii?"

He nodded. "She's basically living with me over there. She's great. She's really saved my life. I feel better than I've felt in—shit, I don't know—since New York."

"You going to stay over there?"

"Nah. Nice weather, nice beaches, but you get sick of it after a while. Besides, there's nothing to do. It was fine when I was just picking up chicks on the beach, but, you know, now that Olga's over there, I've had to clean up my act."

Inside, we could hear Michele and our father talking about Annie, his hunting dog. He was bragging, as he always did, that she could smell a pheasant a mile away.

"Michele's a feisty bitch, isn't she?"

Bitch, I knew, in this context, was a term of affection. It meant, paradoxically, that he respected her, that he thought she was tough and intelligent and attractive.

"Yeah, I'm really crazy about her," I admitted.

"By far the coolest chick I've ever seen you with," Jerry said.

"You didn't like Karisa?"

He rolled his eyes and let out a long, painful growl. "Oh, god, she had such a pole up her ass. If you didn't dump her soon, I was gonna have to seriously consider shooting her myself. I mean, I'm your brother. I wasn't going to watch you go down in flames with a wench like that."

"Thanks," I said, smiling.

He gave me a serious look. "You'd do the same for me, right?"

"Of course," I said, but his words gave me a chill.

19

On New Year's Eve, Michele and I left my father's house and drove north for four hours to Los Molinos, a small town near the Oregon border where my mother's parents had moved after Pop retired from the landscape-contracting business about fifteen years earlier. It was a different California up there. There was no commute traffic, no smog, no condos. The Sacramento River wound through the center of the valley, and walnut orchards lined the sides of the road. In the distance, clouds danced around the triangular peak of Mount Shasta, an inactive volcano. "What a romantic landscape," Michele crooned.

I don't remember what inspired this trip except that I wanted to get Michele out of Silicon Valley and show her what I thought was the real California. (Now I understand that I had it all wrong—the Valley is the real California, and the orchards and rivers of the north are just a landscape waiting to be subdivided.) I also wanted her to meet Nan and Pop. They were old, I was afraid they would die soon, and I wanted everyone I cared about to get a glimpse of them before they were gone.

In Los Molinos, Nan and Pop lived in a small, white bungalow in a poor residential neighborhood not far from the river. Bad investments had left them with very little money to live on, but they never complained. It was surrounded by fruit trees and several giant camellia bushes, all of which grew like crazy in the rich river-washed soil. When we pulled up, Pop, as usual, was sitting in his green leather chair, smoking a Macanudo, while Nan was perched on the couch in a spot that gave her a good view of the window so that she could spot our car the moment we pulled up.

"Come in, come in," Nan said, holding the door open, her light blue eyes burning bright, even now, in her late seventies. She was a strong, sturdy, earthbound woman. You could tell at a glance that she loved to garden. But you could also tell that she still thought of herself as a real lady. She always wore a fake pearl necklace and ear-rings, and frequent trips to the beauty parlor guaranteed not a trace of gray in her dyed-gold hair.

I gave her a kiss and introduced her to Michele, then walked over to say hi to Pop, who was just rising out of his chair, ashes from his Macanudo drifting down over his red flannel shirt. Unlike Nan, who seemed to get younger and giddier and more childlike every time I saw her, Pop was aging in a different way, gently acquiring the wisdom and authority of an old Indian chief—a man who has tracked many buffalo, seen many moons, and feels no urgency to re-veal his secrets. I loved Pop, and every time I saw him—and saw that he was still alive—I felt blessed.

Nan poured us all some ginger ale, and we headed out for a gar-den tour. Pop talked about how the Chrysler Imperial roses hadn't bloomed well that year and how much bigger the redwood that my father had given them had grown, and we looked over the carrots and lettuce and garlic in Nan's vegetable garden. As we walked along, Michele kept squeezing my hand and smiling at me. I don't know what she was thinking, but I was suddenly overwhelmed by the contrast between my grandparents' lives and what we'd seen in Sunnyvale. Nan and Pop had known plenty of hard times, but here they were, on the verge of their fiftieth wedding anniversary, still taking pleasure in each other and their garden and their silly dog, Lucy, a dachshund who sat up on her hind legs, looking regal as a member of Parliament, waiting silently for Pop to slip her a cookie. It was obvious to me fifteen minutes after we arrived that Michele loved them, and they loved her, and sometime during those fifteen minutes I had a radical and practically unthinkable thought: Maybe not all marriages are about restraint, suffering, submerged desire, unfulfilled possibility, loneliness, frustration, and betrayal. Maybe there are other ways of doing it.

Later that night, the four of us ate New Year's Eve dinner together. Michele baked an apple pie, Pop's favorite, then she and I walked down to the local Veterans' Hall, where a country-and-western band was playing. We danced like teenagers and swigged cheap champagne out of plastic glasses until 1986 was long gone and 1987 seemed like the most promising year in history. On the way home, snow began to fall—a rare occurrence in this part of California—and by the time we made it back to Nan and Pop's house at about 3 A.M., I'd decided that I wanted to marry Michele.

On New Year's Day, as we drove to Lake Tahoe to visit one of Michele's friends, I considered pulling off on the side of the road and popping the question. Then I thought, *No, all wrong.* My head was suddenly full of elaborate scenarios: climbing to the top of a mountain in the Sierras with her (too much snow), paddling out into the middle of Lake Tahoe (too cold), renting a suite at one of the casinos (too expensive). I thought about waiting until we got back to New York, maybe springing it on her aboard the Staten Island Ferry or on the Brooklyn Bridge. But I didn't want to wait. I didn't want it to be a staged production. Besides, if I thought about it too much, I was afraid I'd never do it.

A few nights later, still in Tahoe, we were on our way out to dinner with friends. Michele and I were riding in the back of the car together, hands clamped around each other, watching snow-bent trees slide by the window, when Michele said abruptly, "Are we going to get married or what?"

It was a joke, but only partly. I made a crack about how I wasn't sure she was the girl for me—I was looking for someone taller. But she rattled me (which was, I understand now, precisely her intention). I was afraid the moment was slipping away, getting ruined by self-consciousness: *Just open your mouth, the words will come out.* Then I'd look at Michele and think: *Is this really the person you want to spend the rest of your life with? How can you be sure? Why not slow down, think it through?*

By the time we got back to our friend's condo after dinner, I was so nervous I was shaking. We took off our clothes, preparing for bed. I felt as if I had lockjaw, and my tongue was cast in lead. Finally I heard myself say, "Let's get dressed and take a walk."

Michele did not question the idea, even though it was well after midnight, and it was snowing hard. We dressed, then I took her by the hand and led her into a grove of big yellow pines near the edge of the lake. Snowflakes swirled down on us, and I heard waves lapping quietly against the shore. I felt reckless and foolish and brave and brilliant all at once, the way I had five years earlier, when I'd come to Tahoe with my bike strapped on the top of my VW and met the man with the pink turban and put all my money on the table and watched the silver ball bounce between red and black—between riches and poverty, comedy and tragedy, the past and the future—and I knew, before the ball stopped, that I couldn't lose.

I wrapped my arms around Michele and brushed the snowflakes off of her eyelids. "Will you marry me?" I said. I watched her face light up and melt the snow away, and thank god, she did not hesitate.

When we returned to Sunnyvale the next day, we broke the news to my father first. He just beamed and hugged us and said to me, "As soon as you brought her home, I knew she was the one." Then we drove over to my mother's condo. When we told her, she ran from the room in tears. Michele looked at me, alarmed.

"She's just happy," I explained.

———

We talked about eloping, but I argued that we should mark the occasion with a proper ceremony and a big party. And I knew exactly where I wanted to do it: Mission San Juan Bautista, a beautiful adobe church about an hour south of the Valley, best known as the church where Kim Novak falls to her death in *Vertigo*. It was a purely aesthetic decision: I liked the setting of the church on a bluff above a wide gentle valley, the thick adobe walls, and the brightly colored wooden altarpiece.

I had not been to a religious ceremony since I was about six years old, when our mother and father used to take Jerry and me to a Methodist church a few miles from our house. That had lasted about three months. Who needed God in a place called Sunnyvale? The only churches that did any business at all in the Valley were Catholic, and they were full of sun-whipped Italian and Portuguese orchard workers who'd pull up for Sunday services in their ratty old pickup trucks. Growing up, the whole idea of going to church seemed quaint and old-fashioned, something that people did before we walked on the moon and split atoms.

Nevertheless, for this occasion, I wanted the blessings of a higher authority. And Michele, a lapsed Catholic, agreed. During a quick visit to the mission, Michele grasped the romance of the place immediately but warned me that because I wasn't Catholic the pastor might not be willing to marry us, or he might ask me to convert. When we dropped by the rectory, however, he seemed more concerned about missing a few minutes of a 49ers game on TV than about our faiths. We picked a date in mid-May, then flew back to New York to tell her parents.

That spring, while we tried to make wedding plans from New York, Jerry was a great help. By then, he had moved back to Sunnyvale and was living in Olga's apartment, about a mile away from my father's house. He helped our father pick out a mariachi band for our reception and took care of renting the tuxedos, as well as other details.

Everything went smoothly until the night before the ceremony, when Jerry failed to show up at the church for the rehearsal. No one knew where he was; no one had heard from him or Olga all day. My father was angry, my mother embarrassed. "It's not a big deal," I said, trying to shrug it off. I knew better than to expect too much of Jerry, but, still, this hurt. I made plans for a friend to fill in as the best man in the likely event that Jerry didn't show up for the ceremony the next day.

But he did show up. He appeared in his tux a half hour or so before the ceremony was to begin, looking like he'd had a couple of shots to even out the day, but otherwise he was sharp and sweet. He stood beside Michele and me as we said our vows at the altar, following the direction of the Irish priest, who looked like he'd had a few belts himself. I glanced over at Jerry while a friend read a Yeats poem. He gave me a small smile—more of a nod, really—that said, "I'm here with you, my brother, I did not let you down." And he didn't. He presented the ring on cue, and I was conscious of his eyes upon me as I said, "I do," and then leaned over to kiss Michele with enough happiness to rip her dress. We turned around and walked down the aisle, flashing past four generations of family faces, the great warmth beaming from my father, my mother's tears, my sister with a bouquet of flowers in her hand, Pop in his white jacket and a western string tie, Nan snapping pictures, Michele's mother and father and relatives from Germany, uncles and aunts and nephews and second cousins, many of them strangers to me, but all of us linked by blood and history.

The reception was held on a basketball court in a nearby community center. The mariachi band tuned up as we poured champagne and filled our plates with red snapper. When the moment for the toast came, I glanced at my father, whose eyes were fixed with concern on Jerry—he seemed poised to jump up and tackle him if he said a wrong word. I knew Jerry had been working on his speech for months. He had called me a half-dozen times in the middle of the night and said, "What do you want me to say?" And I had always told him the same thing: "Whatever you want." I knew that he had looked at books of wedding toasts and quizzed our mother, our father, our sister, my closest friends. I was prepared for anything.

Jerry rapped his spoon against his champagne glass. The room quieted. All heads turned toward him. He rose unsteadily, his glass in hand. He looked around the room. He started to say something, then caught himself. He seemed confused, not sure what to do. Finally he said—no, blurted—"To Jeff and Michele. I love them both to death." He looked like he wanted to say more, but tears began to flow, and he sat down quickly.

20

After the wedding, I thought things were calming down in my family. It'd been eight years since my parents' divorce; the hurt and anger of the split was dissipating. Jerry seemed to be finding his balance; Jill was holding down a good job; my mother and father were both in love again. And I was as happily married as a man could be.

As time passed, I began to see that what had happened to my family was by no means unusual, nor was it particularly nasty, as far as divorces went. And frankly, I was sick of thinking about it. Okay, so my parents split up. Get over it. Whenever I was asked what happened to my parents' marriage—as I often was at parties in Manhattan, where expatriate suburbanites of my generation swapped tales of our parents' divorces as if they were baseball cards—I simply said: "My mother and father got married too young. They didn't know what love was." And that was true enough. But mostly, I was tired of looking backward. I was married now, living on a different coast. It was time to build my own life.

Work was a big problem for me. Once my teaching gig at Columbia was over, my job prospects looked dim. I had no novel to sell, no screenplay, no collection of short stories. I could either continue teaching, probably at some third-rate state college, or apply for a job in corporate PR. Either one was its own kind of hell. Then one afternoon, at a going-away party for one of my professors, I happened to meet Pat Towers, the wife of Robert Towers, who was then the chairman of the writing department at Columbia. Pat mentioned that she was involved with a new weekly magazine in Manhattan and that her husband had suggested that I might be interested in trying my hand at journalism. Where Professor Towers had gotten that idea, I don't know—I'd never so much as covered a high-school soccer game. Nevertheless, I told Pat I'd give it a try.

A few weeks later, I visited her at the offices of the magazine in a loft in the East Village. She introduced me to the city editor, a tall, witty southerner named Eric Etheridge. Pat had given him a couple of my short stories to read—what he thought of them, he didn't say. But he did point to a headline in the *New York Post*. "A twenty-two-year-old cop had his head blown off last night by a drug dealer in Queens," Eric said. "Why don't you go out there and see what you can come up with? Play Jimmy Breslin for an afternoon." Given my total inexperience as a journalist, that was like telling a Little Leaguer to go play Mark McGwire for an afternoon. But I took the subway out to Queens anyway and looked at the shattered glass in the street where Officer Eddie Byrne had been sitting in his squad car, reading the sports pages of the *Post,* when a twenty-three-year-old crack dealer walked up and blasted him in the head. Officer Byrne probably never knew what hit him. I wandered around with a notebook, chatting with the patrolmen guarding the scene, slipping under the yellow crime-scene tape that marked off the house where the shooter had been arrested. I stayed up all night writing 750 words, then turned it in to Eric the next morning. He ran it as the lead story in the city section and paid me $125—my first fee as a writer. That night, Michele and I celebrated by spending an extravagant sum—seven dollars—on a bottle of wine.

I immediately gave up writing fiction, which suddenly felt like an adolescent indulgence, and threw myself into journalism. I loved hanging out with taxi drivers, drug dealers, disgruntled bureaucrats, tenants'-rights activists. Unlike the 7-Eleven world I'd grown up in, the characters I met in New York seemed wonderfully and poetically tormented, vivid, and alive.

Less than a year after Michele and I were married, my mother and Dwight exchanged vows in a small ceremony in my aunt Carole's backyard in California. Jerry and Olga were there, as were Jill and her boyfriend, Ed. I was beginning to see what a good man Dwight was, kind and bighearted, and tried my best to be happy for him and my mother. It wasn't easy. Nothing feels quite so unnatural and strange as watching your mother take vows with a man who is not your father. And it's your new stepfather, of course, who carries the burden of those unsettled feelings. I know Dwight certainly did. He wore them like a crown of thorns.

My mother's wedding could have been a devastating moment for my father, but a few days before the ceremony he announced, in what I thought was a sad and deliberate way, that he and Bev were going to get married, too. Despite the awkward timing of the announcement and my mixed feelings about Bev, I was glad for my father. It was weird thinking about him remarried, too, but I knew that he would never find peace as a single man. If Bev was the woman he chose, that was okay with me.

At my mother's wedding, Jerry seemed happy. I still wasn't sure about the dynamic of his relationship with Olga, but she seemed to steady him, to give him comfort. I'd always heard that alcoholics needed to hit bottom before they straightened up. I wasn't sure where Jerry's bottom had been, but it seemed to me that he'd bumped into something. The most important news was that, for the first time in his life, Jerry had found a job that he was good at. He had talked his way into a job as a salesman at one of the largest motorcycle dealerships in the Valley and was making—or so he told me on the phone—three grand a month in sales commissions. This didn't surprise me. When Jerry wanted to turn it on, he had more charm than a giggling baby. "God, it's nice to be making money for once!" he crowed to me on the phone one night. "I actually bought myself a hundred-dollar pair of tennis shoes yesterday. Do you know how bizarre that felt?"

Jill seemed to be hitting her stride, too. Ed, whom I'd met briefly at my wedding, was a little slick, but he seemed harmless enough. He was a hard-drive engineer and said the words *hard drive* as if they referred to a part of his anatomy. He was a few years older than Jill, and he always wore tight shirts and seemed to be romantically involved with his own biceps, even thought they weren't all that spectacular. At my mother's wedding, he treated Jill with an excess of civility, pulling chairs out for her, opening doors, refilling her wineglass. Jill enjoyed being fussed over like this and smiled like a princess.

It was a very huggy time. We were all in the mood for reconciliation and forgiveness—even my grandfather Leonard, who was pushing eighty now and was considered an irredeemable shit by pretty much everyone who had ever loved him, with the exception of Elaine.

Divorce hadn't slowed Leonard down a bit. A year or so after he dumped Edie and his three sons, he and Elaine ran off to Carson City and got married and started a family of their own. They had two sons: The older was two years older than me, the younger was my age. It was as if Leonard had decided that there was a flaw in the manufacturing of his first family, so he cast them aside and started from scratch.

I'd never had much feeling for the old man. When I was a kid, he and Elaine and their kids often dropped by during the holidays for perfunctory gift swapping. By that time, Leonard and my father had worked things out so that they had a functioning if superficial relationship. I don't think they ever talked about much but the weather and the 49ers' latest draft pick, but they did speak to each other.

To me, Leonard was a cold and scary guy. He was clearly one of those men who had zero rapport with children and saw them as mewling midgets who shit and eat and breed chaos. Still, I was fascinated by him; he was cool, yet so precise, so brainy. I could see it was hard for him to be around regular people, whose clock speeds were not as fast as his. I was also interested in the fact that my grandfather had two kids about my age. It took me a while to figure that one out, and when I did I understood why my father tensed up whenever Leonard was around.

There was no question where my father got his love of building things, though he preferred to work in wood, brick, and mortar, while Leonard's projects were 100 percent electronic. Leonard often claimed to have built the first Walkman, back in 1924, when he was fifteen years old, using a pencil, a crystal, a piece of wire, and an earplug. He'd built it, he claimed, because he was bored on his long walks to school. By twisting the crystal on top of the pencil, he could tune in WBZ out of Springfield, Massachusetts. "My walks became a lot more enjoyable after that," he once told me.

Leonard always had some bizarre project going on in the garage of his Los Altos home. For a while, he was fashioning clocks out of old PC boards, using circles of red and green LEDs as the hour and minute hands. But his real pride and joy was an electric car he built out of an old Ford Pinto. In the late 1970s, an electric car was still a dreamy sci-fi idea. But Leonard, tight old Yankee that he was, got tired of paying high prices for gasoline and decided there had to be a better way. So he stripped the internal-combustion engine out of this old Pinto and installed an aircraft generator under the hood. Then he mounted five car batteries in the trunk, another four where the radiator used to be, and another seven in the area that had formerly been the backseat. Presto, his own homemade electric car. It'd go sixty-five miles without recharging, with a top speed of about 35 MPH— the ideal commuter car. He'd come gliding by our house in Sunnyvale once in a while, his blue and white Pinto rolling silently down the street like a ghost, the old man peering out the window with a big, proud smile on his face.

I was not impressed. By the time I was in high school, I'd pretty much decided that Leonard preferred machines to human beings. That was fine with me. Between the ages of seventeen and twenty-seven, I don't think I exchanged ten words with the guy. Not surprisingly, Leonard was the only family member who had not come to my wedding, even though he was in fine health and lived an hour away from the church. My father said it was because he didn't want to run into Edie. That figured. Forty years after he'd dumped her, he still couldn't bear to look her in the eye.

Not long after Michele and I were married—maybe it was the winter of 1987–1988—an odd thing happened. Jill told me that Leonard had stopped by our father's house in Sunnyvale three times in the last month to visit. "He just knocks on the door, and when I answer it he just stands there in his hat and his raggy sweater and says he just wants to say hello," my sister told me. "I invite him in, but he never accepts. He asks me about Dad, about you, about Jerry. Then he leaves. It's really weird."

Michele, who had never met Leonard, urged me to call him.

"I don't have anything to say to him," I told her.

"Maybe he has something to say to you."

I doubted it. Leonard meant nothing to me, and I doubted I meant anything to him.

A few months later, Michele and I planned a trip to California. Before we left, I found myself asking my father for Leonard's phone number. I was, I admit, curious about what was on the old man's mind. I wondered if he had some confession to make or perhaps some family secret to reveal.

I dialed the number my father gave me. "Leonard Goodell," a voice answered, gruff and impatient.

"Hi, it's Jeff."

Silence.

"Your grandson," I added.

"Oh. Yes. Jeff. How are you?"

I told him I'd like to stop by when I was in California and introduce him to my wife.

"Great," he said, sounding genuinely surprised. "Why don't you come by and pet the robots?"

———

The company where Leonard now worked, Adept Technology, was out in the north San Jose flatlands, near the bottom of San Francisco Bay. Mustard bloomed in a large field across the street, and the parking lot was full of Toyotas and Hondas, the favored vehicles of midlevel engineers. The building itself was a typical low-slung Silicon Valley tilt-up with concrete walls and tinted windows. As Michele and I got out of my father's Blazer, I wondered what the hell I was doing there. I didn't really want to see the old man and had no idea what I'd say to him—or what he'd say to me.

We signed in and were given magnetic identification badges—standard fare in the Valley—and in a few moments Leonard appeared from behind a door. He was as lively and alert as ever. Patches of skin on his face were splotchy and red, a reminder of troubles he had had with skin cancer, and his hair was thin on top but not altogether gone. He was dressed in the only clothes I'd ever seen him in: dark slacks, white shirt, and a thin, dark tie. He'd been wearing this uniform for fifty years, and it never varied except on weekends, when he sometimes went tieless and threw on an old, moth-eaten cardigan. All in all, the old man looked like the primal nerd, which was exactly what he was.

He shook my hand warmly and said hello but was immediately more interested in Michele. "Welcome to the family," he said, shaking her hand and giving her a devilish smile. Now I knew where my father, brother, and I got our flirty ways.

Michele seemed flattered by the attention. "Nice to finally meet you."

After a few minutes of polite chatter about family matters, he said, "Let me show you around."

We followed him down some hallways and through some doors until we came to a large, open warehouse about the size of a football field. In the center of the room was a large oval track, maybe a hundred feet across, with half-built machines stationed along it that looked like big milkshake blenders. Inside the oval were several dozen men and women, surrounded by boxes of sophisticated mechanical parts and electrical equipment. You could tell important work was going on here because everything was so clean: the floor, the air, the machinery, the workers' hands and clothes.

"This is the assembly line," Leonard explained.

"What are they building?" I asked.

He shot me a deadly glance, one that suggested that if he were king, people who asked stupid questions would be executed. Then he remembered who I was, and he just looked bemused. "Those are the robots," he explained.

"They don't look like robots to me," I said.

"Well, you've seen too many movies," he said. He walked us along, explaining how these startlingly primitive-looking machines worked.

Leonard was right—outside of the movies, I'd never seen a robot before. I'd expected cute little humanlike machines, like R2D2. There was nothing human about these machines at all. No faces, no eyes, just one big mechanical arm. They were industrial drones, capable of repeating infinitely precise movements millions of times over—assembling tiny electric motors, etching computer chips.

Leonard's job seemed to be to mentor the nerds. He introduced Michele and me to a few. They were about my age or a little younger, and as they shook my hand they said things like, "Your grandfather is quite a character," and "Hey, lucky to have an old man like that as a grandfather." It was strange, seeing this man who was so despised by his own family so respected at work.

But it was not as strange as seeing an old man surrounded by robots. High tech is a young person's game. Age forty is considered over-the-hill; at fifty, the only question is how they'll put you down: lethal injection or sledgehammer to the forehead. And here was Leonard, a man born the same year Henry Ford introduced the Model T, shuffling around like some kind of engineering icon in a room full of MIT grads too young to remember Neil Armstrong's moon walk.

"How long have you been working here?" Michele asked.

"Just a couple of years," Leonard said. "I get restless if I stay in one place for too long." He winked at her and added, "I like to play the field."

"I bet you do," Michele replied, blushing a little but not missing a beat.

We walked around for about ten minutes. Leonard showed us his cubicle, where he kept a desk and a phone and not much else, and then we wandered down the hallway, past the Coke machines and microwave oven. I asked to see a demonstration of the robots in action, but he waved his hand and said, "I don't think there's anything up and running right now." By then, we were standing in the front lobby of the building. The tour was over, but Leonard insisted that we allow him to buy us a drink at a nearby hotel. "Follow me," he said, and so we wandered out into the parking lot and watched him stoop into his big American sedan. (He'd retired his electric car a few years earlier.)

We drove a few miles down the Bayshore Freeway to a sorry old gravel-roofed hotel that had been built during the glory days of Formica. The cocktail lounge was full of red Naugahyde furniture and veneered cocktail tables. As soon as we sat down, Leonard started waving over his pals. He introduced us to Joe from Philco, and Steve, whom he'd worked with at Shugart, and Ben from Applied Materials. I realized that he wanted to show us his world; he wanted us to see that, in his domain, he was a big man.

Between introductions, he asked me about my work. I could see that he judged others by their titles and ambitions. He seemed impressed that I was living in New York and earning a paycheck as a journalist.

"New York is a tough city," he said, looking at me with obvious pride, like I was a chip off the old block. It was so unexpected and unjustified that it was almost touching.

As we talked, I was surprised at how curious he was about my life. He asked me about the kind of stories I'd worked on and the magazines I wrote for. He asked about our apartment in New York and whether we were happy there, and if we saw ourselves living there for long. The odd thing was, he wasn't asking about this as chitchat; it seemed to me that he was genuinely interested in what I'd been doing with my life in the last half-dozen years. At times, it felt like I was catching up with a guy I had gone to high school with, rather than a man fifty years my senior; he was up-to-date with everything that was happening in the world. An old fart Leonard was not.

What struck me most, however, was not Leonard's brains or his curiosity but the way I'd catch him looking at me sometimes. It was not exactly a warm or affectionate look. It reminded me of the way a scientist might look at a creature he had brought to life in his lab—a cloned sheep, maybe, or a special breed of mouse. It was a mixture of pride and satisfaction and responsibility, a look that suggested that he believed he had made some meaningful contribution to the world, even if no one in his family gave him credit for it.

He loved Michele. They hit it off immediately. He liked the fact that she had gone to Yale and that her mind worked even faster than his. And that wasn't all he liked. "Such kissable lips!" he said to her. And then he looked at me and winked, as if to say, "It's great fun being a dirty old man."

Michele thought he was great. "I see a lot of him in you," she said as we drove back to my father's house through rush-hour traffic. "You're both tall and thin. You both have brains. You both like women. He's a little brattier than you, but I'm sure you'll grow into it."

"You're joking, right?"

"Not at all. Why do you think I'm joking?"

"Because Leonard . . . well, I hardly know him."

"So? He's still your grandfather."

We drove along in silence for a while. I was having a hard time computing this. I'd always thought of Leonard as such a shit, such a cold bastard, so inhuman.

"The weird thing is, I see a lot of Leonard in you," Michele continued, "but I don't see anything of him in your father. It's strange to think of them as father and son."

"I think my father wanted it that way," I said.

"Why?"

"Because he hated him. After Leonard ran off with Elaine, I think my father decided that he wanted to be everything that his father was not."

"Well, he succeeded," Michele said bluntly.

21

I knew my father and Bev were having trouble. My father dropped cryptic hints about weekends at the beach that ended badly and tears after dinner in restaurants. Still, I was stunned when he called one night and said, "I canceled the wedding."

"What happened?"

"She's a gold digger," my father announced.

A gold digger? I wanted to say. *Then why is she going out with you?*

Instead, I said, "What do you mean?"

"She's got debts," my father explained.

"What kind of debts?"

"Big ones. If we get married, her debts become my debts. I'd be underwater for years. I've worked too long and hard to end up living like that." Well, I understood that. My father might never have made more than forty thousand dollars a year in his life, but he was proud of his financial independence. From the sound of things, Bev had puked a nasty financial hairball into his lap without warning. Apparently, she had not planned to reveal her debts to him until after they were married. But in a moment of weakness—or was it strength?—she confessed, hoping, presumably, that my father was so enraptured with her that the possibility of bankruptcy wouldn't bother him. It did. It bothered him a lot. But he might have been able to get over it had Bev not added that after they were married she hoped to quit working and write poetry full-time.

A few weeks later, my father flew out to New York for a visit. He looked exhausted. His face was saggy and pale. He'd put on weight. He still smoked like a chimney. In fact, if anything, he was smoking more. We drove out to New Jersey to see Michele's parents, who lived in a big, suburban house in a woody development that was very different from Sunnyvale. There were no blue-sky promises here, no booster spirit. Northern New Jersey is all about vanity and striving, with each house larger and ornamented more grandly than the next. Whereas Sunnyvale says, "I have a dream," northern Jersey says, "I have arrived."

My father seemed to enjoy the change. Although he didn't have much in common with Michele's father, who was a computer programmer and movie buff, he got along well with her mother, a rugged German woman who wore a lot of gold around her neck and arms and who shared his belief that cleanliness was next to godliness. She and my father walked around the yard and talked about the beech trees and the azaleas, but I could see that it was just his mouth that was moving—there was something missing inside. We had borrowed a friend's Cadillac, and the five of us squeezed into it and headed up toward Cooperstown, New York, where we planned to stay at a country inn and visit the National Baseball Hall of Fame. My father sat in the backseat next to the window, chain-smoking all the way, oblivious to the fact that we were all gagging. As I drove, I glanced back at him in the rearview mirror, noticing a thousand new wrinkles in his face and the dullness in his beautiful green-gold eyes. Somewhere on Interstate 90 west of Albany, I had an uncomfortable thought: Maybe my father had loved only one woman in his life—my mother. Now, after her marriage to Dwight, he finally realized he had to live without her, and he could not.

———

Next it was Jill's turn to take a fall. Not long after our mother's wedding, she decided to dump Mr. Hard Drive. At the time, I hadn't heard the whole story about what had happened between them, but she called once in a while to tell me what a jerk he was and how he was always pushing her around.

Instead of moving out to her own apartment, however, she moved back into the condo with our mother and Dwight. It was an odd decision, I thought, given the troubles she'd had living with my mother before, and given that she had a full-time job and could presumably afford to pay for a place on her own. When I asked her about it, she said, "Because I'm broke, okay?" It was that old fuck-you-big-brother-keep-your-nose-out-of-my-business tone. That Halloween, Jill went to a costume party with some friends at a club in downtown Los Gatos. She was twenty years old, a year under the legal drinking age in California, but thanks to the fake ID that I'd helped her procure on a trip to New York, she was usually able to slide by. For the party, she dressed up as a prom queen who had been in a car accident (a costume which, it occurs to me now, was unintentionally symbolic). She applied plastic scars all over her face and splashed fake blood on her dress. She looked horrific, which was exactly what she wanted.

When she left the club around midnight, she was not too drunk to walk, and it seemed to her that if she could walk, she could certainly drive. It was only a couple of miles back to our mother's condo. And she almost made it. A block from the driveway, a red light flashed in her rearview mirror. Next thing she knew, she was in handcuffs and on her way down to the Santa Clara County jail. The drunk tank at the county jail is not a pretty place on Halloween night. It was crowded and smelled of puke and there was a two-hundred-pound Mexican woman in a devil costume—red leotards, horns, pitchfork, and all—passed out on the floor. Jill was outraged that she'd been hauled down there like some kind of criminal and ranted and raved about how they had taken away her cigarettes, goddamn it, until a prostitute with a pockmarked face and running mascara took her by the arm and said, "You better drop the attitude, girl, or you're gonna be in trouble."

When my mother arrived at around 4 A.M., Jill learned that cigarettes were the least of her problems. Unbeknownst to Jill, Mr. Hard Drive was a serial check-bouncer, and Jill had signed her name on several checks on their joint account that had never been paid.

She was charged with fraud; a warrant had been issued for her arrest as well as his.

My mother posted bail, and Jill was released. She picked up her keys and wallet from the desk and stepped out into the waiting area in her bloody prom dress, plastic scar tissue peeling off her face, her hair matted and tangled. She took one look at my mother, and they both burst into tears.

I saw Jill a couple months later when Michele and I flew out to the Valley for the holidays. She looked like a whipped puppy. It was profoundly obvious to her that, for the next year or so, her life would suck. A judge made her pay several thousand dollars in restitution for the bounced checks; he also sentenced her to several hundred hours of community-service work.

So Jill had a right to sulk. Her favorite expression that Christmas was "Jeff, I don't want to talk about it." The holiday was unbearably bleak—a total contrast to the year before, when we had all been so bubbly. Besides Jill's sulking, my father was still chain-smoking and gaining weight. The whole reason he'd started smoking again, he'd once told me, was to help him lose weight. Now he was pulling off the dubious feat of smoking two packs a day and gaining what looked like five pounds a week. So I sulked, too. Even Michele sulked, trapped as she was in this sad-sack family holiday. My mother and Dwight were cheerful enough, but my mother was always cheerful on Christmas, so that hardly counted.

Amid all the sulking, it was Jerry who gave off the weirdest vibe. He and Olga came over to my father's house on Christmas Day. In Jerry, I expected to see a man on the rise. There had been no late-night phone calls recently, no drunken outbursts, no audible regrets about not having pursued a career in music, no more "I'm either a genius or an idiot." He seemed to have put all that behind him and was now, for better or worse, cruising down the middle lane of life.

When I saw him walking up the driveway, however, I hardly recognized him. He'd lost fifty or sixty pounds, his cheekbones jutted out like icebergs, and his eyes lurked in spooky hollows. He was also jittery. He got up five times during breakfast to go to the bathroom and was constantly wiping his nose. I thought he had a cold.

Olga was not in much better shape. Jerry had told me on the phone that she'd been in the hospital recently. She had colitis, Jerry had said, and when it flared up she sometimes needed to spend a few days on an IV. She still looked weak. She was barely able to stand on her own and was constantly leaning on Jerry for support. Nevertheless, she had obviously taken pains to look her best. She wore a medium-length blue skirt and a blue blouse with a big bow across the chest that made her look like a librarian.

Afterward, I asked her how she was feeling. "Oh, I'm okay," she said in a way that suggested she was something less than okay. "Fortunately, your brother is taking good care of me. He is really a good nurse, you know. He won't even let me change the TV channel for myself."

"That's nice," I said.

"I don't think you realize what a good man he is," she said.

I felt a stab of anger. Who was she to be telling me this about my brother?

"Of course I know what a good man he is," I barked.

"He talks about you all the time, you know. He is very proud of you."

I nodded. "And I'm proud of him."

"You should tell him that."

"I do. All the time."

"Well, tell him again," she said urgently, as if it were something I must do before sundown. "Jerry is a love sponge. He soaks up everything you give him."

————

Jerry and I made plans to go to a movie the following night. He called about 6 P.M. however, and said, "I'm not up for a flick."

"Fine," I said. "What do you want to do?"

"I don't know. . . ." He sounded like he was ready to jump through the phone line, he was so edgy and nervous. "I was gonna stop by, but I decided I'm not in the mood for any more family talk, if you know what I mean. So why don't you just meet me out in front of the house in about a half hour. We can go for a drive somewhere."

"Sounds good," I said, then hung up.

My father, who had walked into the room when he heard the phone ring, gave me a penetrating stare. I knew what he was thinking: *Jerry's fallen off the wagon, hasn't he?*

"How does he sound?" my father asked.

"Okay," I said, shrugging.

"I don't like this," my father said. "I noticed something in him yesterday, but I didn't want to say anything about it. I was hoping it was just my imagination."

"I'm sure he's fine," I said, even though I had my doubts, too. When I walked out of the house a half hour later, Jerry's maroon Toyota Celica was parked at the curb, engine idling. I could hear *Some Girls* blasting on the car stereo. I opened the passenger door and the music blew my hair back. Jerry nodded and smiled but made no move to turn the volume down. He looked like he'd just emerged from a twelve-hour Dumpster dive. His face was unshaven, his thin gold hair greasy and a mess, his eyes bloodshot and dry looking. He was wearing dirty Levi's and his beloved Diadora tennis shoes.

I turned the music down.

He turned to me with mock outrage. "Hey, man, what are you doin', messin' with my tunes?"

"Sounds great," I said. "But I thought you wanted to talk."

"I do, man," he said. He threw the car into gear. "Let's go for a drive."

We headed north up Wolfe Road to El Camino Real.

"So, do you have a destination in mind, or are you just driving?"

"I want to go down to the shop and see if this guy took delivery on a Ninja. If he did, they owe me four hundred bucks. It was the last bike I sold."

"What do you mean, the last bike?"

"I quit my job."

"Why? I thought you were making good money. I thought you were happy there."

"Ah, they hassled me too much. I decided I'm not going to spend my life as a salesman. I can sell water to a duck, but so what? I have other talents. I don't want to look back on my life in fifty years and realize that I wasted it selling motorcycles to guys who are just going to go out and kill themselves on them anyway. Do you realize I've had four customers who've died in the first twenty-four hours after I sold them a bike?"

"That's brutal," I said, "but it's not your fault."

"I didn't say it was my fault. I just don't want to be around anymore when it happens. It got to the point where every time I sold a guy a motorcycle, I'd have this weird hallucination of him lying with his eyes closed in a casket. It was weird shit, man. It's like death has just infiltrated my mind."

By this time, we'd arrived at the dealership. It was a typical glass-fronted showroom; inside, we could see rows and rows of shiny new motorcycles, everything from trail bikes to highway cruisers. The hottest machines—the ones with the rocketlike cowlings and fat tires and thinly padded seats—were set above the others on rotating platforms. The dealership was closed, but Jerry pulled up in the parking lot and turned the car off and walked up and peered into the window. I walked up beside him. "What are you looking at?"

Suddenly he reared back and said "Fuck!" so loudly that I thought he'd been electrocuted. He slammed his fist against the huge pane of glass; it vibrated like a giant eardrum.

"What's wrong?" I said, alarmed.

"Fuck, fuck, fuck!" Jerry cried. He slammed his fist against the glass again. "Those fuckers! They must have blown the fucking deal! The bike is still there. The guy was supposed to take delivery last fucking Friday. And it's still there! I know they blew it. They probably blew it on purpose, just so they wouldn't have to pay me the four hundred bucks they owe me." He pounded on the door and screamed, as if talking to someone inside, "You're not going to get away with this, you peckerheads! I had that deal signed! I had it done! I worked on that guy for a fucking month!"

I said, "Jerry, cool it. Maybe the guy changed his mind. Or maybe he did buy the bike, and your check is in the mail. Why don't you just wait until they're open tomorrow and call the sales manager and ask him about it?"

"Yeah, like they're going to give me a straight fucking answer," he said.

"Have you tried?"

"What do you think I am, *stupid?* Like anybody in this fucking place is going to be *honest* with me? When has anyone ever been *honest* with me? Fucking never. It's the story of my fucking life." With that, Jerry's rage dissolved as quickly as it had flamed up. I presumed he was crying, because he looked away. He wiped his eyes with the back of his wrist.

"God, how did everything get so fucked up?" he muttered.

"What do you mean? I thought things were going pretty well for you."

"Yeah, right," he said sarcastically.

"Aren't you and Olga—"

"Olga's a witch," Jerry said. "If I don't get away from her, she's gonna wreck me. She thinks because she has all the money and because the apartment is in her name, she can control me. She has me on a fucking leash, man. I hate it." By now, his nose was running ferociously. He leaned into the car and got a box of Kleenex. He blew hard into a tissue.

"That's a nasty cold you have," I said sincerely. My brother is rail thin, wildly emotional, broke, angry at his girlfriend, had just lost his job, his nose is reamed out wider than the Holland Tunnel, and I still believe he has a cold. Who says emotion doesn't alter perception?

"I just want to do one thing in my life," Jerry said, his face shadowed by the flickering glow of the streetlights. "Just one simple fucking thing."

"What's that?" I asked.

"Play music."

"Then do it," I said encouragingly.

"It's the only thing that matters to me. It's the only thing that gives me pleasure. It's the only thing that gives me peace. I don't care about sex or money or anything else. I just care about music. I just want to play." He took a folded-up piece of yellow legal paper out of his pocket. There were a few bars of music written on it. Since I don't read music, it meant nothing to me.

"What is it?"

"The beginnings of a song."

"What kind of song?"

"Well, it's not really a song. Just a beat, really. Wanna hear it?"

"Of course," I said.

He dropped his hands onto the fender of his Celica. A look of clarity and concentration eased onto his troubled face. He started pounding out a beat on the fender as if it were a bongo. It started simply, then built into a more complex riff that seemed to dance and vibrate in the air between us. It was beautiful and moving, but to my ears it wasn't music. It was a kind of tonal code Jerry was using to communicate something that he could never put into words. What that something was, I couldn't say, but that night, I felt some approximation of it, similar to the way you pick up a Christmas package and shake it and guess what's inside. At one point, the beat seemed to reverse itself suddenly, then perform a double twist and a somersault. "See that, that's one hot fucking paradiddle. I don't quite have it down yet. I'm still working on it." Jerry smiled hugely. He knew it was good. "Wanna hear it again?"

22

In the weeks after I returned to New York, there were many late-night calls during which Jerry sounded amped up or hungover as he talked about how much he loved music or how he couldn't pursue it as long as he was with Olga. When I suggested he leave her, he said things like, "She left her husband for me. I can't just dump her." And I told him predictably brotherly things such as, "Jerry, you have to do whatever makes you happy. If Olga is in the way, you have to leave her. Whatever happened between her and her husband is not your problem, and it's not your responsibility."

These words were laced with impatience and exasperation and, worst of all, expeditiousness. I was working ten or twelve hours a day, running from plane crash to murder scene to taxi scandal. I loved the hustle of reporting—the deadline pressure, the thrill of the chase, the private ego jolt of seeing my name on the cover of a magazine at every newsstand in New York City. But it meant that I had less and less time for Jerry's rambling late-night conversations. Or, to be more honest about it, I was not willing to work less so that I could talk to Jerry more. I'd done what I could for him, I thought. I'd lived up to my responsibilities as a brother, I'd listened to him and talked with him and counseled him and been achingly sympathetic with him and brutally frank with him until I was, as my mother would have put it, blue in the face. The effect of all this, as far as I could tell, was less than zero.

It was time to end this nightmare of codependency and draw a sharp line between his life and mine.

It worked for about three months. During that time, Michele and I were finally booted out of my Columbia-subsidized apartment in Manhattan to make way for the next crop of grad students. We moved into a small one-bedroom in Carroll Gardens, a Brooklyn neighborhood that was full of aging Italian mobsters and lovely brownstones. Michele and I were still unpacking our clothes when my father called one night. "Just wanted to give you a heads-up," he said. He used this phrase all the time when he was referring to Jerry. It meant trouble.

"Your brother's in jail," he said.

"What happened?"

"Arrested for possession of cocaine," he said. "He just called. He wants me to bail him out."

"Cocaine?"

"Are you surprised?"

I was. My elaborate wall of denial had held until exactly that moment. "What are you going to do?" I asked.

"Nothing. I think it might do him some good to sit in there for a few days. Give him time to think."

I didn't disagree. I knew that, over the past few weeks, Jerry had been screaming at my father for various offenses he might or might not have committed, from not being properly respectful of Olga at Christmas to not being supportive enough of his talents as a musician. I knew, too, that my father had indeed bailed Jerry out many times before. On the night of Jerry's senior prom, after he had been arrested for driving while intoxicated, my father had driven up to San Francisco at 3 A.M. to haul him out of jail. A year or so later, when Jerry was arrested for drunk driving again, my father posted bail. My father drove to Santa Cruz to pick him up when his car broke down and to the Oakland airport when he missed his flight because he was hungover. As far as I know, my father had never turned his back on him.

My mother had been an even softer touch—which was remarkable, given the amount of abuse she'd taken from him lately. He frequently accused her of marrying Dwight only for his money, of neglecting Jill, and of not loving him enough as a child. That was like a knife in my mother's heart. Still, when Jerry called her from jail, she was torn about how to handle it. She agreed with my father that it might be a good thing for Jerry to spend a few days behind bars. But she couldn't just turn her back on him completely.

So she went to visit him. She thought she was doing a good deed, showing her son that she had not forsaken him. Jerry later told me that when she walked into the visitors' lounge, she was smiling. Why she was smiling later became a subject of much dispute. To Jerry, the smile meant that she was happy to see him in jail; to her, the smile meant that she was happy to see him off the street, where he couldn't hurt himself or anyone else.

Then Jerry learned that she did not come to post bail but to visit. "You're not going to get me out of here?"

"Not right this minute," she told him. They were separated by a Plexiglas wall and spoke via telephone. "I think it's a good way for you to sober up." They talked for a few more minutes; when she left, my mother said, Jerry seemed disappointed. But the way he recounted it later, he was berserk with anger. "My own mother wouldn't even bail me out! How do you think that made me feel? And that smile—it was like, 'Ha, ha, you're finally getting what you deserve.' "

Olga finally got him sprung a few hours after my mother left. This did not surprise me. What did surprise me—and I didn't find this out until several weeks later—was that she had gotten him arrested in the first place. She and Jerry had gotten into a fight, and for good reasons or bad she had called the police. When they arrived at her apartment, they found several ounces of cocaine in one of Jerry's shoes in the closet. Why they were poking around in his shoe was never explained, although Jerry did tell me once that he had no idea the coke was there and thought that Olga had planted it to ensure that he'd be arrested.

Whatever happened, this coke bust was a turning point in his feelings for Olga. He was not angry at her for calling the cops on him; he did not feel betrayed. Quite the contrary. In Jerry's eyes, our mother and father were the ones who let him down. They were will-ing to let him rot in jail. Olga, on the other hand, was the only per-son in the world who loved him enough to post bail.

In the weeks after his release, Jerry fell apart. When we talked on the phone, he often referred to "that fucking smile on our mother's face." His fury was of a different tone than it had been before he had been arrested. At least before his rage had been articulate; now it was just a quick machine-gun shot of anger and resentment and self-pity. Olga apparently caught some of it, too, because not much later she threw him out of her apartment and changed the locks. Why she did this so soon after posting his bail was never clear to me.

Desperate for cash, Jerry sold his car to Jill for a couple thousand bucks, payable on a monthly installment plan. I don't know what he did with the money—more coke, I presume—but it never lasted. Be-fore long, he confessed to me that he'd spent several nights in a homeless shelter in Sunnyvale. "What a weird scene," he said. "All you hear are guys snoring and beating off all night long." Days passed when no one in the family heard from him. Sometimes he'd call from San Francisco, where he said he was sleeping in some flop-house in the Tenderloin. Sometimes these random calls were full of the usual anger at my mother and father, sometimes he ranted about what a spoiled child Jill was or how my path in life was "strewn with roses," but I often felt that the point of these calls was not to torture us but to stay in touch. It was his way of demonstrating affection.

But it was torturous. Jerry had been down-and-out before, but nothing like this. I spoke with my mother and father every night, hoping someone had heard from him. My mother felt responsible for this breakdown; she cried on the phone. "I thought I was doing the right thing, leaving him in jail. I thought it was good for him. I thought he understood that." My father tried to play it tough, say-ing he was sure Jerry would turn up somewhere, that he was a ca-pable kid. We all talked to Olga, who was friendly enough and claimed she hadn't heard from him, but I wasn't sure that she would tell us if she had. Despite the new locks on her apartment, her loyalty remained with Jerry.

At night, I lay in bed imagining my brother sleeping under an overpass or in the bushes in a park. I knew he wasn't sleeping on a friend's couch, because by this point Jerry had no friends. He'd never grown close to the members of the various bands he'd been in. Most of his other friends, uncomfortable with the violent personality changes he underwent when he was drinking, had long since distanced themselves. His one great and true pal, a guy named Rolf—whom he'd gone to high school with and with whom he'd been so close that people often wondered if they were brothers or lovers—had finally abandoned him after Jerry made a sexual advance on his wife. Besides family, Jerry had nowhere to turn.

About a week later, at 3 A.M., the phone rang. I knew immediately who it was.

"Hey, bro."

My first read: calm. Everything was okay.

"Jerry! Hey, good to hear from you."

He sounded puzzled. "Why?"

"Nobody's heard from you in a week. Nobody knows where you are."

"I'm in San Diego."

I could hear traffic in the background. He was calling from a pay phone.

"What are you doing down there?"

"I'm in love," he announced.

"What do you mean you're 'in love'?"

"I mean I've found the girl for me."

I had a sudden fantasy that I'd been all wrong, that I'd underestimated him again, that while I was imagining him sleeping in park bushes, he was in fact nuzzling with some tender soul on the beach in San Diego.

"Who is she?"

"Her name is Kathy."

"Where did you meet her?"

"I worked with her at a restaurant a few years ago."

"Oh." Already this was not making sense. "What inspired you to look her up again?"

"I was just thinking about her. She was really sweet. I regretted never pursuing things with her. So that's what I came down here to do. I'm going to tell her I love her."

"What do you mean you're 'going to tell her'?"

"I'm calling you from a gas station around the corner from her house. I'm going over there now."

"Is she expecting you?"

"No."

"When was the last time you talked to her?"

"Couple of years ago," he said blithely.

"She doesn't even know you're in the area?"

"Nope. I'm gonna surprise her."

A smoke detector screeched in my head. "Jerry, I'm not sure that's a good idea."

"Why not, man? Why should I fuck around? Why shouldn't I just tell her what I feel? Women respect that. I'm tired of all this repressive shit. I just want to lay it out for her and see what she says. If she's the kind of woman I think she is, she'll understand. I think it will blow her away."

"How do you know she's not married?"

"So what if she is?"

"Maybe she's happily married."

"I doubt it," he said.

"But what if she is? What if she has kids, a dog, a loving husband, and a minivan in the garage?"

He hesitated. I could tell he had not even considered this idea.

"I think you should call her first," I said, adopting a graver tone. "Invite her out for coffee. See how it goes."

"Nah, I don't want to fuck around. I just want to tell her I love her and let her deal with it."

"But how do you know you love her? You haven't even seen her in two years—"

"Believe me, I know," he said.

"Really, Jerry. No bullshit. You should think about this. If you just ring her doorbell and announce that you're in love with her, you might scare the hell out of her. She might think you're some kind of crazy person."

Jerry didn't miss a beat. "Do you think I'm crazy?"

"No, but I think you're drunk."

Wrong thing to say.

"You think I'm drunk?"

"I think you've had a few beers—"

"You think that's what this is about?" I could tell he was deeply offended, which didn't mean I was wrong. In fact, it probably meant I was right.

"Look, Jerry," I said, trying to be as direct with him as I could, "I don't doubt your feelings for this woman. I just think you should take a walk and think about it before you go over there. I just don't think it's a smart thing to do—"

"You don't know shit, man," he snapped.

"Jerry, I'm just—"

He slammed the phone down.

I didn't hear from him for about twelve hours. Then the phone rang again.

"You think I'm gay, don't you?"

I knew instantly that Jerry was on a different planet than he had been on the day before. "I think you're . . . *what?*"

"You think I'm gay." He said it in a tone of macho aggression— like if I said yes, he'd beat my face in. I could hear traffic in the background—a pay phone again.

"No, I don't. The truth is, I haven't given your sex life much thought. You can have sex with whoever you want, it makes no difference to me."

"Fuck you. You're a liar."

Click. I looked at Michele.

"Jerry?"

I nodded.

"What's going on with him?"

Before I could answer, the phone rang again.

"I just want you to be fucking honest with me," Jerry said, suddenly sounding close to tears. "For once in my life, I want someone to be honest with me."

"What do you want me to be honest with you about?"

"Do you think I'm gay?"

"Who cares what I think? Do *you* think you're gay?"

"Fuck no," he said reflexively. But then he added: "What does *gay* mean, anyway? Does it mean you only want to fuck other guys? If that's the case I'm definitely not gay. I love women. I've fucked more women than most guys on this planet. But does that mean I've never looked at another guy, or that if I was broke I wouldn't let some guy—"

I interrupted. "Jerry, where are you?"

"San Diego."

"What are you doing?"

"I told you, I came down here to see this woman."

"Did you go see her?"

"Yeah."

"What happened?"

"I don't want to talk about it," he said proudly. "Let's just say she's not the woman I thought she was, okay? As far as I'm concerned, there's only one woman in the world, and that's Olga." He suddenly started sobbing. "That woman . . . you wouldn't believe the things she's done for me, talk about an angel on this earth. . . ." Then all of a sudden he shouted, "I know *some people* who could take a lesson from that woman! I know *some people* who don't even *understand* what the word *love* means! I thought mothers and fathers and brothers were supposed to give each other *unconditional* love! Do you know what the word *UNCONDITIONAL* means? It means *ALL THE TIME. NO MATTER WHAT. UNDER ANY CIRCUMSTANCES. FOREVER.* Maybe I should buy everyone in my family a *FUCKING DICTIONARY* for Christmas!"

He banged down the phone.

I stood in the living room of our apartment in Brooklyn, stunned.

Michele looked at me. "What?"

"My brother," I said, "just snapped."

For the next several days, I was never not on the phone. The particulars of Jerry's rants—his sudden obsession with my opinion about his sexuality, his feeling that he had not been loved enough by his family—were pushed aside by the more practical concern of how he was living and whether or not he might do something to hurt himself or someone else.

My father was adamantly against any rescue mission. "Jerry has to get through this on his own," he kept saying. "We've given him money before, we've bailed him out a thousand times. What good has it done? At a certain point, you just have to say, 'It's up to you, Jerry. It's your life.' " I could tell by his tone that this was not a decision he came to casually—in fact, it sounded like it was tearing him up inside. My mother wanted to agree with him, but by this time she was such an emotional wreck—she could hardly talk on the phone without crying—that it was hard for her to think clearly about anything.

I knew my father was right: It was Jerry's life. But this didn't seem like the time to start practicing tough love, and I told my father that if this went on I was going to fly out to San Diego and track Jerry down and . . . well, I didn't know what I'd do. Hoping to get some advice, I called several substance-abuse centers and talked to counselors. They all told me the same thing: Do not send him money. Do not go rescue him. Tell him you love him and that you will help him get into a program when he's ready. You can do all the paperwork ahead of time and make it very easy for him to say yes. You can give him a ride to the front door. But you cannot open it for him. "It's his journey," one counselor told me. "He has to take the first step."

The hardest moment came when Jerry phoned and said he had no money and hadn't eaten for several days. He always called my mother first, thinking she was the most likely to give in; when she either didn't pick up the phone or refused, he called me; when I refused, he tried my father as a last resort. One night, my father's tough love went soft, and he wired Jerry two hundred dollars. Jerry promised my father he'd use it for a bus ticket to get home; he didn't, of course. Forty-eight hours later, he was calling again, begging for more.

This time, he sounded truly desperate.

"You gotta help me, man. I haven't eaten anything but a bag of hamburger buns in a week," he said. "Can't you send me, like, a hundred bucks?"

"I can't, Jerry," I said.

"Come on, man. I'll pay you back. I promise."

"No."

"Jeff, man, you're my brother. I'm telling you. I need this money."

"You're just going to use it to buy more blow. We both know it."

"Fuck you, man. You don't believe a word I say, do you?"

"Not when it comes to drugs and money."

"Well fuck you, Mr. Sobriety. You don't give a shit that I'm starving, do you?"

"I do give a shit, Jerry. That's why I'm not sending it to you."

"See, this is what I'm fucking talking about. This is what I mean by unconditional love. Or the lack of it."

He knew exactly how to push my buttons. "That's a cheap shot, and you know it."

The anger suddenly left his voice. "Jeff, man. I'm telling you, I'm starving. I need a meal. I need some food. I'm asking you, as my brother and my best friend, to please send me some money. Even twenty bucks. Anything."

I could ignore an angry demand, but I couldn't ignore a desperate plea. I told him to go to a restaurant nearby and have them call me, and I'd pay for whatever he wanted to eat with my credit card. I also offered to buy him a bus ticket back to Sunnyvale using the same method.

He seemed genuinely grateful. "Thanks, bro. I knew you'd come through for me."

A few minutes later, however, he called back. "They won't fucking do it," he said.

"Who?"

"The restaurant."

"Then try another one."

He acted as if it were my fault. "Yeah, maybe I will. Or maybe I'll just go beat the shit out of some old man and take all his money. You'd like that, wouldn't you?"

I didn't hear from him for a couple of days. The silence was corrosive. I was unable to sleep or work and barely able to hold a conversation with Michele. She had gotten a few blasts of Jerry's anger when she made the mistake of picking up the phone and accepting his calls. He'd said some ugly, sexually suggestive things to her that, in a different situation, I would have wanted to strangle him for; now, it was just another offense among many. It was after one of those calls, however, that I saw something change in Michele's face, and I knew that she had decided that Jerry was not just an alcoholic and a coke addict going through withdrawals but had had some kind of psychological breakdown that was not reversible. She thought he was mentally ill.

Although I often talked about how Jerry had snapped or lost his mind, I didn't really believe it. I thought cocaine had a lot to do with his troubles, as well as guilt and shame about his sexual identity. (I wondered if the woman he'd gone down to see was indeed a woman.) But I still believed that this was just a particularly desperate episode, that he was going to hit bottom and have some kind of revelation, and everything was going to be okay again. In fact, the idea that Michele had written Jerry off seemed like a kind of disloyalty on her part; I was angry at her for it.

Nevertheless, I called several mental-health centers and asked for help. Everyone told me the same thing: It's impossible to make any evaluation of a person's mental health until they are stone sober.

But beyond putting him in shackles, I didn't see any way of getting him clean. I feared that the only way to save his life was to lock him up. "Unless he causes himself or someone else serious bodily harm," I was told by every mental-health professional I spoke with, "that's just not possible."

For his part, my father mostly stuck with his "we gotta let Jerry sink or swim on his own" philosophy. My mother had no idea what else to do and was so stressed she began to get a skin rash. We all knew that this couldn't go on much longer, that Jerry's situation was too desperate; he was heading downhill too fast.

And we were right. Again, the call came at about 3 A.M. I heard the familiar rush of traffic in the background and the operator asking me if I'd accept a collect call.

Then Jerry said, "I've had enough."

"Enough what?"

"You don't understand, do you?"

"Jerry, I just woke up. What are you talking about?"

"I'm standing next to an overpass. How would you like it if I jumped?"

"Hey, come on, settle down—"

"I'm not fucking joking, man."

"I didn't say you were joking—"

"I'm going to jump."

"No, you're not. Come on, take it easy. You're okay. What's going on?"

"Don't tell me what I'm feeling, okay?"

"I didn't mean to tell you what you're feeling—"

"I don't see the point. I just want to get this shit over with. It's gonna end this way anyway."

"What are you talking about?"

"You don't understand shit, man."

"Talk to me, Jerry. Tell me what's going on."

"What's going on? You want to know what's going on? I'm living on the fucking streets, that's what's going on. My family has fucking written me off—"

"No one has written you off—"

"*Listen to me, asshole.*"

"Okay. I'm listening."

"My family has written me off. Olga is. . . ."

"What?"

"Never mind."

"Tell me."

"Nothing, man. This isn't about Olga. It's about me."

He started to cry.

"Jerry, I love you. Mom loves you. Dad loves you. Jill loves you. Don't do this to yourself."

"Those are just words. Just fucking words."

"Words have meaning."

"Oh, fuck you and your intellectual bullshit."

"Jerry—"

"Just fuck you, okay? This is my decision. If I want to jump, *nothing* you can do or say is going to change my mind. NOTHING. *You hear me?*"

"I hear you," I said quietly.

"This is my life."

"That's true."

"I swear to *God* I want to jump off this *fucking* overpass. *I swear to God I want to do it. I am this fucking close. . . . You don't know how fucking close.*"

Yes, I did know. I felt like he was on a high wire—one gust of wind, and he'd be gone.

"Are you still there?"

"Yes," I said.

"Have you heard a word I said?"

"I've heard it all," I said.

"And?"

"If you want to jump, then jump."

He laughed suddenly, uncontrollably. "You're telling me to jump? What kind of reverse-psychology bullshit is that? Man, you're a trip. . . . You're hilarious."

"I wasn't trying to be funny," I said.

"Oh, you don't know how fucking funny you are. . . . I'll see you on the other side, man."

After he hung up, I sat there for a while in our dark Brooklyn apartment. I could hear sirens wailing in the distance and an occasional taxi blasting up Court Street. I thought of Jerry on the other side of the country, standing on an overpass, staring down at the passing cars. Oddly, I did not feel any panic or desperation. In fact, I felt terrifyingly calm—the calmest I'd felt in months. It's the same kind of calm I often feel in a jet accelerating down a runway on takeoff. My fear of flying is replaced by a kind of relief that whatever happens, the waiting is over.

Jerry did not jump off the overpass that night. I don't know how close he came. But something must have happened, because the next time I heard from him—maybe three days later—he was back in the Valley. He sounded sober and sad and completely beaten up. Olga had given him the keys to her apartment again, and they were—I thought—working on another reconciliation. Several weeks went by at a stretch and I'd hear nothing from him, nor would my mother or father. And by the perverse logic we'd acquired over the past few months, that was now good news. If nobody heard from Jerry, it usually meant that things were okay.

At one point, Jerry called to tell me that Olga was in the hospital again. As usual, Jerry was elusive about the details, but he told me that she was at Stanford Medical Center and that he was spending every day with her. I presumed her colitis was acting up again.

Then a few days later, I picked up the phone and Jerry said, with his usual directness, "Olga just died."

"What?"

"Olga died."

"What happened?"

"Her heart stopped beating. She died."

"I didn't know she was so sick."

"She was."

"I'm sorry, Jerry."

Long silence. He was not crying.

"Where are you?"

"In her apartment."

"What are you doing?"

"Lying on the floor."

"You okay?"

"Yeah, I'm okay."

More silence.

"She died of AIDS," he said.

"AIDS?"

"Yeah. I have it too. I'm HIV-positive."

I felt like a safe had fallen on my head.

"Oh, God, Jerry, why didn't you tell me?"

"You didn't ask," he said coolly.

23

I dropped everything and flew out to California a few days later. Jill met me at the airport, though I hardly recognized her. Her blond hair had grown out, falling over her shoulders, and the last vestiges of the red and orange dyes were gone. Her green eyes were steady and clear, and the sullenness she'd displayed at Christmas had mellowed; she seemed sober and serious and direct. Not long after her arrest, she'd decided it was time to go back to school and had enrolled in a couple of night classes at a local junior college. She also had a new job at a company called CalComp, which made digital scanners and printers. On weekends, she did her community-service work, donning an orange vest and picking up trash along the highways side by side with other petty criminals, scofflaws, and drifters. She never complained about her punishment and as far as I know never missed a weekend of work.

On the way down the peninsula to Sunnyvale, Jill and I talked about Jerry. Although I had several friends who also were HIV-positive, I didn't know anyone personally who had contracted AIDS. Most of what I knew about the disease was the result of an article I'd written about ACT UP, which was at the time clamoring for more federal research funding for AIDS and quicker approval of drugs for treating its symptoms. Not that there were, at that time, many hopeful possibilities. In 1989, AIDS was more or less regarded as a death sentence. The only question was how long it would be until symptoms first appeared.

"Despite his drinking, Jerry has always been a very healthy guy," I said to Jill. "He might live ten years. And by then, they might very well have found a cure. There are lots of people working on this. All the best scientists in the country."

"Uh-huh."

"He needs to start taking care of himself," I said.

"What he needs is to stop drinking," Jill said.

"Well, of course."

We drove along in silence. In Redwood City, we passed a glassy new office tower rising near the bay. I noticed it because previously new buildings in the Valley had tended to be laid out horizontally. There had always been plenty of new orchards to knock down, plenty of elbow room. Vertical building was a sign that things were getting crowded. It was also a sign of new money. The traffic, I noticed, was heavier than I'd ever seen it; every other car on the road was a Lexus or a BMW. It was as if someone had turned on a spigot and the Valley was filling up with cash. It made me feel lonely and hyperconscious of the passing of time.

"Could Olga have given it to him?"

"Possibly," I said. "I really don't know. And it really doesn't matter where he got it. The point is, he has it."

I stared out the window at the dusty oleander bushes in the median.

"Dad's freaked," Jill said.

"Why?"

"AIDS, you know."

I waited. "What?"

"Dad thinks only homosexuals get it."

"That's not true."

"*I* know that. Explain it to him."

———

The first thing I noticed about my father was how gray he looked. The second thing I noticed was his lung-scraping cough. It worked up from the depths of his chest and brought up wheelbarrows full of mucus, which he spit into the sink or into a wad of Kleenex. His doctor diagnosed pneumonia and prescribed antibiotics. I presumed it was related to the stress of the past few months. "I just need to take it easy for a few weeks," he told me.

That night, my father, Jill, and I went out to dinner at a nearby Chinese restaurant. We talked about Jerry, but only in the most general way. My father had not seen Jerry since Olga had died, or since he'd been back from San Diego, for that matter. He'd spoken to him a few times on the phone and knew that he was living in a hotel. My father was never dispassionate, but when he talked about Jerry now he was surprisingly cool. "I'm ready to do whatever I can to help him," my father said, "but only if he quits drinking. Until then, there's nothing I can do."

"What about getting him into a detox center?"

"That would be great. But he has to make the decision to go. And nothing I've heard suggests he's ready."

"Maybe Olga's death will have an effect," I said, eternally hopeful.

"Fat chance," Jill said.

"Why do you say that?"

"If all the bullshit he's been through hasn't convinced him to stop," Jill said, "what makes you think Olga's death will?"

My father started to say something but then began coughing. It was several minutes before he could speak again. By that time, plates of chow mein and kung pao chicken had arrived.

"Let's eat before it gets cold," my father said.

The Maas Hotel, where Jerry had moved after Olga's kids booted him out of her old apartment, reminded me more of East L.A. than Silicon Valley. It was a sagging three-story stucco building near the railroad tracks in downtown Mountain View, a couple of miles from nicely landscaped industrial parks where engineers at Sun Microsystems and Silicon Graphics toiled over the design of the latest superfast computer workstations. The Maas Hotel, however, barely had running water. Most of the windows were held together with duct tape, and it was impossible to enter the building without the consent of a Filipino man who sat behind an inch-thick slab of bulletproof glass watching soap operas on a nine-inch TV.

"I'm here to visit Jerry Goodell in room two-eleven," I said.

Without turning his head or showing any sign that he'd heard me or in any way registered my presence, he buzzed the door open.

Inside, the air was old and heavy and unbreathable. I headed toward the concrete stairs at the end of the hall. The cinder-block walls were painted banana yellow, and portions of the Sheetrock ceiling were sagging and water-stained. TVs blared from behind closed doors. I heard gunshots and bits of Spanish soap operas.

Jerry's room was at the top of the stairs. Before I knocked, I listened—no sounds. I rapped on the door. "Hey, Jerry, you in there? It's me."

"Hey," he said, then opened the door.

I don't know what I was expecting, but it wasn't this. He was wearing baggy plaid boxers, black socks, and a tight, white T-shirt that was stained in the front, as if he'd spilled soup on it. His face was swollen and chalk-colored, his eyes glazed like a Christmas ham. He looked—and smelled—like he hadn't had a shower in several weeks.

I said nothing. But I must have communicated something of the shock I felt because he immediately looked away and said, "Hey, it's the emergency-rescue squad. What took you so long? I thought you said you were going to be here an hour ago. I coulda died in here."

"I called Michele, and we talked for a while."

He sat on the edge of the bed and hung his head between his knees.

"Sorry, man. I've got the D.T.'s."

I noticed his hands shaking. I sat down next to him.

"I've been watching little green men run around the room for the last two days. Why is it always little green men? Why isn't it little red men or little green cats or even big green men?" Then he stood up suddenly, slowly, and leaned over the small, cracked, white sink beside the bed. He made a violent choking sound. A rope of yellow bile hung from his bottom lip.

"I've been puking all day," he said apologetically. "There's nothing left to come up."

He wiped off his mouth with a filthy towel and sat back down. He could hold his head up for only a moment, then it dropped down between his knees again.

"What can I do for you? Can I get you some food? Some juice? Water?"

He looked at me with bloodshot eyes. "You can get me a pint of Jack. It'll help take the edge off."

"I'm not gonna buy you booze, Jerry."

He laughed, a deep chuckle that suggested how little I understood not only about his life but about life in general. "I'm not gonna get drunk, you dumb fuck," he said, shaking his head. "Why do you think I'm going through this shit? I want to get *sober*. But to get sober, I gotta go through hell. A few sips of Jack just makes the reentry a little easier. Besides, I don't even *like* Jack. When I ask you for a quart of Stoli, *that's* when you should worry."

Something in the tone of his voice precluded argument. I simply obeyed. I walked to the liquor store down the street and bought him a bottle of Jack. I also bought a liter of mineral water, a quart of orange juice, some peanuts, and a Snickers bar.

When I arrived back in his room, he was lying on the bed in a fetal position. His entire body trembled; sweat beaded on his forehead.

"Did you get it?" he asked.

"Yeah, I got it."

"Well, open the fucker up."

"I got water, too. And juice."

"Very nice. Just give me the Jack, okay?"

I did. He spun the top off and took a couple of quick sips. He made a pronounced *ahh* sound, as if he were in a Diet Coke commercial. The shaking continued.

He handed the bottle back to me. "Okay, you've done your duty. I don't mean to be rude, but there's really no point in you hanging around any longer. I'm not in the mood to chat, if you know what I mean. I just need to lie here for a few hours, okay? Come back tomorrow, and I'm sure I'll be feeling better."

"I've got nothing better to do."

He smiled. "I appreciate it, bro. But I'd rather go through this alone, if you don't mind."

I stood up to leave. I held up the bottle. "What do you want me to do with this?"

He eyed it for a moment. "Give it to me," he said.

I handed it over. He smiled and took one long gulp. I felt like I was watching him stick needles in his eyes.

He started to hand the bottle back to me, then changed his mind. "I want to keep it here, just in case. Just to prove to myself that I can kick Jack's ass."

He looked at me, expecting me to argue with him, but I didn't. I'd suddenly lost the will to fight him any longer. Not so much out of apathy but out of respect.

I said, "Up to you."

By the time my father got home from work at 6 P.M., he could hardly stand up. He had been on his feet all day at a job in San Jose, where he was overseeing the construction of a new city park. He looked exhausted. He flipped through the mail and then poured himself a lemon-lime soda and headed for the couch. With his pneumonia, he clearly should have been in bed, not out hassling with subcontractors, but he said, "The work's gotta get done, and I'm the only one who knows what's going on."

We talked about nothing for a while, then he asked, "So, did you see Jerry today?"

I told him I had and gave him the general picture of things, minus a few details. "It's important for him to take care of himself now," I said, moving the conversation in a different direction. And from the way my father looked at me, it was clear that he knew exactly where I was headed. And it was also clear that he didn't want to go there. I went anyway.

"Just because Jerry is HIV-positive, it doesn't mean he'll get

AIDS," I said. (At the time, I didn't know that, with rare exceptions, HIV always leads to AIDS.)

"I know that," he said tentatively.

"There are people who've been infected for five or six years who still have no symptoms."

"I know that," he repeated.

"But it's really important that he quits drinking."

My father seemed not to hear me. "Do you think he got it from Olga?"

"I have no idea," I said.

"It's possible, isn't it?"

This was my father's way of saying, "It's possible that my son isn't gay, isn't it?"

"It's possible," I said. "He could also have gotten it by using a dirty needle. Or from homosexual contact. There are other ways, but those are the most likely."

"I never liked Olga," he said. "I knew she was trouble."

My father, it seemed, had made up his mind.

I let his fantasy live. We could talk about this later, I thought. I moved on to a more practical concern. "Jerry's going to need a place to live, Dad."

At the time, Jill was living in one bedroom of my father's house, a boarder had rented out another, and my father was in the lonely master suite upstairs. That left one bedroom open.

My father coughed. His face turned crimson from the effort. He grabbed a Kleenex and spit into it. He said in a raspy voice, "As long as he's sober, the door is always open."

"Even if he's not sober, he needs a place to live."

"I've been through this with him."

"I know, but now things are different," I said firmly.

He seemed to consider the implications of this while he wadded up the Kleenex and tossed it into a paper bag beside the couch. The bag was nearly full of used tissue, which he eyed as if it were a monument to all that had gone wrong.

"You don't have to tell me what I owe my son," he cautioned me.

That night, I went for a drive in my father's Blazer. I had no destination in mind, I just wanted to get out of the house. I considered a movie, but when I got to the theater the line was too long. So I drove to a bookstore and browsed for an hour or so. I'd been going to this bookstore for years and could mark time by the growth of the computer-books section. In 1980, when I'd worked at Apple, all the computer books were on a single shelf. Now they took up an entire wall: *The Conquest of the Microchip; Programming in Pascal; Taming the Tiger: The Struggle to Control Technology.*

I bought a copy of *Great Expectations,* which I intended to give to Jerry the next day. It was his favorite Dickens novel, and he had mentioned something to me a few weeks earlier about wanting to read it again. Then I walked out to the Blazer and sat in the parking lot and watched the headlights on Stevens Creek Boulevard and tried to distract myself from the darkness that was rising within me. I thought about going to visit a friend, but I had no close friends here any longer, just a few acquaintances and former work buddies. Everyone else had long since been pushed out of the area by sky-rocketing real-estate prices and the promises of simpler lives elsewhere. My family had more or less fled, too. Nan and Pop were the first to go; then my aunt Carole (my mother's sister) and her husband sold their house in Sunnyvale and moved north to Danville; both of my father's brothers had long since left the area.

A month or so earlier, even my mother had decided to jump ship. She was tired of the traffic and the constant deadlines at Apple and the never-ending rush to build the next hot product. She had worked at the company for nine years, watching it rise from a shaggy little operation in one small building in Cupertino to a global enterprise with a brand name as recognizable as Coke or Nike. And she had gotten what she wanted out of it: a career, self-confidence, the chance to start a new life after the divorce. But the increasingly frantic pace of life at Apple, coupled with Jerry's breakdown, was too much. "I need to get out of here," she told me one night on the phone. Before long, she and Dwight bought a house in a wild rural area in far northern California, near where Nan and Pop lived. They hoped to raise a few head of cattle, plant a big vegetable garden, and slow down.

As I drove toward my father's house, I happened to pass a bar across the street from the old Apple offices and directly adjacent to a thirty-acre parcel the company had just acquired for a new corporate campus. The Peppermill was one of the few drinking establishments in the area that wasn't a pickup joint or sports bar, where you could sit alone with a drink and be fairly certain no one was going to try to ruin your evening with happy talk.

When I walked in, the lounge was nearly empty. I took a seat at the bar and ordered a Jack Daniel's on the rocks. I considered it a gesture of solidarity with Jerry, who was, I presumed, at that very moment curled on the bed in his room a few miles away, sipping the very same lovely brown liquid. I wouldn't drink with him, but I would drink to him. I understood how hypocritical this was, but I didn't care. I wanted a drink and was determined not to let Jerry's troubles make a monk out of me.

I spent the next hour or so staring into the ice cubes, thinking about my brother. I had been thinking about my brother for many years now, and I had come no closer to understanding what had happened to him or who was responsible for it. First I blamed the divorce. Then it was my father's failure. Then it was alcohol. Then it was the combination of alcohol and Olga. Then it was the layered misery of divorce, alcohol, coke, and Olga. I arranged these ideas in my head like puzzle pieces, trying to figure out how one interlocked with the next and what larger picture they revealed. But I still couldn't see it. My brother talked a lot about feeling as if he'd never been given unconditional love. He used that phrase as if he'd been raised in an orphanage in Belgrade. Yes, my father yelled at him a lot about not eating his peas, and, yes, he never took as much interest in Jerry's musical talents as he should have, and, yes, I was clearly his favorite son. But the road from these crimes of negligence and stupidity to the Maas Hotel was not at all clear to me.

The same went for the idea of honesty, which Jerry talked about a lot. My parents never told us the whole truth about things. But so what? Who tells the whole truth about anything? Nobody I know— including myself. I don't even know anybody who believes a whole truth exists.

I ordered another Jack Daniel's, and as I watched the bartender refill my glass I thought about what Jerry often said about the limits of rationality. I knew he would laugh at my attempts to find a neat explanation for his troubles. He didn't really believe in explanations— he believed in feelings. In this way, he was an old-fashioned romantic and completely at odds with the reigning faith of the world we grew up in, which held that everything can be reduced to the ones and zeros of computer code. Jerry believed that anything truly important or moving or alive can't be explained in a rational way. I wondered if his troubles were themselves an articulation of those unsayable things. Instead of trying to explain them or deconstruct them or wonder which parts made sense and which parts didn't, maybe the trick was to think of it all as a kind of terrible music. Maybe the best thing to do was just listen closely.

24

When I returned to the Maas Hotel the next day, I was fully prepared to launch a one-man intervention. First, I'd get Jerry out of this dive and into something less wretched, which I would somehow pay for with my already maxxed-out MasterCard. Then I'd sit on his head for two or three days and refuse to let him leave the room, no matter how many little green men tortured him. Then I'd give him a speech about how he was in the grip of something more powerful than himself, how he could not possibly beat it on his own, and how it was time to seek help. We would discuss treatment options, from the county detox program to the Betty Ford Clinic. I knew exactly what Jerry would say: The county program was for street people and losers, and he wasn't a street person or a loser. And Betty Ford was for rich whiners who didn't have the guts to face their own problems.

And I knew exactly what I would say in response: I don't give a shit. You're going. Somewhere. Now. You're HIV-positive. Getting sober is not an option anymore. It's a matter of life and death.

When Jerry opened his hotel-room door, however, my plan flew out the window. Gone was the sweaty, foul-smelling, little-green-man-haunted brother of yesterday; he stood erect and fairly clear-eyed. He was dressed in black jeans and a semiclean yellow Ralph Lauren polo shirt. Since there was, as far as I could tell, no shower or tub in his room or down the hall, he had apparently washed up in the sink. He'd shaved and combed his hair.

He proudly held up the bottle of Jack. "Jack is a wuss," he said. "I kicked his ass."

Then he made a big show of spinning off the cap and pouring the amber liquid into the sink. When it was empty, he opened the window and tossed the bottle in the general direction of a Dumpster below.

"This is a happy sight," I said.

"I had a bad night, but I survived. And now I'm never going back. Never."

I hated to hear him say that—it sounded like a reverse prophecy.

"Did you sleep?" I asked.

"A couple of hours. You saw me at my worst. It got better after you left."

I noticed a Snickers wrapper in the wastebasket. "Your appetite's back, I see."

"Fucking-a it is. I'm *starved*."

"What are you in the mood for?"

"Pepperoni pizza. I was dreaming about it all night. I haven't had one in months."

"It's only eleven A.M.," I said.

"So? There's a place down the street that opens at eleven-thirty. We'll get the first pizza out of the oven."

Jerry reacted to the sunlight like Dracula, shielding his eyes. As we walked, we talked in a general way about the hell he had been through in San Diego, although he never mentioned his threat to jump off the overpass, and I never brought it up. He spoke of that time as if it had been nothing more than a misadventure. He explained his motivation by saying, "While Olga was sick, I was starving for affection. I just felt this hole in my heart. So I decided to go down and see this woman. It was a dumb thing to do, but hey, when you're fucked-up, you do dumb things."

I was heartened by Jerry's sobriety and by his cool appraisal of his actions, but it didn't last long. We paused at a red light at a fairly busy two-way intersection on Castro Street; but instead of waiting for the light to turn green, Jerry blithely stepped out in front of traffic. He did this not out of absentmindedness or because he was in such a hurry to get to the other side of the street, but with a kind of arrogance—as if by stepping out in front of passing cars, he was forcing the drivers of the passing cars to acknowledge his existence.

One guy in a red BMW was not in an acknowledging mood. He did stop, tires squealing, but then leaned out his window and yelled, "You're supposed to wait for the light, you moron."

Jerry froze. He turned and stared. "What the fuck did you say to me?"

"I said, 'Wait for the light, asshole.' "

Jerry's eyes narrowed. The driver of the BMW—in his early forties, I'd guess, wearing a crisply pressed blue shirt and a fat digital watch—continued to glare at him. Jerry approached the car. I grabbed his arm, saying, "No big deal, Jerry, let's get out of here," but he pulled himself away. Fear bolted across the driver's face as Jerry charged toward him. He rolled up his window just as Jerry's fist slammed against it.

"You think just because you're rich," Jerry screamed, "you don't have to stop for pedestrians?" The guy mouthed something to Jerry—it looked like "you're a psycho"—then punched the accelerator and sped off.

When Jerry's pizza arrived, he ate like a starving man, consuming most of a large pepperoni by himself, and washing it down with three large Pepsis. By the time he was done, the table was littered with wadded-up napkins and his chin was shiny with grease. But the weight in his belly seemed to do him good; it relaxed him, made him groggy. We talked about our father and Jill and about my mother's recent decision to quit Apple and move north.

At some point, I made the unfortunate mistake of bringing up Olga's death. I asked him why he hadn't told me she was sick, and especially why he hadn't told me she had AIDS.

When I said *AIDS*, he blinked, as if startled to hear the word spoken out loud. "What difference would it have made?"

"Well, that was a lot for you to handle on your own. It might have helped if we'd talked about it."

"Like you really cared about her," he said sarcastically.

"I care about you," I said.

"But you didn't care about her, did you?"

"I hardly knew her, Jerry."

"There wasn't exactly an outpouring of grief in our family when she died," he said.

"She was close to you—she wasn't close to us."

"Tell me the truth. You didn't like her, did you?"

"I didn't think she was good for you," I said stupidly.

"Why?"

"Drugs, drinking—it all seemed to get worse after you met her. She discouraged you from following your interests as a musician. She made you feel guilty for breaking up her marriage. You told me this yourself a thousand times. She may have been a sweet person, but I don't think she had your best interests at heart."

If I have ever said a wronger thing at a wronger moment, I can't recall it. All the pizza-inspired mellowness immediately vanished from Jerry's face. If I wasn't his brother—his *only* brother—I'm absolutely sure he would have leaped across the table and torn my throat out. Instead, he bit his lip for a moment and turned away, and I could almost hear the inner dialogue—the good angel reminding him to cool off, the devil wanting action.

Then he said, in a slow, deliberate tone, "Do not ever, *ever* say anything bad about Olga in my presence again. You did not know her. You do not know the things she did for me. You do not know the hell she went through with me. And you have no fucking idea how much I owe her."

I finally understood. He was not just grieving for Olga; he believed he was responsible for her death. He believed he had given her the virus. He had no way of knowing for sure, of course. It had certainly not been deliberate—he hadn't known he was HIV-positive until Olga got sick. Nevertheless, in his own ferocious judgment, he was a murderer.

I did not know what to say, where to begin.

"I'm sorry," I muttered shamefully. "I didn't mean any disrespect."

The next day, Jerry and I drove up to see the forty-acre ranch our mother and Dwight had recently purchased in Red Bluff, a hundred and fifty miles south of the Oregon border. He was in a brighter mood that morning and still sober. He seemed happy to get out of the Valley—"This place is full of ghosts," he said as we headed up the freeway. We cruised across the Bay Bridge, then headed north through Berkeley and Walnut Creek and into the flat, wide central valley. Jerry brought along a couple of cassettes, including a Frank Sinatra compilation with "Summer Wind" on it, which Jerry argued was the greatest of all Sinatra songs. It suited our drive, anyway, given that it was an uncharacteristically hot June afternoon. The rice fields shimmered in the heat, and the green flanks of the coastal mountains were already fading into their midsummer khakis.

Maybe it was just being on the road, in motion, going somewhere, but I felt cautiously hopeful about Jerry's turnaround. This was day two of stone-cold sobriety—not much, but it was something. "A journey of a thousand miles starts with a single step," as they say in AA. Although I never said it to anyone except Michele because it sounded so heartless, I wondered if Jerry's discovery that he was HIV-positive might have been a blessing. Yes, the virus would kill him, but drinking and drugs would kill him faster. Ten years with the virus beat two or three years with a failing liver. As for the guilt he bore over Olga, I presumed it was an expression of his deep grief, and that as time passed he would find a way to live with it. He would see that it was not his fault, he had not known he was carrying the virus, and that whatever the circumstances that led Olga to have an affair with him and end her marriage, they had been set in action long before she met Jerry.

In the late afternoon, we pulled up in our mother's dusty driveway on a secluded hillside outside of Red Bluff. My mother and Dwight's miniature schnauzer, Tina, immediately started barking and dancing around the Blazer. It was a modest house with a large redwood deck on three sides. The land had a rugged, open, big western feel, with dramatic rock outcroppings and gray-green oaks. To the east, Mount Lassen loomed in the distance, rising out of the buttes like a sand castle on a beach. Its peak was still capped with snow.

Our mother gave us big, warm hugs. When she embraced Jerry, there were tears in her eyes. The stress of the past few months had obviously taken a toll on her, too: She was twenty or thirty pounds heavier than she'd been the last time I'd seen her, and her brown eyes seemed darker, as if they had been permanently blackened by worry, even in joyful moments like this. Dwight remained up on the deck, as if to underline his separateness from our family. I was growing fonder of Dwight, largely thanks to Michele, even if Jerry wasn't. And Dwight, it was clear as we shook hands, had some fond feeling for me. In Jerry, all he could see was a drunk. But I had faith that that would change once he spent more time with my brother.

My mother, Dwight, and Tina gave us a tour of their new spread. Sunlight slanted through the oak trees, and the air smelled of manzanita and sagebrush. As we walked the land, my mother and Dwight talked in an excited, almost childlike way about where the horse barn would be and how they wanted to get some livestock to graze the land and the turkeys they had seen on the hillside behind the house. It was a big, western dream, full of wide-open spaces and the promise of a new beginning.

During the tour of the property, Jerry grew quiet. Maybe it was the idea of seeing our mother so deliberately staking out her turf in this new world; maybe he was just uncomfortable around Dwight. Whatever it was, it worried me; I didn't want to do anything to upset his hard-won psychological balance.

My mother went all out for dinner, breaking out the place mats and candles, but was careful not to open any wine. The entire house, I noticed, was clean of alcohol. No six-pack of beer in the fridge, no dark bottles of zinfandel on the counter. If Jerry noticed this, he didn't remark on it. He washed down his lasagna with several cans of Diet Coke, then ate a bowl of ice cream for dessert. All in all, it was a fine, peaceful meal. Dwight and Jerry avoided looking at each other, but how many American dinner tables don't have a little tension between stepsons and stepfathers?

While my mother cleaned up, Jerry and I went outside to sit on the deck and look at the full moon, which lit up the hillside like the headlight of God's Harley. It was a warm, clear evening, bullfrogs croaking down by the pond, an occasional whinnying of a horse in the distance. Whatever uneasiness Jerry felt was gone now; he was as lively and loose as I'd ever seen him. I wish I could recall what Jerry and I talked about that night, but I can't. Whatever it was, it was trivial, and I was profoundly grateful for that. It had been a long, long time since I'd had a simple, carefree conversation with my brother. I felt like I'd inhaled nitrous oxide, I was so high and buoyant. All the mean words between us, all the hurt and despair—it was all gone, vanquished like a bad dream. When I looked at Jerry, I saw not the man in the filthy T-shirt at the Maas Hotel but the bright-eyed kid I remembered from years ago, the kid with the great, rolling belly laugh, the one with the smooth, beautiful skin and the fragile hands, the kid I'd shared my secrets with, my bunk mate, the thief of my coloring books, and Robin to my Halloween Batman. *Jerry, my brother, my soul mate, my coconspirator, my partner in crime—I missed you!*

Jerry and I had been out on the porch for some time, maybe an hour, when I heard the phone ring in the house. It was after midnight, but I thought nothing of it. A few minutes later, my mother slid the screen door open. I looked over. In the darkness all I could see was her silhouette. She hesitated.

"Jill just called," she finally said, her voice breaking. "Your father just threw up blood. He's on his way to the hospital in an ambulance right now."

I looked up at the full moon. *Cancer.* The word leaped into my mind like a fact. I glanced over at Jerry. He looked like a grenade had just gone off in his hand. I kept the *c* word to myself, and we consoled each other with vaguely hopeful words. Mostly we sat in silence, listening to the toads down by the pond, and waited for more news. The moonlight seemed to brighten, and the oak trees cast blue shadows across my mother's garden.

A half hour later, Jill called back. My father was at the hospital.

He was okay. They weren't sure what happened. They would do tests in the morning.

Jerry and I decided to try to get a few hours' sleep before driving back to the Valley. My mother cooked us breakfast, which we ate in silence. I wondered what she was feeling, but she revealed little. I asked her if she wanted to drive down to the hospital with us, but she said no, she'd call him later, "after things settle down."

Jerry hardly spoke during the four-hour drive back to Sunnyvale. He just stared out the window at the rice fields and grain silos. He looked numb, as if he were deliberately shutting down as many neural receptors as quickly as he could to prevent a systemwide overload. I felt myself filling not with sympathy for our father or worry about his condition but with fury—why did he have to get sick now, at precisely the moment when Jerry was least prepared to deal with it? Although our father obviously had no choice in the matter, it still seemed grotesquely unfair. Why couldn't he have waited a month, after Jerry'd had some time to steady himself?

I dropped Jerry off at the house. He said he just wanted to lie down for a while and get some sleep. I said that was fine, and told him that, if everything was okay at the hospital, I'd be back in time for a late dinner. I went directly to the hospital. Jerry promised to visit the next day.

When I returned that night, my father's liquor cabinet was open. Jerry was long gone.

25

Two days after my father was admitted to the hospital, he was officially diagnosed with lung cancer. He vowed to fight it. Indeed, when I visited him in the hospital the day he got the news, he looked perfectly healthy and ready to go sixteen rounds with his tumor. His suntanned, leathery face stood out against the clean white sheets. He said, "I'm not ready to die yet. I want to walk my daughter down the aisle and see my grandchildren." I held his hand and told him that he wasn't going to die, that lung cancer is often treatable, and that I would help him find the best possible doctors.

Jill was a steady presence at his bedside, but Jerry did not visit my father at the hospital that day or the next or the next. I had no idea where he had gone, what he was doing, where he was sleeping and eating, or how to get in touch with him. I explained Jerry's absence by telling my father that, after Olga's death, just walking into this hospital—the one in which Olga had died—was too difficult for him. My father nodded and said he understood.

My father was fifty-three when he was diagnosed with cancer. I don't think he'd ever been to a funeral in his life—certainly not one of anyone close to him. Both his parents were still alive, as were both his brothers, and all his children, nephews, and nieces. The same was true for my mother. Pop's brother, Phil Schromm, had been blown up in a tank in France during World War II, but my mother was two years old at the time—it hardly registered with her. We never visited his grave, we never visited anyone's grave. There was no history of tragedy in my family, no holocaust, no suicides, no starvation, no murder victims. It was as if by moving to a town with a deathless name like Sunnyvale, we had somehow found a loophole in life's mortality clause.

Our days as immortals were over now. As if my father's and brother's diagnoses weren't enough, when I went back to work in New York, my editor immediately assigned me a story about a tenants'-rights organizer in Harlem named Bruce Bailey who had been found cut up into a half-dozen pieces by a chain saw. No arrests had been made in the case, but it was widely assumed to be the handiwork of an irritated slumlord who tired of Bailey's insistence that tenants deserved heat and running water. Rather than fix the plumbing, the slumlord fixed him.

It was a gruesome crime, but it suited my mood. In fact, it was downright exhilarating to think about—now *this* was death. I soaked up every detail, as if there were some greater truth to be discovered in the splatter and gore. I interviewed detectives who had spent hours digging through the Fresh Kills landfill in search of Bailey's head—the only part of his body that had not been recovered. I quizzed forensic pathologists about how one goes about cutting up a body with a chain saw, how big a mess it makes, how easy it is to dispose of, how long it takes before the body parts begin to smell. I climbed the stairs in a tenement on 108th Street in Manhattan to interview Bailey's widow, a heavy black woman who was still in a blank-faced state of shock about what had happened to her husband.

"What does death feel like?" I asked her at one point during our conversation. I was as startled by the question as she was.

She looked at me for a moment, and I saw a flash of fear in her eyes, like maybe I wasn't a journalist at all but some psycho who gets his jollies harassing the survivors of murder victims. She said, "That's a very strange thing to ask me." I apologized, but the damage had been done. Not long after that, she ended the interview and asked me to leave.

Although I knew in my bones that my father was a goner, the optimist in me wouldn't give in. During his initial stay at the hospital, my father was told that his tumor was sited at the branch in his bronchial tubes, making surgery all but impossible. Then a lung specialist mentioned a highly risky surgical procedure that involved more or less removing both lungs, cutting out the tumor, and then stitching the lungs back in. "It's a brutal operation, one that only a few doctors in the country are willing to perform," he told us. My father's eyes lit up. A few weeks later, I tracked down the surgeon at the University of California at San Francisco School of Medicine who had pioneered this procedure, and he agreed to see my father. It was a brief visit, however. He examined my father's chest for about twenty seconds, looked over his X rays for another ten seconds, then said brusquely, "Sorry, can't do it" and left the room.

Except for his persistent cough, my father felt pretty good at first. A little tired, maybe, but that was about it. A month or so after his diagnosis, he began radiation therapy, which he hoped might stun the tumor and keep it at bay for a few years. He considered chemo but decided against it after he was told that the chance of it curing him was less than 1 percent, while the chance of him suffering horrific side effects was near 100 percent.

As the summer passed, the cancer began to sap his strength. It was a slow, gradual withering. He often found that he did not have the energy to take his dog, Annie, for a walk in the evenings, or to do the grocery shopping on Saturday mornings, or to carry the garbage cans out to the curb every Thursday.

And so my father began relying more and more on Jill. She did her best, but it was obvious that she was terrified that the entire burden of care would fall on her. I jetted to and from New York, staying for a week at a time, but she was stuck with the daily grind of cooking and dishes and laundry. She didn't know much about cancer, but she had heard stories about bedpans and bedsores and daily morphine injections. She imagined that was our father's future, and she knew she wasn't going to be able to handle it. I tried to reassure her that we'd get plenty of help when the time came, that she wouldn't bear the burden of it all, but I don't think my assurances did much to allay the basic horror of the situation.

It was during this time that we all felt the gaping hole divorce had left in our lives. My father needed his family—it was that simple. Jill could be expected to do only so much. Jerry, of course, was out of the picture. That left me and my mother.

Had my mother and father remained married, taking care of him would have been her job. They had, after all, spent nearly twenty years together and raised three kids. Looking after each other in old age is part of the deal. But she had a new husband now, a new life. The deal was void.

So, understandably, she kept her distance. She had called him in the hospital after the diagnosis, and she checked in every week to see how he was doing, but she did not drive down and volunteer to do his laundry, much less sit at his bedside and talk to him about dying.

As for me, the limits of my duties were far less clear. I knew he needed me. With my mother gone, the chain of responsibility led straight to me, his oldest son. I knew that I should be making plans to move out to California to take care of him, but I was reluctant to give it serious consideration. My father certainly never encouraged it. More than anything else, he did not want to think of himself as a burden to me; he would have kept me away at gunpoint. But that doesn't mean that moving home to take care of him wasn't the right thing to do. I knew this cancer would kill him. My job had enough flexibility so that as the disease progressed I could spend some time in California with him. But I loved my work, and my life in New York, and did not want to abandon them. I'm ashamed to admit that this was not even a difficult decision for me.

With Jerry, the situation was more complicated. There was no question that Jerry was in no shape to help care for my father, but there were things he could do. As you might imagine, my father had a lot he wanted to talk to Jerry about. But mostly he wanted forgiveness. Although my father never talked about it explicitly, he knew very well that he had failed to give Jerry the most essential thing a parent can give a child: the confidence to make his or her own way in the world. For whatever reason, Jerry didn't have that. Maybe no man could have given it to him. Maybe Jerry was doomed by a clump of disfigured receptors deep in his hypothalamus. But that did not make my father's sense of responsibility any less acute.

Jerry, however, was in no mood for reconciliation. My father's diagnosis had pushed him back to the bottle, and he had been drifting around the Valley in a semihomeless state, spending a few nights at the Maas Hotel, then moving on to a shelter, then back to the Maas. He worked in restaurant kitchens or bused tables or sold magazine subscriptions via telephone. None of these jobs lasted more than a few weeks. He'd always have a run-in with his boss, or he'd miss a day of work and they'd fire him. When we talked on the phone, he often seemed angry about all the sympathy and attention my father was getting for his disease and, as a result, how little sympathy and attention he received. It was as if my father had deliberately one-upped him: *You* may be HIV-positive, but *I* have lung cancer.

Whenever I'd suggest that he stop in and visit Dad, he'd say, "Yeah, sure" and leave it at that.

For some reason, Jerry became obsessed with my father's relationship with Jill. He often talked about how spoiled Jill was, how my father gave her more than she deserved, how my father showed her a level of attention that he had never shown Jerry.

"All true," I said to Jerry.

"He's guilty about the divorce, so he indulges her."

"Absolutely right. If you'd stay sober for a few weeks, maybe he'd indulge you, too."

I was tired, emotionally wrung out. I'd coddled Jerry enough.

"Oh, it's all *my* fault."

"No, it's not your fault. But whatever mistakes Dad made, I'm sure he's sorry, and I'm sorry, and I know you're sorry. We're all fucking sorry, okay? The whole fucking world is just weeping with fucking sorrow. But the truth is, you have one problem right now, and only one problem—alcohol. Until you recognize that, there's nothing I can do, or Dad can do, or anyone can do, to help you."

After a moment of silence he said, "You really think it's that simple?"

"I do."

He laughed. It began as a chuckle, then rolled into a full-throated rumble. "Man, you crack me up."

At first, Michele was a real angel. She flew out to California with me several times in the months after my father's diagnosis. She cooked my father meals, she sat beside him while he coughed up blood-flecked mucus, she laughed at his lame jokes. That was great, but as my father's condition worsened, I often thought she was not disturbed enough by what was happening to my family. She could laugh at a joke on TV two minutes after Jerry called in a rage; she could talk about my father's cancer without breaking into tears. I thought she was taking it all a little too easily—as if, because she happened to be my wife, she was duty bound to suffer to an equivalent degree. I took the fact that she didn't as a kind of disloyalty.

Worse, she demanded that once in a while I pay attention to her. She demanded that I sit through a meal maybe once a week and not muse about What Had Gone Wrong. She demanded that if I was going to spend every penny we both earned flying back and forth to California once a month that I not give her a hard time for spending fifteen dollars on a tube of lipstick. She demanded that I not ignore our second wedding anniversary. She demanded conversation, gestures of concern, affection.

"I'm not asking you for much," she said when we were lying in bed one night.

"I'm doing the best I can," I replied.

"I feel like you're married to your family, not me."

"That's a ridiculous thing to say."

"It's the truth."

I rolled over, stared at the wall, and tried to push myself off the dark cliff into sleep.

I never knew where Jerry was when he called. One day he'd say he was sleeping in a homeless shelter, the next he'd proudly announce he had a job delivering pizza. Then I'd hear from Jill that she thought he'd slept in the backyard; a week later, I'd get a call from my mother, who told me that Jerry had been thrown off a bus on his way up to visit her. When she drove down to pick him up, she found him drunk and covered with mud—he'd slept in a field the night before.

It was obvious to us all that Jerry couldn't go on living like this; it was equally obvious that there wasn't anything that I or anyone else in the family could do about it. Worse, it was clear that Jerry and my father were headed for some kind of collision. Jerry started showing up two or three times a week at our father's house, sometimes breaking in when no one was home to take a shower, other times stopping by for no other reason than to verbally assault him. This was not the reconciliation any of us had hoped for.

My father had always been able to handle himself fine around Jerry, even when Jerry was in his darkest, most abusive moods. But as summer ended, my father grew more and more fragile, both physically and emotionally. He often had pains in his chest. The radiation made him nauseous, his appetite declined, and his weight dropped fast. He worked only half a day and spent most of the rest of the time on our green plaid couch, the cushions of which now retained the shape of his body. Even the briefest encounter with Jerry took an immense toll on him. It wasn't just the words Jerry said but the simple fact of seeing his son drunk and knowing that drunkenness would kill Jerry just as surely as the tumor would kill *him*. I sometimes wondered if this sense of their connected fates contributed to Jerry's anger—they were going down together, father and son.

Still, I assumed that as my father's weakness became more apparent, Jerry's feelings would change. I thought sympathy for a dying man was a natural force, immutable as gravity. It is not.

One Saturday evening in October 1989, just before my father was about to leave on what he knew would be his last deer-hunting trip, I happened to call home. Jill answered. I could tell by the tone of her voice that all was not right.

"What's going on?"

"Jerry and Dad are out in the backyard screaming at each other," she said coolly.

"What are they fighting about?"

"I don't know. Hunting, I think."

"Hunting?"

"I don't know. I'm trying not to listen."

"Let me talk to Jerry," I said.

She dropped the phone. I heard her open the sliding-glass door and call to Jerry; a moment later, he picked up the phone. "Hey, bro," he said.

"What's going on?"

"Not much. Just stopped by to talk to Dad."

"Jill says you're screaming at each other."

"That's her opinion," he said.

"What are you and Dad talking about?"

"Killing animals. What a selfish thing it is to do. But then, our father is a selfish person."

"Since when did you get so interested in animal rights?"

"I'm not," he said. "I'm interested in communicating to our father what a wimp he is. How he needs to carry a gun to feel like a big man. That's why he kills things, you know. To feel big, to feel tough. To make him feel good despite the fact that he's raised such a *slut* for a daughter."

"What are you talking about?"

"Oh, nothing. Forget it."

"Leave Jill out of this, okay?"

"You should see how she's dressed."

"Who made you the enforcer of public morality? It's none of your goddamned business how she's dressed."

"Yeah, okay, right," he said, obviously humoring me. "Hey, I got the book you sent me." A few weeks earlier, I'd mailed him a copy of *Tropic of Cancer*. "I'm about half done. Henry Miller writes like Miles Davis plays his horn."

"That's true," I said, eager to change the subject.

I'd learned that the best way to handle Jerry's anger was to distract him—often, after a few minutes of trivial banter, he'd completely forget what he was so upset about. And that happened now, or so I thought. He told me he was staying at the Maas Hotel again and that he was starting a new job in the kitchen of an expensive Italian restaurant in Palo Alto on Monday morning.

"That's great," I said. "I'm happy to hear that."

"Yeah, I'm doing okay," he said. "I'm fine. I'm handling this shit the best I can."

"I know you are," I said affectionately. "I know how hard this is on you."

I considered asking him to leave my father's house but decided against it. He seemed calm enough, defused. I was so confident of that, in fact, that I didn't ask to speak to my father or Jill; I just said good-bye and hung up.

I went to the little grocery store down the street and bought some soup for dinner. When I returned, the phone was ringing.

"This may be the last time you ever talk to me," Jerry said as soon as my ear hit the receiver.

"What?"

"I just slugged Dad."

"What are you talking about?"

"I punched him in the face."

"Jesus Christ, Jerry. Why?"

"Because I felt like it."

"Because you fucking *felt like it?* What an asshole you are. I can't fucking believe this. You're kidding me, right? Dad is so sick he can barely get off the couch, and you *punched* him?"

"Yeah, I did. I'm sure Jill will fill you in on all the details. Just remember one thing—the son of a bitch deserved it. Okay? Remember that. That's all I ask."

That night, I dreamed I was sitting on an enormous pile of wood, just waiting for someone to strike a match. I waited and waited. Finally, a stranger came along. He said, "Are you ready?"

I said, "I'm ready." When the match flared, I woke up.

26

"I'm afraid Jerry is going to kill Dad," Jill confessed to me. It was about a week after Jerry had slugged my father—no one had heard from him, knew where he was, or knew if he was drinking or sober, detoxing or guzzling.

"Don't be crazy."

"I'm serious."

"He slugged him—he didn't take a gun out and point it at him."

"You didn't see the look in his eyes or hear the way he screamed at him."

No, I hadn't. By now, however, I'd been able to piece together a fairly clear picture of what had happened: Not long after Jerry had hung up the phone, my father stepped into the kitchen. He said to Jerry, "I think you better leave. You're welcome to come back when you're sober." He was still fuming about whatever Jerry had said to him in the backyard. Jerry said, "Fine," and walked toward the front door. My father followed. As he reached the door, Jerry glanced at Jill and said to my father, "You must be real proud of yourself for raising such a slut." Jerry was always an expert at pushing our emotional hot buttons, but this time he had pushed a little too hard. My father exploded. He grabbed Jerry by the shirt collar and slammed him up against a mirror hanging on the wall. How he found the strength to do this, I have no idea. My father hardly had the strength to stand up, much less lift his 190-pound son. The mirror crashed to the ground, shattering. My father said, "You will *not* talk about your sister that way in my house." Jerry's fist was already flying. It landed on my father's jaw, sending him sprawling back against the stairs. Jill screamed and ran to call 911. Jerry did not pause to see if my father was hurt; instead, he opened the front door and took off up the street.

When I talked to my father afterward, he was shaken up but not hurt. Not physically, anyway. There was no anger in his voice, none of the usual bewilderment and frustration and despair. He just said, quietly, "I think Jerry got a little carried away. It's not a big deal. I think we should just let it go, forget about it."

Jill was less forgiving. In fact, she was freaked. "I don't think you quite grasp what is going on here," she said, her voice rising. "You don't understand what this is like for me—or for Dad. You're not living here. You're not dealing with this face-to-face."

She was right, of course. I wasn't lying in my bed at night, listening to every creak in the house, every tick of the heating ducts, and wondering if Jerry was trying to sneak into the house to grab some booze or take a shower or exact justice from our father. I wasn't Jerry's little sister, a woman now but still smaller and weaker than Jerry; I didn't feel vulnerable the way she did. I also didn't have to deal with the rough sexual language that Jerry used when he was drunk—he wasn't calling *me* a slut. To me, Jerry was still just a kid who had lost his way; to Jill, he had become a kind of family stalker who, as she said to me once, "seems determined to take someone down with him."

I told her I understood her fear but thought she was making too much of it. The only time Jerry might be dangerous, I thought, was when he was drunk, and when he was drunk he was too physically uncoordinated to do much harm. "Besides, you're a tough girl," I joked with her. "You can kick his ass, can't you?"

Jill did not laugh.

———

A week or so later, Jerry turned up at my father's house again. This time, before any blows could be exchanged, Jill called the cops. Jerry split immediately, but instead of running up the block he crawled into the back of the Blazer and passed out. When the police arrived twenty minutes later, Jill was distraught. She told them about the punch Jerry had thrown last time and added in no uncertain terms that she was afraid Jerry was going to kill our father. The cops explained that fear wasn't good enough; unless Jerry had physically harmed my father or my father had a restraining order prohibiting Jerry from visiting the house, there wasn't much they could do. They did, however, wake Jerry up, handcuff him, and transport him, spitting and screaming, to Valley Medical Center for a so-called psychological evaluation. It was not an exam at all, just an excuse to lock him up without filing charges; he was back on the street in twenty-four hours.

For the next three weeks, no one heard from Jerry. I learned later that he'd stolen a leather jacket, sold it to some woman in a parking lot, and used the money to buy a bottle of Stoli and a bus pass. He spent his days riding up and down El Camino Real between San Jose and Palo Alto. I think he was as lost and scared and despairing as he'd ever been, because for the first time in his life he enrolled in a detox program, one run by the Salvation Army in San Jose. When he arrived, he'd signed a document that more or less allowed the Salvation Army to keep him locked up for the next six months. In effect, Jerry threw himself into jail.

Jill, however, was not taking any chances. With our father's permission, she drove down to the Santa Clara County courthouse and filed for a restraining order against Jerry, citing his past violence against my father and repeated threats on both his and her lives. It was processed without question. Now, if Jerry came within three hundred feet of the house, he could be arrested. My father seemed desperately sad that it had come to this, but he was too weak to put up much of an argument.

27

When Michele and I flew out to California a few weeks later for a visit, I didn't bother writing Jerry to tell him I was coming. I had received a brief letter from him just before we left, telling me that he was doing fine, that the program at the Salvation Army was rigorous but that he was grateful for the discipline. I saw no point in disturbing his routine with news of my visit, which I feared would only make him anxious. In fact, I considered not even visiting him at all while I was out there. Distance might do us all good.

I had second thoughts, however, when I arrived in Sunnyvale and got a look at my father. His back pain was severe—he could hardly get off the couch. I knew as well as he did that this was not a good sign; it probably meant that the cancer was spreading into his spinal area. His face had taken on the otherworldly color of a person who had spent too many hours under a sunlamp. His stomach was swelling even as the muscles in his arms and legs wasted away. The day after Michele and I arrived, I insisted that he call his doctor; he went in for an exam the next morning and returned with a prescription for the painkiller Percodan. He popped a couple of pills, and within two minutes he was a new man. And the new man wanted to go shopping. "I need new shoes and a ladder," he said.

"Why shoes and a ladder?"

"Shoes for my feet, and a ladder to reach the gutters. The old ladder is falling apart, and the gutters are clogged with leaves. I want to get them cleaned out before winter."

The cancer is spreading to his spinal cord, and he's worried about the leaves in the gutter. Okay.

"Where do you want to go?" I asked.

"Let's start with Home Depot."

"Are you sure you're up for this?"

"I'm fine," he said. "Let's just do it quickly."

So we drove off to Home Depot. I held his arm as he walked across the parking lot and through the zippy sliding-glass doors. He moved with an odd tilt, holding his back at an angle to the left, his eyes locked on the middle distance—the same deliberate separation of mind and body that you see in the eyes of marathoners at around mile sixteen. I pushed the cart beside him, moving at the same slow pace, careful not to seem impatient or to wait for him, which would have only dramatized his weakness. He walked down rows of screws, nuts, and bolts, then into the tool section, past racks of screwdrivers, a dozen different kinds of hammers, pliers, and Allen wrenches: tools to fix things, to build things, devices that suggested the world was made up of interlocking pieces that could be replaced as needed. At Home Depot, there is no such thing as death, only refurbishment.

We came to the ladders. My father looked them over briefly, then nodded to a deluxe fifteen-foot-extendable aluminum model. Rubber feet. Nonskid treads. It was the most expensive ladder on the rack. "That'll do."

We paid for it, wheeled it outside on a cart, and wedged it in the back of the Blazer. Four feet of ladder hung out the rear window. I tied a red flag on it.

My father looked like he was about to drop.

"You okay?"

"I just need to sit down for a few minutes," he said.

He practically fell into the Blazer.

"You don't look good," I said.

He looked at me severely. "What's wrong?"

"You just look pale," I said.

"How pale?"

Like a ghost, I wanted to say. "Just . . . not your usual self."

He lay there for a moment with his eyes closed. Behind him, out the passenger window, I watched a man emerge from an electronics store, carrying a big white box with the happy, rainbow-colored Apple Computer logo on it.

"Let's go get some shoes," my father said, his eyes still closed. "I need some decent shoes."

The next day, I went to see Jerry at the Salvation Army shelter in San Jose. We sat on the grass in a small yard behind the lobby. There were butts from hand-rolled cigarettes everywhere, like the droppings of some nocturnal animal. Jerry looked surprisingly good. He wore an orange University of Miami sweatshirt, clean jeans, and a pair of Tiger running shoes that he told me he'd bartered for with another inmate. He had the air of a man trying very hard to pull himself together.

I knew that what I had come to tell him would not make that job any easier.

As we sat in the afternoon sunlight, he described his daily routine: up at 6:30 A.M., a half hour of exercise, breakfast, a half hour of "meditation," four hours of work—he was currently on laundry detail, in charge of manning seven washers and six dryers. Lunch at 12:30, another four hours of laundry, more exercise, dinner, then counseling sessions and group meetings in the evening. In bed at 10 P.M., lights out an hour later. I could tell by the way he described all this that he liked the discipline and rigor of it. "There is no room for any bullshit, which is nice," Jerry said. A tabby wandered out from the lobby; Jerry picked it up, stroked it, and yanked its tail. "This is Alfonso. He is one tough-assed cat. I've seen him kill ten mice just in the last month."

We talked about football for a while—college rankings, Joe Montana, the 49ers' chances at the Super Bowl. He watched all the games on the big-screen TV in the lobby and read the sports pages front to back.

Then he said, out of nowhere, "My T-cell count is two-ninety."

T cells are a type of white blood cell that trigger the body's immune system and are key indicators of the progress of HIV. A T cell count of about twelve hundred is normal; people with full-blown AIDS usually have counts between zero and fifty. Two months earlier, in a rant on the phone, Jerry had told me his count was one hundred. Now he was telling me it was almost three times that.

"That's good news," I said.

He gave me a hard look. "It was five hundred two months ago."

"I thought you said it was one hundred."

"No, I said it was five hundred."

"Well, then that is not good news."

I understood what he was doing: He was saying, remember me, I'm sick too.

"How are you feeling otherwise?"

"Good. Strong. I do fifty push-ups a day." He flexed his bicep. "Feel that."

"I believe you."

"No, really. Feel it."

I felt it. A rock. "What a stud," I joked.

"I'm taking care of myself. Eating right. Exercising. Sleeping. It's a weird feeling."

"What?"

"Being normal. I'm not sure I like it."

"You'll get used to it."

"I'm not sure I will. If it wasn't for my counselor, I'd probably be outta here."

"Outta here—to where?"

"I don't know. Just out. I don't want to spend the rest of my life caged up."

"Six months. Five now. Less than that."

"It's still a long time," he said mournfully.

"What is it you like about your counselor?"

"She's honest. You know what she said to me the other day? She said, 'You feel like you killed Olga, don't you?' It was great to hear someone be so direct like that. I loved it. She says stuff like that all the time. Nothing scares her."

I nodded. He fished a cigarette butt out of the grass. "So I'll probably stay. At least for a while. I don't want to get so that I'm afraid of the outside world. I'm not mentally ill, you know. You might think I am, but I'm not."

Eventually, I moved the conversation around to our father. I did not tell Jerry about how he needed to pop a Percodan just to get out of bed or about how soft his hands had become, or about the pain and regret I'd seen in his eyes that morning.

I simply said, "Dad's dying."

Jerry looked away and bit his lower lip. It was the gesture he always used when he was trying to suppress some powerful urge; it was as if he were grunting from the strain of physically moving his mind in another direction. I'd learned to be careful when it came to lip biting—it was sometimes a prelude to explosion. But not this time. The impulse passed, and he relaxed the clench of his jaw.

"I know you don't want to talk about this, but I'm going to talk about it anyway. If there's anything you want to say to him, you should do it now."

He gave me a look that was just this side of aggressive. "What would I want to say to him?"

"That's up to you," I said.

"I think he understands where I'm coming from."

"All the same, you might want to visit him."

"I'd get arrested if I tried."

"No, you wouldn't."

"There's a fucking restraining order on me, remember? Thanks to our darling sister, Jill."

"No one would call the cops if you wanted to visit. I guarantee it."

"Doesn't matter anyway," he said. "I'm not allowed to leave."

"Can't you get a one-day pass?"

"Nope."

"I bet you can. Want me to talk to the person who runs the place and see what I can do?"

He stared up at a palm tree that was growing in a nearby yard, its fanlike fronds waving against the bright winter sky. I could not tell if it was pride that kept him from speaking to our father, or if it was shame, or anger. Whatever it was, the force of the emotion within him had an effect on the mechanics of his face. His jaw began to work as if he were chewing gum, and his left eyelash fluttered like a bee's wing.

Finally he said, "Maybe I'll give him a call."

"That would be good," I said. "He'd like that."

Later that night, I helped my father up the stairs to his bedroom. It took twenty minutes to ascend twenty steps. Along the way, I had plenty of time to think about the days when he built those steps. It was right about the time of the divorce. My father apparently thought that if he added a new master bedroom suite onto our house, giving my mother a big, new bathroom, a huge walk-in closet with a cedar floor, an enormous bedroom with a rear balcony that looked out over the Sunnyvale rooftops toward the Santa Cruz Mountains—if he built her a palatial suburban suite in the sky— that the problems in their marriage would be solved. Or if they weren't solved, they might just disappear into the woodwork. I thought about him pounding those nails, the dirty white nail pouch tied around his waist, sweat rolling off his nose as he fit each tread into place. I remembered him telling me how difficult stairs were to build correctly. "You can't fake it with stairs," he told me. "If you don't build them right, they squeak."

Ten years later, they still didn't squeak. As we reached the landing, my father said, "Get me a pitcher full of water, will you?" I went into the bathroom, refilled his yellow plastic pitcher with fresh water, and placed it on a tray beside his bed.

It took him five minutes to get into bed, another couple of minutes to get settled. When he finally got comfortable, my father said, "Tell me more about your visit with Jerry."

"I told you everything," I said. "He looks good. Sober. I think he's doing fine."

My father stared at the photos in a collage I'd given him for Christmas, which was now leaning against the wall near his bed. I'd gone through old shoeboxes full of pictures and tried to pick out a handful of happy shots of Jerry and me and Jill as kids. There was one of Jerry and me dressed up as cowboys, another of Jill toddling through a pumpkin patch at Half Moon Bay, another of my father holding me in his arms just after I was born. I'd also included a picture of Jerry, age six or seven, with his fingers in his ears, making a face at the camera.

Looking at it, my father smiled weakly.

"That's the Jerry I remember best," he said.

"He was wild sometimes, wasn't he?"

"He was. Crazy temper. Bad as mine."

"He had a great laugh. Still does."

My father looked away and started to cough. It was a monstrous cough. His lungs seemed to want to expel themselves through his mouth. I poured a cup of water and offered it to him, but he waved me away. The coughing continued. He spat blood into a Kleenex. His eyes watered.

Finally, he settled down. He lay back on the pillow and stared up at the ceiling.

"Someday, I want to understand what happened to him," my father said abruptly.

"I don't know if there's an answer to that," I said.

"I should have been better to him. More patient."

"You have been a good father," I said to him.

"Not good enough," he said simply.

A week or so later, Michele and I were home in Brooklyn. I'd been assigned a story about Gay Men's Health Crisis, a major AIDS advocacy and treatment organization in New York. I had lunch one afternoon in the organization's cafeteria, surrounded by men with hollow eyes and lesions on their cheeks. I tried to imagine Jerry in this condition but couldn't. On the way home, rattling through the New York subway system, I thought about the difference between my life and Jerry's: I was writing about the disease, and he was living it. I thought about my years in Tahoe. I hadn't heard of HIV then, even though it was already well established in bathhouses on

Castro Street in San Francisco, and elsewhere. Given that Tahoe was only four hours away from San Francisco, it's likely that the virus was beginning to make the rounds in the casinos as well. Many of the women I slept with—and they were, alas, all women—were not exactly prom queens. It was just luck that I hadn't picked up the virus myself. A spin of the roulette wheel. A random bet.

Not long after I walked into our apartment, the phone rang. It had a distinctive quiver, a panicked tremble, that meant it was not bringing good news. Phone calls never did anymore.

"I'm going down," Jerry said, drunk again.

"Down where?" I asked stupidly.

"Down and out."

"Where are you?"

"What difference does it make?"

"You left the program," I said.

"You know what my T-cell count is?"

"No, I don't."

"Of course you don't. You never ask."

"What's your T-cell count?" I asked quietly.

"Eighty-five."

I let this sink in for a moment. Then I said, "Jerry, why don't you come out and stay with me for a while. Go to the airport, I'll buy you a ticket. I think it would be good for you—good for both of us. You can get away from things, we can hang out together and talk—"

"Fuck that," he said. "I'm singing on the street corner here in S.F. Made six bucks in two hours. Banging on a pot, singing 'Wild Horses'? See, I told you I had musical talent. I told you I was a genius. Even people on the street know it."

I said nothing, just listened to the distance crackle between us on the phone line.

"I'm thinking of joining an AIDS support group," he said, the sarcasm evaporating from his voice.

"Good for you," I said.

"They have a bunch of them up here in S.F. I've been looking into them."

"I think that's an excellent idea."

"Maybe I can meet a nice woman at one of the meetings. Seems like a good place, right? I can't live without physical love, man. I can't do it."

When Jill found out Jerry was loose again, she freaked. She figured out where all my father's hunting guns were in the house, and she knew how to get out the window, and she made sure that her new Dalmatian pup, Tyler, slept in her bedroom with her every night.

"What are you afraid of most?" I asked her one night.

"Everything," she said.

28

It was only after Christmas, when my father's death became imminent, that I began to pay attention to my wife again. I'd like to say that there was a tender moment that reawakened me to her Jersey charm and wit, but in fact it was more selfish than that. I understood that my father was going to die soon, and I didn't want to go through it alone. I had no idea how violent or disturbing my father's final days would be, nor did I know how I would bear up when the time came. After all these months of melodrama, I was exhausted; I felt at once fragile and combustible.

To begin to make amends, I suggested to Michele that we take a road trip to Atlantic City. On a recent trip to Washington, D.C., which I'd recently visited to cover a gay-rights rally, I had been given a coupon good for a complimentary one-night stay at Trump Plaza hotel and casino. I hated to let any freebie go to waste—particularly one that offered us a bed on the Jersey shore. Michele and I had spent a wildly romantic weekend there the summer before we were married, drinking Wild Turkey on the beach at night and playing Whack-A-Mole at the Wildwood boardwalk. Now seemed to be a good time to remind ourselves of that happy trip. And so in the beginning of February, Michele and I threw our suitcases into the backseat of our Honda Civic and headed south for a three-day weekend.

I was a little uncomfortable about going away. I had not seen my father in almost a month but had spoken to him on the phone every day, usually twice or three times. Sometimes, I was amazed by the

energy and spirit in his voice and was sure that he would live another six months; other times, he sounded so weak that I doubted
he'd make it through the day. I called his doctor several times in the
weeks after Christmas to get a frank appraisal, and I always asked
him how long he thought my father had left. "I have no way of
knowing," he said wisely. Once, when I pushed him to be more precise, he said, "When's your father's birthday?"

"July first," I said.

There was a long hesitation; perhaps he was running numbers in
his head. "I would be very, very surprised if he was around to celebrate it," he said.

That was four months away. I figured my father had a month,
maybe two.

About a week before our trip to Atlantic City, my father lost
feeling in his legs. It happened so suddenly that it scared him. He
called an ambulance, and they rushed him to the hospital. They
took X rays and the usual battery of tests and determined that the
cancer had spread to his spinal cord. This was not a surprise—his
doctor had warned us of this possibility as soon as my father began
suffering severe back pain.

I wanted to jump on a plane immediately, but my father talked
me out of it. "I'm doing fine," he said from his hospital bed. "There
is nothing you can do here."

I told him I'd recently received an assignment from a glossy
men's magazine to write a story about the police chief of San Jose.
This was a big break for me, and I was grateful for it—not just because for the first time in my writing life I was being paid a decent
wage, but because the magazine would pay for my airfare to California and give me an expense allowance. I planned to spend a
month out there working on the story and taking care of my father.

"I'll be out there in ten days," I told him. "Then you won't be
able to get rid of me."

For Michele and me, it was a tense, largely silent drive south
through New Jersey. It had been at least a year since we'd had any

time alone during which the phone didn't ring, there was no family emergency, and I was not on some harrying deadline. We hardly knew what to say to each other. Icebergs of resentment and bad feeling drifted beneath our simplest conversations.

We spent the first day at the Winterthur Museum in Delaware. This side trip to Henry Francis du Pont's old country house was Michele's idea, and although I didn't know a Chippendale chair from a Chippendale dancer, I liked the sparkle that old furniture put in Michele's eyes. Du Pont had been a great collector of early American antiques, and Michele was a kindred spirit. She loved old silver, old chairs, old houses. Unearthing a coin-silver spoon at a garage sale in New Jersey lifted her mood for weeks, just as it took her months to recover from the day when she missed out on a particularly beautiful hand-painted eighteenth-century blanket chest because another woman saw it ten seconds before she did.

Of course, Michele and I couldn't afford any fine antiques ourselves. If we spent fifty dollars on a faux-Hepplewhite dresser that was missing its brass pulls and desperately needed to be refinished, that was a big deal for us. By far the most exquisite object in our possession was our cat, Joe, whom Michele had found as a kitten, abandoned in a snowstorm outside the Court Street subway stop.

At Winterthur, we moved from period room to period room behind a white-haired docent in soft shoes. Michele attempted to explain the glory of Chinese porcelain to me and the difference between a real Queen Anne table and a nineteenth-century knockoff Queen Anne. I took it in with glazed eyes. I just kept thinking about my father, lying on his green plaid couch (Ethan Allen showroom, circa 1976). Was he okay? Was he in pain? Did he need me for anything? Michele generously ignored my funk and kept prodding me to see the elegant curve of a particular chair leg. I resisted, thinking to myself, *What the fuck am I doing here?* But eventually I gave in. I understood this was Michele's way of reminding me of something I was in danger of forgetting: that along with suffering and death, there is beauty and grace in the world, as well as a lot of nice furniture.

After the tour, I felt better. The moat between Michele and me seemed a little less forbidding. As we pulled out of the parking lot, I put my hand on her thigh. It was the first time I had touched her with any tenderness in months. Michele smiled and put her hand on mine. We drove across southern Jersey and made it to Atlantic City just after sundown.

The flashing lights of the casino had about the same effect on me as a Wedgwood vase with white-jasper snake handles had on Michele. I felt an unexpected spurt of adrenaline, a slight tingling in my hands, a heightened clarity of vision. It was by far the gaudiest casino I'd ever been in—there were mirrors everywhere, and trompe-l'oeil marble columns, and baccarat tables cordoned off by red velvet ropes. We checked in at the front desk, ignoring the slight but nevertheless detectable change in the clerk's voice after we presented her with our two-nights-for-the-price-of-one coupon, and stepped into the red-carpeted elevator that took us up to a room on the twelfth floor. I called my father immediately.

"Hey old man," I said cheerfully when he answered the phone.

"Hi," he replied, and I immediately knew he was having a rough day.

"How are you feeling?"

"I've been better," he said. Then he asked, in too sudden of a way, "Where are you?"

"Atlantic City," I reminded him. "Remember I mentioned to you that Michele and I were going away for the weekend? We just checked into the hotel."

"How long are you going to be there?"

"Tonight and tomorrow," I said. "Why?"

"I hate to ruin your party," he said weakly, "but I think you should come home."

My heart jumped. "Why? What's wrong? Has something changed?"

"No, nothing's changed. I just think you should."

"You're still in the hospital, right?"

"Yes. They're thinking about discharging me later this week. We'll see."

This wasn't making sense. "Is there something you're not telling me?"

"No, there's nothing I'm not telling you. I have no medical news to report. I'd just like you around, that's all. I think this would be a good time for you to visit."

"I'm coming out next Friday, remember?"

"You should come sooner," he said, point-blank. He sounded scared.

"I'm not sure I can get a plane tonight. It's already late."

"No, no, not tonight. Enjoy your visit. Take your beautiful wife out for a nice dinner. But then Monday . . . maybe you could come out on Monday?"

"Yes . . . absolutely," I said. "I'll call the airline right now and make a reservation."

There was a moment of silence. I looked over at Michele, who was in the bathroom, leaning toward the mirror, tracing her lips with a tube of bright red lipstick. I could feel myself turning toward her and away from my father. It was as if he were already gone and this voice I was talking to on the phone was just an echo from the past.

"I'm starving, I need to get some dinner," I told him. "I want you to call me immediately if anything changes."

"I will," he said. "I have your number right here next to the phone. I'll see you the day after tomorrow. Give your sweet wife a kiss for me, will you?"

I promised him I would.

29

My flight to San Francisco that Monday was terrifying. I knew I was going home to watch my father die.

Somewhere over the Midwest, I opened my backpack and pulled out the book I had brought with me: *The History and Memories of Leonard Newton Goodell.* He had sent it to me a few weeks earlier, but I had not had time to read it. It was a typewritten manuscript 123 pages long, bound between sheets of clear plastic like a quarterly sales report, with lots of badly photocopied pictures scattered throughout the text: Leonard standing in front of a cyclotron he'd helped design; Leonard in his homemade electric car; Leonard standing in his driveway in a white shirt and tie, looking like a very important man.

I was not exactly surprised to see that my father's name hardly appeared in Leonard's autobiography, nor was there much about Leonard's other four sons. It was all about the glory of his work. He offered a detailed account of his many inventions, including his beloved Walkman and his electric car. His rise through the ranks at Westinghouse got lots of space, as did his trials and tribulations at various start-ups. The final pages were a delightfully corny ode to Elaine, in which he raved about her sewing ability and a mosaic of the Golden Gate Bridge she once made out of scraps of ceramic tile.

As for family history, there wasn't much of it. For Leonard, time began the moment he was born. There was not a word about his grandfather or great-grandfather, both of whom had been prominent Methodist ministers, nor about the larger movement in his family from God to engineering. He never mentioned church or spiritual matters at all. In fact, the book is a masterpiece of doubtlessness. It is a portrait of a man who viewed life as a mathematical equation, who believed that if you keep the numbers straight and the decimal point in the right place, everything will be fine.

Still, there were a few human details to glean from the book. For example, I learned that he had lived in and around Pittsfield, Massachusetts, until he was nine years old, when his family moved to New Haven. I learned that his mother, Helena, kept a rhubarb patch and that his father, Newton, raised Belgian hares and made his own wine and worked as an engineer in the coil department at General Electric. This was all fine and interesting, and while I was winging my way back to California that day it kept my mind out of the shadows.

But then I found something in the book that made my heart jump. In 1928, when Leonard was nineteen and his brother Murel was thirteen, their father suddenly disappeared. After several weeks of desperate searching, Helena somehow discovered that Newton had moved to Cincinnati. She packed up the car, along with Leonard and his brother, and drove out to Ohio. They were able to track Newton down through a friend. Leonard wrote: "Dad saw me for a minute but didn't want any part of us." Helena later learned that Newton had fled because he had been caught stealing a piece of copper tubing from General Electric.

I felt a small burst of sympathy for the old man—he, too, knew the loneliness of a missing father. But more than that, my perspective on our family troubles shifted. It reminded me that what had happened to us was more complicated than I'd ever know. It had been shaped by a long accumulation of forgotten triumphs and sorrows, and any understanding I came to about the precise dynamics of our family story was bound to be full of shadows and half-truths.

On the other hand, after I read Leonard's book, if I wanted to be really simpleminded about it, I realized I could draw a straight line through four generations of men in my family: Leonard's father had dumped him, so when the going got rough, he felt compelled to dump his family in a similar way; which led to my father's anger and loneliness; which led to his deep desire for his marriage to succeed; which led to his devastation when it didn't; which played itself out in his relationships with Jerry and Jill and me; which left my brother with rage in his heart and my sister without a high-school diploma and me with lots of guilt; and which, finally, left my father himself stretched out on a bed in the hospital with cancerous tumors twisting around his internal organs. All because of a piece of stolen copper tubing.

Leonard's rosy, skin cancer–splotched face brightened when we met at the airport. He had called before I left New York and insisted on picking me up. He was wearing his usual dark pants, white shirt, and moth-eaten cardigan, but he'd added the stylish touch of an old fedora that he wore at a jaunty angle. It made him look debonair. I wasn't sure how to greet him. A handshake would have been enough, but I was in such an emotional state that my instinct was to go for the hug. Leonard, too, felt this, I guess, because as I approached he opened his arms wide.

"How is he?" I asked immediately.

"Not good," he said soberly, looking away.

"What's wrong?"

Leonard shrugged. "He just doesn't look good."

"Any news from the doctors?"

"Not that I know of."

I followed Leonard out to his car, I noticed that he tended to weave back and forth as he walked, as if he were forever catching his balance. It did not occur to me then that this characteristic might also carry over to his driving.

It did. In fact, his driving was worse. The forty-minute ride from the airport to my father's house in Sunnyvale was sheer white-knuckle terror. Leonard drove like a bat flies, veering from object to object at the last moment. On the freeway, he floated from lane to lane, oblivious to whether anyone was beside him or behind him or trying to pass. High beams flashed, horns blared, but Leonard did not register them. On one occasion, he drifted so close to the concrete barrier in the median that I closed my eyes and prepared for impact.

Somehow, we made it to my father's house. It was close to 11 P.M. All the lights were off. I dreaded going in. Leonard seemed to understand this. After he pulled into the driveway, he threw the car into park and turned off the headlights, leaving the engine idling in the darkness.

"I read your book on the way out here," I said.

"Oh really?" he replied, sounding pleased.

"I'm curious about your father, Newton."

Leonard began picking at a loose thread on his slacks. "He was an engineer," he said, as if that was all anyone needed to know about the man.

"Were you very close to him?"

Leonard shrugged. "Not really."

"Why not?"

"He wasn't a people person," Leonard explained.

"Why did your mother and father split up?"

"They didn't get along," he said.

"Didn't get along in what way?"

"I really don't know," Leonard said. "It was a long time ago."

"Your father just disappeared, right?"

"He moved to Cincinnati," Leonard said. He continued pulling at the thread on his pants. "I don't know why, except that he'd been accused of stealing some copper tubing."

"You say 'accused'—does that mean he didn't do it?"

"I have no idea."

"Why Cincinnati? Did he have a girlfriend there or something?"

"I can't tell you that, Jeff."

"Did you ever ask him about it?"

"No."

"Why not?"

"When we went out there to talk to him, he slammed the door in my face. I never saw him again."

"Why not?"

Here, Leonard snapped. "Why would I want to?"

"I thought you'd be curious."

"Well, I wasn't," he said curtly.

"So what became of him?"

"I have no idea," he said, as if we were talking about an old high-school classmate. "About fifteen years later, I heard he died. He's buried in Connecticut. I was going to fly out for the funeral services, but I had too much work to do."

That night, I sat for a long time on the small balcony outside my father's bedroom. It had a view of our neighbors' triangle-shaped pool, covered now for the winter, and the branches of the mulberry tree in our backyard. The jutting limbs of the tree, one growing out of another, made me think of Leonard and my father, what different paths their lives had taken, and how they were guided by different definitions of success and failure.

With Leonard, the equation had always been simple: work first, life second. He'd had a long and successful career as an engineer, and although he never became rich or famous he took some satisfaction in having been an important cog in the great wheel of American enterprise. He talked proudly of his work on the Trident submarine and the cyclotron he designed with Enrico Fermi. Leonard believed he was contributing to the greater good, and if someone told him that America wouldn't have won the cold war without the electrical firing harness he designed for Polaris missiles, he would have believed them.

But in the end, Leonard's single-mindedness led to ruin in everyone around him and begged the question of whether his worldly success, such as it was, was worth the high price that he and everyone else had paid for it. His kids—all five of them, by both Elaine and Edie—were damaged goods. Even as adults, their lives were still colored by the anger they felt toward their father. Learning that Leonard's father had ditched him, too, gave me sympathy for him, but it also made his failure more acute: Leonard had done to his kids what had been done to him.

SUNNYVALE

By now, I think Leonard understood how much he had missed in life and how much pain he had caused, and I think he regretted it. But he was eighty-one years old. How does one go about making up for a lifetime of negligence and carelessness?

My father, on the other hand, had made the opposite choice that Leonard had. At every turn, he had chosen family over work. It was a choice that might have worked out fine in Portland, Oregon, but in Silicon Valley it was like choosing to breathe water rather than air. But my father's failures, profound as they were, were offset by one simple deed whose significance, until that moment, sitting on the balcony of his empty bedroom, I had not quite grasped. Unlike Leonard and Newton and who knows how many generations of fathers before them, when things got rough, my father never walked away.

30

I arrived at the hospital at 7 A.M., just as orderlies were beginning to wheel silver carts loaded with breakfast trays down the hallways. My father was on the fifth floor—not the cancer ward, I was grateful to discover. When I stepped into the room, it was dark. There were two beds in the room; my father was in the one closest to the door, and the curtain had been pulled between his bed and his neighbor's. It took my eyes a moment to adjust. He looked terrifyingly peaceful, and for a moment I thought I was too late. But then I saw his chest move: He was asleep. His breathing was shallow and fast. He had an oxygen tube up his nose, but no IVs, no heart monitor. When I got over the shock of seeing him unconscious, it was really a rather peaceful scene. I felt a surge of relief.

His eyes fluttered open. He seemed startled by my presence, and in the half light I saw his eyes zoom in and out, like a camera lens pulling focus. Then he said, abruptly, "You made it."

"I did," I said. I walked over to the edge of his bed and grabbed his dry, bony hand. It felt disturbingly reptilian.

He squeezed and smiled weakly. "How was your flight?"

"Fine. I got in late last night."

My father pushed a button in the box that controlled his bed; his head and shoulders rose slowly. I flipped on the light and pulled an orange plastic chair to the foot of his bed. His face looked grayish-yellow against the clean white sheets, and I noticed that his lips were badly chapped. The thing that struck me the most, however, was his upper arms. The muscle had vanished, and his skin hung off the bones like drapes off rods.

It was obvious that he was happy to see me. He asked about Michele and our weekend in Atlantic City and asked how much money I lost (only fifty dollars!). There was a forced normalcy to our talk, a deliberate attempt by each of us to make this visit just like any other. I asked him if there was any news from his doctor; he said no, they had done some tests, and a specialist was coming to see him that morning. He was still having difficulty moving his legs. He wiggled his toes for me and pulled the sheet up to expose them. I saw that he was wearing tight white hose that extended up to mid-calf. They looked oddly feminine on him. "Maybe it's just my imagination, but it does feel like I have a little more movement this morning," he said hopefully.

There was the usual hustle and bustle of hospital activity—nurses darting in and out to check his blood pressure and heart rate, change his bedpan (he could get up to go to the bathroom with some help, but it was a long, difficult process), clear his breakfast tray, take his lunch order.

Then a middle-aged man in a blue suit and a red tie walked into the room. He looked like a banker. He seemed excessively well scrubbed and hygienic.

My father's eyes brightened. "Dr. Walsh. Good to see you."

Dr. Walsh introduced himself to me. He was about my father's age and had the cool, cocky reserve of a fighter pilot. I knew he was my father's last, best hope. He had taken MRIs a few days earlier of my father's back and was here now to give us his verdict on what the problem was and what could be done about it.

I also knew that my father felt a special connection to this doctor. As it turned out, he was the son of the surgeon who had performed the adrenal-gland surgery on my father thirty years earlier. It was sheer coincidence that he was under the son's care, but my father, desperate for hope, took it as a good omen.

Dr. Walsh dispensed with small talk quickly. In a passionless but not unkind way, he told my father that the MRIs had revealed an orange-sized tumor near his spine and another in his abdomen. He said, "These tumors won't kill you," but he made it clear that they would make it difficult for him to walk and to control his bowels. Dr. Walsh told him he could either have surgery to remove the tumors or let them go—"But if you decide to have surgery, I must tell you it won't prolong your life."

I watched my father's face. He did not look sad or shocked; rather, he looked almost relieved. Here was the hard truth, the inevitable facts, the end of false hope.

"Without surgery, what do I have—a month?"

"I have no way of knowing," Dr. Walsh said, then apologized for bringing such bad news and left. Before my father and I could exchange more than a glance, his regular doctor, Dr. Alan Chausow, arrived. I'd gotten to know him fairly well during the course of my father's disease. He was a small, carefully spoken man with wire-rimmed glasses who seemed more interested in my father's well-being than in the glory of saving his life.

But Dr. Chausow's view of my father's condition was even bleaker than Dr. Walsh's. "Surgery is not a good option," he said.

"Why not?" my father asked.

"Because it will cause you a lot of pain, and it will not prolong your life."

My father nodded. I knew he wouldn't choose surgery anyway. Not at this point.

"It's important to me that I die with some dignity," my father said.

Dr. Chausow nodded and patted his leg in an affectionate way. "That's a very good point, my friend. I'll talk to Dr. Walsh later and see if there's anything else we can do to make you more comfortable, okay? Now hang in there. I'll be back to see you this afternoon, and we can talk more."

When Dr. Chausow left, the room was silent. I stepped closer to my father, and my eyes welled up. The man in the bed beside my father stirred uncomfortably and cleared his throat, as if to remind us that he was just on the other side of the gauzy curtain and that he'd appreciate it if we kept all this uncomfortable talk about death and dying to a minimum.

"I knew this was coming," my father said, dry-eyed and almost wistful. "As soon as my legs went numb, I knew it."

As I grasped my father's hand, I felt a rough spot on his ring finger. It took me a moment to understand what it was—the callus from his wedding ring. I had no idea when he had stopped wearing the ring or what he had done with it, but he had worn it long enough that it had almost become part of his body.

For the next hour, there was hardly a quiet moment—nurses running in and out, visitors for the guy in the other bed, the phone ringing. An excessively bubbly redheaded nurse danced in—"Okay, Ray, time to brush those great whites of yours"—and then went into the bathroom, grabbed his toothpaste and toothbrush, and handed them to him. My father smiled at her in a flirty way—oh, how happy I was to see that flash of sexual energy!—and said, "You don't let me get away with anything, do you?" and then started to brush his teeth. It seemed to take him forever, one small stroke at a time, up and down and sideways over each tooth. The nurse stood beside him the entire time, making sure he didn't skip a single tooth. It was kinda hopeful, actually. Dead men don't fear plaque.

When the nurse finally left us, my father stared at the wall for a moment, and I could see that he was gathering his thoughts. He finally said, "I've been thinking about my will."

My father had told me a few months previously that he was leaving Jerry a lump sum of twenty thousand dollars, with the rest of his property—the house in Sunnyvale and a few thousand dollars in retirement savings—to be split between Jill and me. I argued against this, saying Jerry was the one who needed the money the most. He had no health insurance, no disability, no savings. I told my father that if he was worried about Jerry blowing all the money, he should put it in a blind trust.

Nevertheless, my father had resisted—partly because he had worked very hard for every penny he had and couldn't stand the idea of Jerry drinking it away, and partly because he genuinely believed that a big lump of money might not only do Jerry no good but even kill him. I had disagreed and had asked my father to reconsider.

And apparently he had. "I want you to call the lawyer and tell her I want to change my will. Jerry is my son. I want to be fair to him. I made a rash decision, and I want to correct it."

"I'm very glad to hear that," I said.

"So let's call the lawyer and let's get this done." My father seemed energized by having a piece of business to take care of.

"You want me to call her now?"

"Yes," he said. "See if she can come by this afternoon."

So I did. She was not available, but her secretary said she might be able to stop by the next morning. I said that was fine and hung up.

When I relayed the conversation to my father, however, he seemed uneasy. His eyes jumped and wandered. "Couldn't she come any sooner?"

I didn't understand his panic. "That's the best she could do."

"Call back and ask again."

"Her secretary said she's in court all day."

"Ask her to come by tonight, then. On her way home."

I thought my father was being slightly hysterical. Yes, time was short, but what difference did a few hours make? Nevertheless, I said I'd call again. Instead of calling from his room, however, I walked out and used the phone in the hallway. I wasn't sure how I was going to explain the urgency of the situation, but I thought it would be easier to do it out of his earshot. As it turned out, it wasn't necessary.

"Say no more," the secretary said, stopping me before I even had a chance to explain the situation. She said she would make arrangements for that night.

I was extraordinarily grateful for this small act of understanding. She probably dealt with the relatives of dying clients all the time, and to her I'm sure it was no big deal. To me, however, it was a remarkable gesture. It recognized the dignity of a dying man, even if he was a total stranger to her. It was sympathy without judgment, which I was beginning to understand is the only sympathy that's worth anything.

I returned to my father's room and told him the news. He seemed relieved and visibly sank into the bed. He stared at the ceiling for a while, his breathing shallow but easy, and then his eyelids began to drift down. He slept for a few minutes, then his eyes opened again. I touched his hand and said, "While you take a nap, I'm going to get some lunch."

He smiled faintly, chapped lips cracking, revealing tiny plateaus of dead white skin. "Good. Go. Enjoy yourself."

I was suddenly afraid to leave. "I'd be happy to stay if you want."

"No, go. I'm fine."

"Can I get you anything while I'm out?"

"No, just get out of here," he said, waving at me, trying to shoosh me out of the room.

It was a gray day, threatening rain. I drove mindlessly down El Camino Real, grateful to be out of the hospital room. I thought I'd go back to my father's house—I knew Jill would be home for lunch soon, and I could update her on our father's condition. Along the way, I passed a sagging red and white plywood shack that slouched like a tired old dog amid the strip-mall splendor of El Camino Real. It was Olson's cherry stand, a Valley landmark that I had presumed had collapsed long ago.

We visited Olson's all the time when I was a kid; my mother and father would buy big green cartons of Bing cherries, which grew in the orchard behind the stand. To me, they were the most luscious evidence of our bountiful life in Sunnyvale. I ate them by the pound. I became an expert at rolling the pit around inside my mouth, sucking it clean of fruit, then shooting the clean yellow nugget from my mouth like a bullet.

I knew it was too early in the year for cherries, but I pulled up at the curb in front of Olson's anyway. I just wanted to go in and look around, maybe buy a bag of dried apricots to take back to my father as a gift. If he didn't eat them, I certainly would.

The stand hadn't changed much from what I remembered. Still the same old dilapidated structure, corrugated aluminum roof, white-painted tables set out to hold the fruit. On the walls were cobwebby black-and-white photographs of women in white aprons slicing trays and trays of apricots, and of Charlie Olson, the patriarch, receiving various awards and blue ribbons for his cherries. As I was looking at the photos, a tall, attractive woman with a red handkerchief tied over her blond hair wandered out of the back room and struck up a conversation with me. I told her how astonished I was to see that the stand was still here and that the orchard had not been bulldozed. She said, "We're holding out until the bitter end." As we talked, however, it became clear that it was not sentimentality that was keeping the business alive. The Olson family still owned a good hunk of the old cherry orchard and planned to hold on to it as long as they could. "The value of this land will only go up," she said. Then she told me that a thirty-acre orchard less than a mile from my father's house had sold recently for forty million dollars—or about $1.3 million an acre. She did not roll her eyes in amazement; instead, she had the cool, intelligent look of a woman who knew exactly what game she was playing.

I grabbed two bags of dried apricots and handed them to her. She rang them up on the register, then opened her hand for the money. "Thirteen eighty," she said.

I thought I heard her wrong. "I'm sorry?"

"Thirteen eighty," she repeated coolly.

"You're kidding."

"No, I'm not. They're very good. Worth every penny."

⸻

Jill was already home when I arrived. She was sitting at the kitchen table eating a piece of bread and some canned minestrone and flipping through a magazine. She was in businesswoman mode, blond hair held back with a hair band, Filofax on the table beside her, along with a textbook from an economics class she was taking at a local junior college. The last few months of hell had had a remarkable effect on her, squeezing every last bit of childishness out of her and turning her into a very direct and straightforward person. She, too, knew exactly what game she was playing now, and the stakes were a lot higher than they were at Olson's cherry stand.

I gave her a peck on the cheek and told her about my visit to Olson's. She shrugged. "Hey, if you can find someone stupid enough to pay the price, why not?"

I let it go, enjoying her buoyant mood, sorry I had to drop a bomb on it.

"Dad got some bad news this morning," I said as evenly and as calmly as I could.

The brightness faded instantly from her face.

"The numbness in his legs is being caused by a tumor near his spine," I continued. "He has another tumor in his abdomen. It's spreading quickly."

Her eyes began to glisten. "How long, do you think?"

"A week. Maybe two."

"The doctor told you this?"

"No, the doctor told us about the tumors. He wouldn't speculate about how long he has left. Nobody really knows. But I'd be surprised if he's alive in a month."

"Well, maybe you're wrong."

"I don't think so," I said.

She buried her face in her hands.

"I'm not telling you this to scare you," I said carefully, trying for some stupid big-brotherly reason to hold myself together in front of her. "I just want to be open with you about this. When the time comes, I want you to be ready."

When I returned to my father's hospital room, he was still asleep. I settled into a chair against the wall and picked up the front page of the *San Francisco Chronicle* and pretended to care for a moment about what was going on in the world.

I looked up at one point, and my father's eyes were open. It was not clear at first if he had registered my presence. Then he said, "Have a nice lunch?"

I told him I had. I told him about my trip to Olson's and about the forty-million-dollar cherry orchard. I don't know why I brought that up or what possible interest I thought my father might have in someone else's good fortune, but I needed words to fill the silence between us, and that's what came to mind.

He smiled with one side of his mouth. "You know what they say about real estate," he whispered.

I did know, but I said "What?" anyway.

"They're not making any more of it."

I nodded and smiled and said, "That's for sure."

His breathing was shallow but noisy—I thought I could actually hear air rushing over the tumor in his bronchial tubes. I had the powerful feeling that my father had been waiting for me to return.

He motioned for me to come closer. I stood up, walked over to the head of the bed, and grabbed the cold steel railing. My hands had suddenly started shaking uncontrollably, and I didn't want my father to see them.

"There are a few things I've been thinking about," he said in a hoarse whisper.

As I bent down to hear him better, the only thing I could think about was how bad his breath was. It was not just unpleasant but as sharp and rancid as if something inside were literally rotting away. It was difficult for me not to pull back.

He said, "I have some money in a real-estate fund, not much, but a little. My broker at Merrill Lynch knows about it. The deed to the house, the car—all that kind of paperwork is in my desk, or in the paper file in my closet."

He lay in silence for a moment, biting his lower lip, tearing at a tiny loose flap of skin. I thought about how strange that was—his body was fighting a losing battle with renegade cells, but his mind was preoccupied with chapped lips.

"Don't worry, I'll take care of everything," I reassured him.

"Oh, I know you will," he said.

I listened to the conversation of two nurses outside my father's door. They were debating who was sexier, Paul Newman or Clint Eastwood.

Then I said, with some urgency, "Do you want me to go find Jerry?"

We both knew this meant, "Do you want to see your son before you die?" I had been wanting to ask him this all morning but couldn't find the words or the opportunity to do it. Now it just jumped out of my mouth.

My father did not react the way I expected him to. Instead of sending me out on a mission to find my brother, he raised his arms above his head and looked troubled. His eyes wandered around the room. I saw fear and suffering in his eyes, but most of all I saw resignation and sorrow. He knew this was the last important decision he would make as a father.

After much consideration, he finally shook his head and said, "Why open Pandora's box? I know how hard a visit would be for him. Maybe the best thing to do right now is leave him alone."

I started to disagree, to say that I thought Jerry wanted very much to see him (which I wasn't sure was true), but I didn't even get to finish my sentence before we were interrupted by a short nurse with dark, schoolgirl bangs who bounced into the room as cheery as a third-grade teacher about to pass out crayons. "How's my favorite patient doing today," she chirped, clutching a metal clipboard to her chest with one hand and grabbing one of my father's toes with the other.

"Must be four o'clock," my father said, smiling. "Shift change."

"Lucky you," the nurse said. "You get to have your blood pressure and temperature taken."

I smiled at my father and said, "I'm gonna step out in the hallway while she takes care of you."

He nodded and gave me the brightest smile of the day. "I'm in good hands here, don't worry."

"You bet you are," the nurse said jauntily as she unwound the blood-pressure cuff. "Now stretch out that big, strong arm of yours and let me go to work."

As I walked out of the room, I ran straight into Leonard. He was more spiffed up than usual, in a gray suit and vest with a red tie. He told me that Elaine had just been admitted to the hospital again because of her asthma; while he was here, he thought he'd stop by to see how my father was doing. He made some crack about finally having all his loved ones under one roof, and he seemed remarkably jolly and bright eyed. It was as if, after all these years, he'd finally gotten the knack of being a husband and a father and was enjoying it immensely.

"How's he doing?" Leonard asked, motioning toward my father's bed.

I pulled him away from the door and said, "The nurse is with him now. He's doing fine. We got some bad news today, though." Leonard's face paled. I was afraid he was going to faint. "Why don't we go sit down," I said.

There were people in the waiting area next to the elevators, so we found an empty room two doors down from my father's. The curtains were open, and there was a view across the Valley—rooftops that seemed to be laced together by telephone wires; spires of redwood trees; shaggy palms; and in the far distance, near the foot of the bay, the humps of the old zeppelin and blimp hangars at Moffett Field.

Leonard and I pulled two chairs up beside the window. I started from the beginning, telling him about Dr. Walsh's visit this morning, but hadn't even spoken three sentences before a nurse burst into the room. She was pink faced, crying, out of breath. She asked if I was Mr. Goodell's son. "Yes," I said, not understanding what was going on. She muttered something about a hemorrhage, about massive quantities of blood, and the do-not-resuscitate order that was written in his medical chart. I still couldn't grasp what was going on. I had just seen my father two minutes ago. He was joking, feeling okay. Surely this had to be a mistake. I stood up, intending to go down to his room, but she grabbed me strongly by the shoulders and said in a panicked voice, "You must stay here. You can't go in there."

I heard scurrying in the hallway. I was beginning to understand.

"Is he conscious?" I asked.

"No," she said.

I sat back down, thinking, "No, not yet. We still have things to talk about." My face felt numb and hot, and tears started to roll down my cheeks.

Time passed. Then the phone beside me rang.

"It's for you," the nurse nodded.

I picked it up.

"This is Dr. Chausow," I heard a voice say. "The head nurse just called me. My condolences to your family."

"So this is it?"

"This is it."

I asked him what had happened, and he said he didn't know, it could have been a perforated stomach ulcer or a ruptured artery. "It happened very quickly," he assured me. "It's a blessing."

I hung up the phone and looked over at Leonard. He was crying—a sight I never imagined I'd live to see. It was like watching a machine weep.

At some point Leonard said, "We should call people. We should let them know. I'll call Bob and Dick."

I watched him reach for the phone to call my father's brothers. He spent a few moments pushing buttons on his digital watch, which apparently doubled as a phone book, but his glasses were so fogged up from his tears that he couldn't see well enough to work the tiny buttons. He finally gave up. To get his own sons' phone numbers, Leonard had to dial information.

31

The night my father died, Jerry called. He said he was just check-
ing in, but somehow he knew. I said, "Dad died at about four P.M.
today." It was probably a mistake to announce it so bluntly over the
phone, but I couldn't help myself. He reacted in a flat, emotionless
way. I did not tell him about the will, or about my father's last
words about him. I asked him if he wanted to come over and spend
the night at the house. He said no. I asked if I could buy him lunch
the next day. He suggested I meet him at a Burger King near our
house. That would not have been my choice, but I didn't argue.

He was slouched in a corner booth when I arrived. His eyes
were dry and bloodshot and seemed too small for their sockets. I
asked him if he was hungry, and he shrugged in a way that suggested
he would eat something if it was put in front of him. I walked up to
the counter and ordered us Whoppers, large fries, and Cokes. While
I watched the clerk load the food onto the tray, I thought about my
father's final moments and wished he had said something more
about Jerry. I wished he had said, "Tell him I love him" or "I'm
sorry." I considered telling Jerry he had said it anyway. What difference would it make to my father? It would be a lie, but a lie that told
a larger truth.

I carried the food back to the table. Jerry immediately grabbed
a few fries and shoved them into his mouth.

I told him about our father's last hours and about how strange
it was that he died just as Leonard walked into his room. Then I told

him about the will. I explained that our father had died before he could legally make the changes he'd wanted to, but that as far as I was concerned he'd get one third of the estate, which meant about one hundred thousand dollars for each of us. "No strings attached," I said.

Jerry looked stunned. "I never expected anything from him."

"Well, he wanted you to have it."

Then Jerry looked at me with such intensity that I almost could not hold his gaze. I knew what he was looking for. He wanted to know if my father had had any final words for him.

I hesitated. I wanted to give him what he so desperately wanted, to speak the unspoken, but I couldn't. Not because I was incapable of lying, Lord knows, but because if I owed anyone in the world the truth, it was my brother.

"Dad loved you," I said. "I hope you know that. When he died, he was not angry at you. I wish he could have talked to you and told you this himself, but . . ."—I didn't know how to finish the sentence. *But what?*—". . . but he ran out of time."

I could see that this was not exactly what Jerry was looking for. He didn't want my words. He wanted my father's.

He looked out the window at the passing traffic for a long time. I have no idea what was going through his mind, but when he looked back at me his eyes were like dark spots on the horizon. All I felt was distance, like every thinking and feeling neuron in his body had fled, leaving a lifelike dummy behind.

I told Jerry about the wake that we had planned for the weekend, and he said that he'd try to make it. I asked him if he needed money, a place to stay, anything.

"I'm okay," he said, then he stood up, and I stood up. We hugged, and he squeezed me so hard I thought my lungs were going to burst. Then he walked out the door toward the bus stop. Watching him go, I had the powerful feeling that I might never see him again.

But as usual with Jerry, I was wrong. He showed up at the wake, which was held on a gloomy day at our house in Sunnyvale. We had a big fire in the fireplace, and about fifty friends and relatives milled around, wet cheeked and sad. Since we had no experience with grief in my family, no one knew quite what to do other than hug whoever was near.

Jerry's presence was a surprise to everyone. Not only did he show up, he looked sharp: He was showered and shaved and wore clean khakis and a crisply ironed blue dress shirt. Where he got this stuff, I have no idea. I noticed that Jill eyed him warily and kept her distance. Several other relatives were cool to him, too, and I could see shame in Jerry's face as well as determination. It was obvious this was difficult for him; it seemed to take every bit of strength he had just to stand in the living room in front of the cobblestone fireplace and accept condolences from our aunts and cousins. But he did it, and with grace and humility. Watching him, I couldn't help thinking about what my father had always said about Jerry: He had to hit the bottom before he'd change his life. What my father didn't know was that his own death would be that bottom.

——◦——

I spent the next month cleaning out my father's house and getting ready to put it on the market. I was sentimental about it at first, spending hours going through clothes, touching and smelling everything—only in love and death is your nose so attuned to every fading molecule of another's presence. After a few days of this, however, I became ruthless. I separated out the few things of my father's that I wanted to keep: his hunting knife, a deer head, his cowboy boots, a couple of 1950s ties, some photographs, and a few other small items. Jill came over and took what she wanted; I'd asked Jerry at the wake if there was anything he wanted, and after a moment of thought he said, "I don't think so."

So I took it all to the Salvation Army. Dozens of short-sleeved shirts from Mervyn's and Sears, Herb Alpert and the Tijuana Brass albums, cuff links, the stereo, dishes, silverware, camping equipment, cameras—I just threw it all into the back of my father's Blazer and hauled it off. I must have made thirty runs, carting off the debris of a generation of family life. What the Salvation Army didn't want or wouldn't take, I dragged to the Sunnyvale dump. I grew sur-

prisingly cold about it, tossing away things that my father had trea-
sured for years. I didn't care. I wanted it gone.

Then I called in the contractors, and we gave the house a quick
makeover. I yanked out the old, dark paneling in the kitchen and
family room, and the painters came in behind me with their spray
guns and brushes, giving the whole interior a clean coat of white
paint. Then they attacked the outside, slapping more white over the
1970s gold stucco and painting the shutters and trim a happy, innocent blue. I repaired doors, hired a plumber to fix some rattling
pipes and install a new toilet in the downstairs bathroom, sham-
pooed the carpets, ripped off the little card with emergency numbers
on it that my father had taped near the phone. Little by little, the evidence of our troubled lives was repainted, recovered, scrubbed
away. By the time I called in a realtor, the house positively sparkled.

My mother and father had paid $19,000 for the house in 1963;
now, in the spring of 1990, the realtor—a smart, forceful, gray-haired
woman who pulled up in a maroon Jaguar—suggested we put it on
the market for $295,000. A week later, a Chinese man and wife, both
recent émigrés from Hong Kong, toured the house with their real-
estate agent, who was Chinese. The man and woman did not speak
English; their realtor was not fluent in English either, but he could
make himself understood. Most of their questions were about practical matters: Did the roof leak, did we have any problem with termites,
had there ever been any earthquake damage. They did not seem to
care much about the details and amenities of American suburban
homes. Nevertheless, I proudly steered them to the fireplace my father
had built. I explained, through the realtor, that he had laid each brick
himself, that the cobblestones were from the streets of San Francisco.
They smiled and nodded, then said something to the realtor, who relayed their question to me: "How big is the water heater?"

A few days later, they bought the house. They did not haggle over
the price, nor did they have any trouble getting a mortgage—they
paid cash. I cleared out the last of my father's belongings, then headed
back to New York. My life in Silicon Valley, I thought, was over.

32

I dealt with my grief by working. I finished the story about the police chief of San Jose, then immediately accepted a magazine assignment that required me to spend several weeks in L.A. Michele came out and stayed with me for a while, and we went out to dinner a lot and began to get to know each other again. I talked to my mother and my brother and my sister on the phone once in a while, but mostly I paid attention to my wife. I often felt numb and dislocated, like a man just home from war.

While in L.A., I met with a well-connected movie director. Over breakfast one morning, I happened to mention that I'd grown up in Silicon Valley. The director raised an eyebrow—it turned out that he was a closet geek himself and had owned one of the first Apple computers. I told him about my adventures at Apple—about Jobs and Woz and the tedium I felt during my brief visit to the center of the new world.

"Have you ever thought about writing a movie about that?" he said, out of nowhere.

"About what? How bored I was?"

"No, about Jobs and Woz. Two guys in a garage and their dream to change the world."

"No," I said.

"Why not? It's a great story."

"I wasn't part of that, I was just a lowly assistant—"

"So? How about if I set up a meeting for you with a producer? Work up a pitch, let's see what happens."

What happened was I called Michele that night—she'd gone home to Brooklyn—and asked her if she wanted to write a movie with me. She was a serious movie buff, and if I was going to plunge into this I wanted to do it with her. "Wow. That sounds like fun, darling," she said. We spent the next several hours working out a story about two geeky teenagers who build a computer in their garage, get rich, and become American heroes before they're old enough to drink. Of course, there was rivalry and bitterness between the characters along the way and lessons about how fame and money don't buy happiness—it was an old, old story, recast for the digital age.

By this time, I had figured out that something extraordinary was happening in my hometown, and I was both fascinated and repelled by it. I also realized that my impulse to become a writer was somehow connected with that drama, that writing was my way of slowing down this rapidly accelerating world and making sense of it. And if I could actually get paid to write a screenplay about it, so much the better.

The next day, I pitched our story to Edward Pressman, a respected independent producer. He and his assistants laughed me out of the building. The next day, I pitched again to another producer—more giggles. Finally, after cutting the pitch down to about ten minutes and playing up a love triangle between the Woz and Jobs characters and a sexy blond Stanford student, I pitched it to a producer at Universal Pictures who did not laugh. In fact, he offered us a modest sum of money to write a Silicon Valley Horatio Alger story.

The movie money, combined with my father's inheritance, meant that for the first time in my life I had a measure of financial freedom. Michele and I decided to do two seemingly contradictory things: Buy a house in upstate New York, then move to L.A. I won't go into the bizarre reasoning that led to this decision, except to say that Michele had been pining to live in the country for a long time, and after what she had been through with my family I felt like I owed her this. We saw our stay in L.A. as a short-term adventure—we'd stay six months or so, until we finished the movie and sold another. Then we'd return to upstate New York and write peacefully amid the sugar maples and pines.

So Michele and I set out on a series of scouting trips upstate, and after peering into many musty basements and driving many miles through neglected and abandoned farmland, we fell in love with the rolling hills near the Vermont border. We bought a big crumbling 210-year-old Georgian house with a wide center hall and elaborate mantelpieces that was set on two acres at the edge of a small town. It had problems: It was too close to the road, the plaster was in bad shape, the yard was overgrown. But we liked it anyway. I was drawn to the squat rectangular shape of the house and the heaviness with which it sat on its stone foundation. I liked wandering around the rooms at night, after Michele had gone to sleep, and thinking about all the lives that had been lived here, all the babies born, all the struggling deaths, all the silent prayers for salvation, all the criminal intentions and dark fantasies. When this house was built, I often thought, California—the idea, not the place—did not exist yet.

It was obviously no coincidence that I, a child of Sunnyvale, the city of the future, ended up buying a house that was rooted so deeply in the past. I felt like I'd overdosed on sunshine and needed a place to sober up. I wanted to live for a while with the illusion that the world really hadn't changed much in the last two hundred years. This old house fit the bill.

Michele and I only lived there a few months, however, before we packed a suitcase and headed for L.A. We drove cross-country in our Isuzu Trooper, rented a small apartment a few blocks above Sunset Boulevard, and proceeded to write about fifty drafts of the screenplay. Three months of work stretched into six months, then a year. After each draft, we'd take a meeting with the director who was attached to the project, and he would say things like, "This is *Citizen Kane* in Silicon Valley" or "This is *Wall Street* with computers." But there was always a problem with the third act, or the love interest, or with making the Steve Jobs character sympathetic enough, or with the montage in the first act that captured the dizzying ascent of our two heroes from garage geeks to pop-culture icons. We wrote and wrote and wrote. And the more we wrote, the more I realized that the story I was writing had very little to do with anything that I'd seen or felt growing up in the Valley—it was all about creating a compelling fantasy. That's hard enough to do in its own right; it was particularly difficult for me because my feelings about the wonders of the Valley and the accomplishments of our movie's heroes were all tangled up with feelings of grief and loss.

We turned in the final draft of the script well over a year after we had begun. We never heard from the producer himself. We did hear from his chief of production, however. She called from her car phone one afternoon and said, "I just read your final draft. You did great work. We'll be in touch." And of course, that was it. The project was shelved immediately, and Michele and I found ourselves unemployed and broke. We had another script we'd half completed, but it still needed a few months of work. I was too tired and discouraged to finish it, and so was Michele. We wanted out of Hollywood altogether.

So we drove back to our big, rambling house in upstate New York. Michele took a job temping in Albany, while I called every magazine editor I knew, trying to drum up work. Suddenly, our gorgeous old house seemed like a monstrous burden—the furnace was ready to explode, the plaster walls were covered with peeling 1970s wallpaper, the kitchen was lit by a bare bulb hanging from the middle of the ceiling. And we had no money or time to fix any of it. Over the course of just a few months, we'd gone from swinging screenwriters taking meetings in Santa Monica to hillbillies who had to shop around for the best price on heating oil.

For Michele, coming back to New York turned out to be a lucky break. After a few months, she found a job in state politics, fell in love with the daily drama of political life, and within a year was writing speeches for Governor Mario Cuomo. I had a harder time. I hung a photo of my father on the bookshelf near my desk and often stared at it during the middle of the day. Movie writing had distracted me from coming to terms with the fact that he was actually gone. Now, I felt absence all around me: the absence of money, work, furniture, friends, and, most of all, him. I felt like I'd fallen into a cave. I understood something of what my father must have felt when his life crumbled around him. My own troubles were not as serious—I didn't have kids, and my career prospects were infinitely brighter than his had been—but I nevertheless got a good look at the wide-open emptiness that accompanies failure.

Worse, I did not expect Jerry to live much longer. I presumed grief would eventually tip the balance of his already fragile psyche and that he would find a way to get himself killed. I imagined him getting beat up in an alley or stepping in front of a bus. In fact, I braced myself for it. I felt helpless to stop it or even delay it. I sat alone on our pink couch in the family room and thought, "How will I survive when Jerry goes?"

Instead, it turned out that my father's death might have saved my brother's life.

Jerry's resurrection began, appropriately enough, in the bar at T.G.I. Friday's a few blocks from our old house. It was exactly six days after my father's death. He had a beer, he told me later, but he was not drunk. Just hanging out and—unusual for him—smoking a cigarette. Nearby, he saw a dark-haired Hispanic woman in a Rolling Stones T-shirt. Jerry happened to have Jagger's solo albums in heavy rotation on his Walkman at the time, so he took her T-shirt as a sign that they had something in common and struck up a conversation with her. Her name was Isabel. She was in her mid-thirties, worked in a photo shop, and was just getting over a bad relationship. Not coincidentally, she bore a striking resemblance to Olga. Jerry later described her as "an angel who had dropped out of the sky to save me."

From that moment on, they were inseparable. I do not know the mysteries of what went on between them, but I do know that Jerry moved into her apartment in San Jose more or less immediately. He stopped drinking, more or less. He convinced Isabel to pack up and move to Seattle with him—a place he had long dreamed of living in. They found a nice apartment with a view of the harbor, and Jerry got a job driving an airport shuttle bus. He was more at peace than I'd ever seen him. He talked often about how much he'd loved our father and how sorry he was that he had not gotten to talk to him before he died. But he seemed determined to move on, to put that behind him.

And for several years, he did. He stayed healthy, even though his T-cell count remained dangerously low. He and Isabel got married in a happy ceremony in Fresno, her hometown. I was his best man and stood proudly beside him while he slipped the ring on Isabel's finger. My mother and I allowed ourselves to wonder if Jerry might be one of these people whose bodies seem to find some mysterious balance against AIDS and never get sick and die. For all the pain he had suffered in his life, perhaps he had earned a free pass on this one. It seemed only fair.

In the mid-1990s, I started writing about Silicon Valley for various magazines. Editors were desperate for anyone who could make sense of this new thing called the Internet, and I often got the call. Unlike writing a movie, writing about the Valley for publications such as *Rolling Stone* forced me to think more clearly and dispassionately about what was going on in my hometown. I spent a lot of time reading and listening to same boosterish babble I'd heard fifteen years earlier at Apple: Computers are going to revolutionize business, politics, media, you name it. Except now, it was *happening*. The Internet was changing everything.

My own life was evidence of this. When we returned to upstate New York from L.A., I felt cut off from the world. I couldn't even get a newspaper delivered, I lived so far out in the boonies, and if I didn't get to the drugstore in town by 8 A.M., *The New York Times* would be gone. I had no one to talk about movies or books with, no way to keep up with media gossip, no way to trawl for story ideas beyond what was blasted out at me on the network news. Then I joined a Bay Area computer bulletin-board system called the Well, and my feelings of isolation eased. I suddenly had a community of friends—and fellow Californians, no less. I spent hours on-line every night, arguing and consoling and joking. In fact, I began to feel more connected with what was going on in the world than some of my colleagues in New York and L.A., who were constantly mocking the pathetic losers who had nothing better to do than sit in front of a computer all night. I knew better. I formed deep and complex connections with some of the people I met on the Well—they began to feel like my extended family. Jon Katz, a fellow writer I'd met online, finally drove up from his home in New Jersey to visit me; he liked the area so much he soon bought a cabin on a mountaintop a few miles away. (He eventually wrote a book, *Running to the Mountain*, about his move upstate.) We both followed the digital revolution the way other people followed the Yankees, and we spent many hours walking in the woods with our dogs, bullshitting about hackers and geeks and other wonders of the Web. Our friendship was itself a product of this revolution and was proof, if any more was needed, about how simpleminded many of my early phobias about technology had been.

None of this made my visits to my hometown any cozier, however. Whenever I returned to the Valley—I returned every couple of months, usually for business, not pleasure—I often felt like a stranger. Almost everyone I had known had long since moved away, replaced by waves of wanna-be entrepreneurs, most of them in their early twenties, all of them thinking that Silicon Valley was Mecca. In my immediate family, Jill was the last to jump ship. After we sold our father's house, she rented a place with a couple of friends in the nearby town of Campbell, but it was expensive, the traffic was miserable, and she was bored with her job at CalComp and wanted to get away from family ghosts. So about a year later, she moved to a small town outside of Denver, where she got a job at a database-storage company.

Leonard, however, had not budged. He still loved the Valley—the football field–sized electronics stores were the Elysian Fields to him. Whenever I was in town, I'd stop in to see him in the deluxe mobile home he'd bought for himself after Elaine died of asthma in 1990. It was posh and huge, with a fireplace and a big master bedroom with a private bath. He turned one bedroom into an office, where he kept his computer and files. We always sat and talked in his office—he behind his desk, me in a chair in front of him, just like it must have been at Westinghouse during the good times.

Leonard had not planted himself in just any mobile-home park. Incredibly enough, he picked the one that Edie and her husband (her third) had been living in for almost twenty years. Even forty years after their divorce, Edie still hated Leonard with a passion and couldn't believe that he had the gall to park himself a hundred feet from her. She lived in dread of running into him on the way to the pool or the rec hall; when she did, she said a cold hello and just kept walking. Leonard never said this to me explicitly, but I think he moved there because he wanted forgiveness from Edie. Edie suspected this, too, and it made her crazy. She was determined to make the old man pay until the day he died for what he'd done to her. She succeeded.

Leonard and I talked a lot, but only in a chitchatty way. He called me in New York about once a month, usually hoping that Michele would pick up the phone so that he could flirt with her. He always wanted to know how my work was going and asked me to send him my latest articles. He also sent me updates to his *History and Memories,* including paragraphs about Elaine's death and an appreciation of her years of fine cooking. The more I learned about him, the more I liked him, and the more curious I became about how he lived with the fact that all of his kids seemed to think he had a silicon chip for a heart.

I knew Leonard wasn't long for the world, so one day I decided to ask him some questions. We were sitting, as usual, in his office. A year or so earlier, he had been diagnosed with Parkinson's disease, and it was clear that the disease was moving rapidly. His hands shook, and he was having difficulty getting a paper clip around a stack of letters he had written to the Santa Clara County Valley Transportation Authority, complaining that the county bus system was hopelessly disorganized.

"Do you have any regrets?" I asked. I'd learned to be abrupt with Leonard—it was the only manner of conversation he respected or paid much attention to.

He looked at me through smudged glasses. He knew what I meant but chose to stall: "What kind of regrets?"

"About your divorce from Edith, maybe."

"No. During the war, I worked very hard. It took its toll on us. After that, we had troubles."

"What kind of troubles?"

"Troubles," he said. And then, to elaborate, he said, "It just wasn't working out."

"Do you feel like you did the right thing?"

"Yes. In the wrong way, maybe. But it was the right thing."

I waited, in case he wanted to say more. He didn't.

"I've always wanted to ask you about your religious feelings."

"What do you mean?"

"Do you go to church?"

"No."

"You come from a long line of Methodist ministers. You went to church when you were a kid, didn't you?"

"Until I was about ten," he said.

"Then what?"

"I quit."

"Why?"

He shrugged. "Didn't have any feel for it."

I loved that response. That was it, the primal geek rejecting God. Why? He didn't have any feel for it. Simple as that. No drama, no doubt, no fuss.

———

Often, when I was visiting the Valley, I stretched my trip out for a few days and flew up to Seattle to see Jerry. By late 1994, it was clear that the virus was beginning to overtake my brother's body. He didn't talk about it much at first, but I could tell when I visited him that he was growing weaker—one flight of stairs and he'd be out of breath. Then the night sweats began. Earaches. Sore throat. Thrush. He called in sick for work frequently, then quit altogether. By the summer of 1995, he was sleeping on an air mattress on the living-room floor and rarely ventured outside the apartment. He used ear candles to help suck the wax out of his ears, and he kept a huge pile of pills beside him in a coffee can. He took twenty pills a day, a different one for each infection, as well as AZT, which at the time was one of the few drugs that offered any promise of slowing the progression of the disease.

By then, Jerry had converted to Catholicism (his wife, Isabel, a Catholic herself, had been influential in this) and kept a Bible beside his coffee can of pills. I once sat in the bedroom while he and a priest met in the living room, and I heard him talking about the sins he had committed in his life and how he believed AIDS was his punishment for that. I strained to hear the priest's response, but his voice was too low. Whatever he told him, it seemed to help, because when the visit was over and I emerged from the bedroom, much of the tension was gone from Jerry's face.

I don't know exactly how much Catholicism meant to Jerry in the end. He was reluctant to talk about it with me. I know he believed in good and evil in the world, and I know he believed he had done evil. Catholicism gave him a structure through which to express that belief, as well as a hope for redemption. It did not, however, give him an easy way to make sense of the apparent meaninglessness of his short life. The last time I saw him, in early October of 1995, we talked about this. By that time, he and Isabel had left Seattle and moved to Chico, California, a college town in the northern part of the state, so that he would be close to our mother as his disease worsened. I spent several hours alone with him in his dark, little one-bedroom apartment, which had brown shag carpet and heavy curtains on the windows. He did not look thinner or sicker than he had a few months earlier, but he was so tired now that he could hardly move without running out of breath. He said, looking at me with eyes that were so much like mine that I felt as if I were looking in a mirror, "I wasted so much time." He did not understand the point of his time on earth—he had accomplished nothing, he said. He told me about a piece of music he had written that had been incorporated into a song that had become part of the repertoire of the marching band at the high school we had attended—"I guess that's a bit of a legacy." His deepest regret, he said, was that he had not had a child.

Nine days later, he was admitted to the hospital because he was having difficulty breathing. Drugs were no longer much help. His liver was failing. I talked to him on the phone and told him that I loved him and that I was grateful that he was my brother and that I would be out to see him again in a few days. Serious as this moment was, I didn't think this was the end. He had been through these crises before and had always pulled out. Not this time. Isabel was beside him when he died; my mother, who had driven from her house in Red Bluff, arrived a few minutes later. I was at my desk in upstate New York, writing.

33

It's the fall of 1999, and the empire has risen now, growing out of the fertile soil of the Valley like a colony of new, cube-shaped microbiotic organisms. As I drive up the peninsula, I have a look at many of the dominant species: the new Apple campus, the new Intel buildings, the new Adobe Systems building, the new Advanced Micro Devices buildings, the new 3Com buildings, the new Cisco Systems buildings. They all have tinted windows that suggest a complex, secret life inside.

I pull into the parking lot of Excite@Home in Redwood City, where my sister, Jill, now works. She recently moved back to the Valley from Colorado and has lately gone through a divorce of her own. At the moment, however, all of her attention is focused on her job at Excite@Home, which offers high-speed cable access to the Internet and is one of the most-talked-about companies in the Valley. When she comes out to greet me in the lobby, she has a direct, let's-get-to-the-point intensity that tells me she's been working very very hard.

"Hey, Gorilla," I say, and we hug, and she, as always, looks a little embarrassed at my display of affection for her.

We stand in the lobby and chat about my flight, the traffic, a recent trip she took to the Sierras. Then Jill leads me back toward her cubicle. Excite@Home's offices are typical Silicon Valley fare: pinball machines in the hallways, mountain bikes hanging from hooks on the ceiling, lots of guys with goatees staring at big monitors. This is one of the fastest-moving companies in America, and yet, inside,

everything is eerily quiet and calm. As we walk around, Jill intro-
duces me to friends and then, when they're out of earshot, says
things like, "He's worth five million," or, "She just bought a big
house in the hills."

I can see that Jill loves this life: the cool machinery, the parties,
the sense of shared mission, the dreams of hitting it big. She's thirty-
one now and feels the biological clock ticking. But for her, family
life can wait. She's riding the big wave. She has stock options that
might soon make her wealthy, work that she loves, and a circle of
great friends. On weekends, she Rollerblades with her dog, Tyler, or
goes to the beach with her boyfriend. It occurs to me that the
teenage girl who wanted to grow up and work at Apple Computer
has achieved her dream—or a version of it, anyway.

Jill and I eat lunch in Excite@Home's new cafeteria. The spread
of food is stunning, even by Silicon Valley standards: five different
kinds of greens for salad, a dozen different low-fat and organic
dressings, chefs in white hats ready to cook fresh fish to order or
steaks or pasta or pizza or pretty much anything you want. There's
a mountain of fruit nearby and a refrigerator case full of dozens of
different mineral waters and fresh-squeezed juices and yogurts. I
grab a juice, make myself a modest salad, and grab a slice of pizza;
Jill orders a Middle Eastern plate.

We find a table outside on the patio. It's a gorgeous California
day, sunny and mild. The sound of progress fills the air—hammers
and air wrenches and jackhammers from across the street, where
construction workers are erecting yet another high-tech tilt-up office building. Jill and I watch Beemers and Lexuses nose in and out
of the parking lot, mingling democratically with Subarus and
muddy Jeeps.

I ask Jill if it feels weird to live here with no family around. She
nods. "I drive up to see Mom a lot, so that's cool, but I do miss Dad.
Every time I look at a tree, I think of him. I used to think it was
nothing: So you plant a tree, big deal. Now, I'm starting to understand that it's not a bad thing to do with your life." She sweeps her
hand toward the parking lot. "At least you're not contributing to
this—the traffic, the chaos, the rat race."

"I thought you loved your job."

"I do," she says. "It's just so—*relentless.*"

Then it occurs to me that Jill and I are sitting directly across the highway from where the offices of Pop's landscape-contracting company once stood. The building is still there, but in the rooms where my father and grandfather once designed city parks, a handful of engineers labor at an e-commerce start-up. I mention this to Jill, and she turns to me and says with wide eyes, "Isn't that bizarre? And you know what else is bizarre? I take the exact same commute every morning that Dad did: I get on 280 at Wolfe Road, go down 85 to 101, get off at Marsh Road. I didn't plan this—it's just the way it turned out. I had been doing this for months before it dawned on me that I'm literally traveling in his footsteps. Sometimes I feel like I'm living in a haunted house."

After lunch, I continue my tour of the Valley. Everywhere I go, I feel like I've slipped through to some parallel dimension that is very much like the world I was familiar with but not exactly. The roads curve in the same places, and the limbs of the live oak trees sway in the wind with the same lovely grace, but everything else is different. The people move fast, have clean hands, and are young and rich and multicolored. There's a throb of energy in the background, a faint vibration in the distance that has no source and seems to come from everywhere at once.

Parked at a pull-out on Skyline Boulevard above Palo Alto, I notice that new houses are rising higher and higher up the hillsides of the Valley, and the buildings in downtown San Jose are growing taller and taller. The entire Valley seems to tremble with energy. You can almost hear voices crackling along the telephone wires and the hum of the transformers as they feed electricity to the millions of tiny silicon brains that are parsing lines of code, shooting electrons through miles of tiny wires, opening this file, closing that one, performing the thousands of discrete operations that go into something as simple as typing the letter *m* on a keyboard and making an *m* appear on the screen. It's a miracle of engineering so profound that you would not know how to describe it to a person who lived a hundred years ago, and yet now no one gives it a second thought.

I feel like I'm looking down into the heart of a vast electronic hive, where the honey is time: faster chips, faster software, faster wires. It's not about efficiency—it is about cheating death. Dreaming of speed is the way engineers dream of immortality.

I see immortality in the faces of my children. If the Valley is all about speed and change, my world is increasingly about constancy and continuity. I've been married to Michele for thirteen years now, and not only do I still get a little jolt whenever I look into her bright green eyes, but my feelings for her deepen and expand in astonishing ways. We still live in the same big old house in upstate New York (we've spruced it up a bit with new paint and installed a new furnace); the new friends we made when we moved up here are now old friends, and the muzzle of my black dog, Lulu, my great pal and Frisbee partner, is turning white with age. We've planted apple and pear trees in the garden, even though they won't bear fruit for ten years, and in the spring, I like to lie in the grass with a book and a beer while Michele tends to her many rosebushes. Best of all, our two kids, Milo and Georgia, born eight minutes apart on a cloudy day in the spring of 1998, are here to exclaim over the bugs and birds and stare up in wonder every time a plane passes overhead.

I can't help but think of them as I sit in this pull-out above Palo Alto, not far from where I sat almost twenty years ago with my father on the day he confessed to me that he was a failure. To Milo and Georgia, Silicon Valley will be a far-off place, sunny and strange. This saddens me, and as I watch the cars slip along the freeway below, I vow to bring them west for a visit as soon as they're old enough to travel. I want them to absorb some of the hope and reckless optimism of the place. I want them to feel the sunshine on their faces and to walk on those beautifully curved sidewalks and to understand the power and the wonder of the technology that has been born here. Then, before they drink too deeply of all this, I want to take them home.

SUNNYVALE

Late that afternoon, I stop by our old house in Sunnyvale. The structure itself is unchanged: a completely unremarkable suburban tract house except for the monumental chimney on the north side. Rectangular aluminum-framed windows with fake shutters hang on each side, an homage to the East Coast colonials that early California ranch houses descended from.

Architecture aside, the neighborhood is unrecognizable. The pale-faced aerospace engineers are long gone, replaced by recent immigrants from Iran, Hong Kong, India, Taiwan, Russia, Israel, and who knows where else, all drawn here by the smell of money and the promise of a bright future. There are iron gates over windows and doors, just as on apartments in New York City, and a welcome disinterest in what had been the holiest of holy objects when this was our neighborhood: the lawn. In front of my father's house, the grass is weedy and unkempt; other lawns on the block have been replaced by rock gardens or paved over entirely.

There are other, less visible changes. A hundred feet below ground, a plume of toxic chemicals—TCE, TCH, arsenic, toluene—floats in the aquifer. Our old house, I recently learned, sits on the edge of a National Superfund site. There are twenty-two of these in Santa Clara County, four in Sunnyvale alone. The toxins here came from a company that was located a few blocks away in a tree-lined industrial park that made chips for digital watches during the late 1970s. The company popped up overnight and grew like crazy for a few years. There was no time or inclination to consider details such as the safe disposal of the highly toxic chemicals used to clean and etch the chips—they were all just dumped in a rusty storage bin out back. Then the fad for digital watches collapsed, and the company vanished.

Now, a pump runs twenty-four hours a day, sucking water out of the aquifer, scrubbing out the most dangerous chemicals, then piping the almost-clean water into the bay. The toxins are then aerated and forced up an innocent-looking silver pipe and released into the sky, where, according to the not-altogether-reassuring logic of the Environmental Protection Agency, they pose less risk to human beings. About a half pound of toxins are spewed out in an invisible cloud over my old neighborhood each day. This process will continue for the next hundred years or so.

I sit in my rent-a-car, thinking about what the Valley will look like in a hundred years. Like midtown Manhattan, probably. I imagine a geodesic dome, flying cars, neural implants. Who knows what's coming? The future is inexorable, the light at the end of the tunnel toward which everything speeds. The past is the darkness behind, useless and scary. In this world, memory is relevant only if it's expressed in megabytes. Human memory is too slow and burdensome, a relic of an earlier time, a vestigial tail. I feel it myself. *Go, go, go,* a voice tells me. *Move on.* I fight the urge. For ten minutes, I just sit in the middle of the street and look. I notice how the trees my father planted are thriving, despite the foul air and water: the olive and a liquidambar out front, the mulberry and the coastal redwood in back. Their trunks are thickening, their branches spreading higher. They are living hourglasses, marking the passage of decades for a world that runs in nanoseconds.

I look at the chimney, that loyal soldier, standing at the side of our old house. I remember the day work began, my father kneeling down over a chalk line beside the house like a man at prayer. A stack of bricks rested behind him, a wheelbarrow full of mortar to his left. There was worry in his eyes. He had laid plenty of bricks before—a brick planter in the front yard and a small brick terrace to the side—but nothing the size and complexity of this. My father knew that a slight cant in the bricks one way or another, compounded layer after layer, can cause tremendous problems later. And with a chimney, there's no hiding shoddy work. A chimney either is straight or is not; it either stands erect like a temple to the gods or tilts and weaves, uncertain of itself, a monument to indecision.

I remember the scaffolding going up and the feel of the fresh bricks in my hands as I passed them up. I was about nine years old at the time and always copped out after an hour or two of work, but my father kept on. At the dinner table, he was often so exhausted it was all he could do to wolf down his food, then stumble to the couch, where he'd be asleep before my mother finished the dishes. Sometimes, he'd wake up with a start, as if some brilliant idea had come to him in his sleep, and he'd walk outside in his socks and just stare at the half-built chimney. He became a ghostly figure, his face perpetually covered in mortar dust, his hands dry and unfriendly from handling thousands of bricks.

Then, one afternoon, I came home from a bike ride, and I looked up, and there was my father on the roof with his palette of mortar, putting the last few bricks around the top of the clay flue. I noticed how quickly he set each one into place. He was nothing like the hesitant, fearful man who had started at the bottom.

I did not, at that time, grasp what an insane, monstrous, passionate project this chimney had been. It was a monument to stability in the middle of a valley that's crisscrossed with earthquake faults and is, down to its very bedrock, one of the most unstable places on earth. Its purpose was to provide warmth, and yet we lived in an almost perfect Mediterranean climate. Talk about a nutty project! Talk about folly! I did not understand that perhaps my father had other reasons for building this magnificent structure, that maybe it was about more than carrying smoke to the sky.

My father's face poked down at me over the rooftop. He motioned over to the ladder leaning up against the eaves. "Come on up." I climbed slowly, pausing on each rung to get acclimated. I finally reached the top and stepped onto the slanted roof. "Just keep away from the edge," my father warned. I followed him toward the chimney, the wooden shingles cracking with each footstep. We were only about twenty feet above the ground, but it felt like we were scaling Mount Everest.

"Since you helped build the chimney, I thought you'd want to sign it," my father said. I'd helped very little, but I didn't argue. I watched him spread a layer of mortar around the top of the flue. Then he used the edge of the trowel as a pencil, scrawling his initials, *RLG,* into the mortar. Then he handed the trowel to me, and I scrawled my initials, *JRG,* next to his.

"Good work," he said, as if he could never have imagined building it without me. I saw that he had built something big and powerful and important, and I was as proud of him as he was of himself. "Now, in twenty years, you'll be able to look up at this chimney and say, 'I helped build that,' " he said. "And your name is right here in the mortar to prove it."

I looked out at the view around us. I saw the shaggy tops of the apricot orchards down the street, and the silvery dome of the observatory at the top of Mount Hamilton on the far side of the valley. Below, in the backyard, I looked down on Jerry's blond head. I saw the flash of his bright white teeth as he looked up at me—he was mad, of course, that I was up on the roof and he wasn't. Beside him, I saw the soft, round face of my mother, her dark eyes full of worry. She warned me to be careful, shingles are slippery, stay away from the edge of the roof. I ignored her. I looked at my father's mortar-flecked face silhouetted against the bright California sky, and I smiled. He clasped his arm around my shoulder. We were on top of the world.

Acknowledgments

Thanks to Ann Godoff, Bruce Tracy, Brian McLendon, Timothy Mennel, Flip Brophy, Pat Towers, Paulina Borsook, Jann Wenner, Bob Love, Will Dana, Stephanie Benkoski, Carol Raban, Valerie Charpentier, and Trudy Hilton. My deepest debts are to my mother and sister, who gave me the blessings and trust I needed to write this story; to Jon Katz, who talked me off the cliff more times than I can count; and to Michele, who not only read and edited many rough drafts but had to live with me while I wrote each one. Finally, thanks to Milo and Georgia for arriving when you did. This is your story, too.

ALL OVER BUT THE SHOUTIN'
by Rick Bragg

Rick Bragg grew up in northeastern Alabama, seemingly destined for either the cotton mills or the penitentiary, and instead became a Pulitzer Prize–winning reporter for *The New York Times*. At the center of this soaring memoir is Bragg's mother, who went eighteen years without a new dress so that her sons could have school clothes and picked other people's cotton to provide food for her children. With artistry, honesty, and compassion, Rick Bragg brings home the love and suffering that lie at the heart of every family.

Memoir/0-679-77402-5

PHOENIX
A Brother's Life
by J. D. Dolan

Phoenix is a memoir of impeccable beauty—funny, sad, wise—about brotherhood, family, and the domestic arc of American life since the shiny-bright fifties. J.D. Dolan grew up in the postwar boom of plenty: Mom at home, Dad at work, the kids tantalized by teenage freedoms. His older brother John was his hero, teaching him to fish and shoot, to ride motorcycles, and to want to be a grown-up, a soldier, a man. But despite all this glorious promise, the Dolans were eventually battered by silence, resentment, misdirection, and, years later, by a horrific motorcycle accident in the desert.

Memoir/0-375-70317-9

HOLE IN THE SKY
by William Kittredge

William Kittredge's stunning narrative is the story of a grandfather whose hunger for property won him a ranch the size of Delaware but estranged him from his family; of a father who farmed with tractors but consorted with movie stars; and of Kittredge himself, who was raised by cowboys and saw them become obsolete, who floundered through three marriages, hard drinking, and madness before becoming a writer. Most hauntingly, *Hole in the Sky* is an honest reckoning of the American myth that drove generations of adventurers westward—and what became of their dream.

Memoir/0-679-74006-6

THIN ICE
Saved by the American Dream
by Bruce McCall

In this subversively funny memoir, the acclaimed *New Yorker* humorist and Canadian expat Bruce McCall describes growing up in a country that revels in second-rateness and within a family that was dysfunctional before the word had even been invented. As a child in Ontario, McCall worships Yankee flash and prizes Yankee candy wrappers as relics of a higher civilization. He endures his father's petty tyranny and his mother's demure alcoholism. And while he fails abjectly at hockey, he learns to draw the outlandishly deadpan cartoons that will eventually provide him with a ticket south.

Memoir/0-679-76959-5

THE FACTORY OF FACTS
by Luc Sante

Born in Belgium but raised in New Jersey, Luc Sante transformed himself from a timid Belgian boy into a loutish American adolescent, who eschewed French while fantasizing about the pop star Françoise Hardy. To show how this transformation came about—and why it remained incomplete—*The Factory of Facts* combines family anecdote and ancestral legend; detailed forays into Belgian history, language, and religion; and deft synopses of the American character.

Memoir/0-679-74650-1

THE DUKE OF DECEPTION
Memories of My Father
by Geoffrey Wolff

Duke Wolff was a flawless specimen of the American clubman—a product of Yale and the OSS, and a one-time fighter pilot turned aviation engineer. But he was also a failure who was passed up for military service, and he supported himself with desperately improvised scams, exploiting employers, wives, and finally, his own son. In *The Duke of Deception,* Geoffrey Wolff carefully unravels the enigma of this Gatsbyesque figure, a bad man who somehow was also a very good father, an inveterate liar who falsified everything but love.

Memoir/0-679-72752-3

Printed in the United States
by Baker & Taylor Publisher Services